Learning Elasticsearch

Distributed real-time search and analytics with Elasticsearch 5.x

Abhishek Andhavarapu

BIRMINGHAM - MUMBAI

Learning Elasticsearch

First published: June 2017

Production reference: 1290617

Published by Packt Publishing Ltd.
Livery Place
35 Livery Street
Birmingham
B3 2PB, UK.
ISBN 978-1-78712-845-3

www.packtpub.com

Credits

Authors
Abhishek Andhavarapu

Reviewers
Dan Noble
Marcelo Ochoa

Commissioning Editor
Amey Varangaonkar

Acquisition Editor
Varsha Shetty

Content Development Editor
Jagruti Babaria

Technical Editor
Danish Shaikh

Copy Editor
Manisha Sinha

Project Coordinator
Manthan Patel

Proofreader
Safis Editing

Indexer
Tejal Daruwale Soni

Graphics
Tania Dutta

Production Coordinator
Deepika Naik

About the Author

Abhishek Andhavarapu is a software engineer at eBay who enjoys working on highly scalable distributed systems. He has a master's degree in Distributed Computing and has worked on multiple enterprise Elasticsearch applications, which are currently serving hundreds of millions of requests per day.

He began his journey with Elasticsearch in 2012 to build an analytics engine to power dashboards and quickly realized that Elasticsearch is like nothing out there for search and analytics. He has been a strong advocate since then and wrote this book to share the practical knowledge he gained along the way.

Writing a book is a humongous task, I want to thank my wife Ashwini for her patience and support during the nights and weekends I spent writing this book. I'm thankful to my parents Govinda Rajulu, Jaya Lakshmi, my brother Sarat Kiran and my in-laws Satya Rao and Suguna for the constant motivation and encouragement throughout the writing of this book. I'm grateful to all my friends and colleagues, whom I couldn't mention by name, for their valuable feedback and inputs.

I also would like to thank my publisher and editors at Packt for the continuous support.

About the Reviewer

Dan Noble is a software engineer with a passion for writing secure, clean, and articulate code. He enjoys working with a variety of programming languages and software frameworks, particularly Python, Elasticsearch, and various Javascript frontend technologies. Dan currently works on geospatial web applications and data processing systems.

Dan has been a user and advocate of Elasticsearch since 2011. He has given several talks about Elasticsearch, is the author of the book *Monitoring Elasticsearch*, and was a technical reviewer for the book *The Elasticsearch Cookbook, Second Edition*, by Alberto Paro. Dan is also the author of the Python Elasticsearch client rawes.

Marcelo Ochoa works at the system laboratory of Facultad de Ciencias Exactas of the Universidad Nacional del Centro de la Provincia de Buenos Aires and is the CTO at Scotas.com, a company that specializes in near real-time search solutions using Apache Solr and Oracle. He divides his time between university jobs and external projects related to Oracle and big data technologies. He has worked on several Oracle-related projects, such as the translation of Oracle manuals and multimedia CBTs. His background is in database, network, web, and Java technologies. In the XML world, he is known as the developer of the DB Generator for the Apache Cocoon project. He has worked on the open source projects DBPrism and DBPrism CMS, the Lucene-Oracle integration using the Oracle JVM Directory implementation, and the Restlet.org project, where he worked on the Oracle XDB Restlet Adapter, which is an alternative to writing native REST web services inside a database resident JVM.

Since 2006, he has been part of an Oracle ACE program and recently incorporated into a Docker Mentor program.

He has coauthored Oracle Database Programming using Java and Web Services by Digital Press and Professional XML Databases by Wrox Press and been a technical reviewer for several PacktPub books, such as *Mastering Elastic Stack, Mastering Elasticsearch 5.x - Third Edition, Elasticsearch 5.x Cookbook - Third Edition*, and others.

www.PacktPub.com

For support files and downloads related to your book, please visit www.PacktPub.com.

Did you know that Packt offers eBook versions of every book published, with PDF and ePub files available? You can upgrade to the eBook version at www.PacktPub.com and as a print book customer, you are entitled to a discount on the eBook copy. Get in touch with us at service@packtpub.com for more details.

At www.PacktPub.com, you can also read a collection of free technical articles, sign up for a range of free newsletters and receive exclusive discounts and offers on Packt books and eBooks.

https://www.packtpub.com/mapt

Get the most in-demand software skills with Mapt. Mapt gives you full access to all Packt books and video courses, as well as industry-leading tools to help you plan your personal development and advance your career.

Why subscribe?

- Fully searchable across every book published by Packt
- Copy and paste, print, and bookmark content
- On demand and accessible via a web browser

Customer Feedback

Thanks for purchasing this Packt book. At Packt, quality is at the heart of our editorial process. To help us improve, please leave us an honest review on this book's Amazon page at `https://www.amazon.com/dp/1787128458`.

If you'd like to join our team of regular reviewers, you can e-mail us at `customerreviews@packtpub.com`. We award our regular reviewers with free eBooks and videos in exchange for their valuable feedback. Help us be relentless in improving our products!

Table of Contents

Preface

Welcome to *Learning Elasticsearch*. We will start by describing the basics concepts and discuss how Elasticsearch handles failures and ensures high availability. You will see how to install Elasticsearch and Kibana and learn how to index and update your data. We will use an e-commerce site as an example to explain how a search engine works and how to query your data. The real power of Elasticsearch is aggregations. You will see how to perform aggregation-based analytics with ease. You will also see how to use Kibana to explore and visualize your data. Finally, we will discuss how to use Graph to discover relations in your data and use alerting to set up alerts and notification on different trends in your data.

To better explain various concepts, lots of examples have been used throughout the book. Detailed instructions to install Elasticsearch, Kibana and how to execute the examples is included in `Chapter 2`, *Setting Up Elasticsearch and Kibana*.

What this book covers

`Chapter 1`, *Introduction to Elasticsearch*, describes the building blocks of Elasticsearch and what makes Elasticsearch scalable and distributed. In this chapter, we also discuss the strengths and limitations of Elasticsearch.

`Chapter 2`, *Setting Up Elasticsearch and Kibana*, covers the installation of Elasticsearch and Kibana.

`Chapter 3`, *Modeling Your Data and Document Relations*, focuses on modeling your data. To support text search, Elasticsearch preprocess the data before indexing. This chapter describes why preprocessing is necessary and various analyzers Elasticsearch supports. In addition to that, we discuss how to handle relationships between different document types.

`Chapter 4`, *Indexing and Updating Your Data*, covers how to index and update your data and what happens internally when you index and update. The data indexed in Elasticsearch is only available after a small delay, we discuss the reason for the delay and how to control the delay.

Chapter 5, *Organizing Your Data and Bulk Data Ingestion*, describes how to organize and manage indices in Elasticsearch using aliases and templates and more. This chapter also covers various Bulk API's Elasticsearch supports and how to rebuild your existing indices using Reindex and Shrink API.

Chapter 6, *All About Search*, covers how to search, sort and paginate on your data. The concept of relevance is introduced and we discuss how to tune the relevance score to get the most relevant search results at the top.

Chapter 7, *More Than a Search Engine (Geofilters, Autocomplete and More)*, covers how to filter based on geolocation, using Elasticsearch suggesters for autocomplete, correcting user typo's and lot more.

Chapter 8, *How to Slice and Dice Your Data Using Aggregations*, covers different kinds of aggregations Elasticsearch supports and how to visualize the data using Kibana.

Chapter 9, *Production and Beyond*, covers important settings to configure and monitor in production.

Chapter 10, *Exploring Elastic Stack (Elastic Cloud, Security, Graph, and Alerting)*, covers Elastic Cloud, which is managed cloud hosting and other products that are part of X-Pack.

What you need for this book

The book was written using Elasticsearch 5.1.2, and all the examples used in the book should work with it. The request format used in this book is based on the Kibana Console and you'll need Kibana Console or Sense Chrome plugin to execute the examples used in this book. Please refer to *Query format used in this book* section of Chapter 2, *Setting up Elasticsearch and Kibana* for more details. If using Kibana or Sense is not option, you can use other HTTP clients such as cURL or Postman. The request format is slightly different and is explained in the *Using cURL or Postman* section of Chapter 2, *Setting Up Elasticsearch and Kibana*.

Who this book is for

This book is for software developers who are planning to build a search and analytics engine or are trying to learn Elasticsearch.

Some familiarity with web technologies (JavaScript, REST, JSON) would be helpful.

Conventions

In this book, you will find a number of text styles that distinguish between different kinds of information. Here are some examples of these styles and an explanation of their meaning.

Code words in text, database table names, folder names, filenames, file extensions, path names, dummy URLs, user input, and Twitter handles are shown as follows: "We can include other contexts through the use of the `include` directive."

A block of code is set as follows:

```
{
    "articleid": 1,
    "name": "Introduction to Elasticsearch"
}
```

When we wish to draw your attention to a particular part of a code block, the relevant lines or items are set in bold:

```
{
    "articleid": 1,
    "name": "Introduction to Elasticsearch"
}
```

New terms and **important** words are shown in bold. Words that you see on the screen, for example, in menus or dialog boxes, appear in the text like this: "Clicking the **Next** button moves you to the next screen."

Warnings or important notes appear in a box like this.

Tips and tricks appear like this.

Reader feedback

Feedback from our readers is always welcome. Let us know what you think about this book—what you liked or disliked. Reader feedback is important for us as it helps us develop titles that you will really get the most out of.

To send us general feedback, simply e-mail `feedback@packtpub.com`, and mention the book's title in the subject of your message.

If there is a topic that you have expertise in and you are interested in either writing or contributing to a book, see our author guide at `www.packtpub.com/authors`.

Customer support

Now that you are the proud owner of a Packt book, we have a number of things to help you to get the most from your purchase.

Downloading the example code

You can download the example code files for this book from your account at `http://www.packtpub.com`. If you purchased this book elsewhere, you can visit `http://www.packtpub.com/support` and register to have the files e-mailed directly to you.

You can download the code files by following these steps:

1. Log in or register to our website using your e-mail address and password.
2. Hover the mouse pointer on the **SUPPORT** tab at the top.
3. Click on **Code Downloads & Errata**.
4. Enter the name of the book in the **Search** box.
5. Select the book for which you're looking to download the code files.
6. Choose from the drop-down menu where you purchased this book from.
7. Click on **Code Download**.

You can also download the code files by clicking on the **Code Files** button on the book's webpage at the Packt Publishing website. This page can be accessed by entering the book's name in the **Search** box. Please note that you need to be logged in to your Packt account.

Once the file is downloaded, please make sure that you unzip or extract the folder using the latest version of:

- WinRAR / 7-Zip for Windows
- Zipeg / iZip / UnRarX for Mac
- 7-Zip / PeaZip for Linux

The code bundle for the book is also hosted on GitHub at `https://github.com/PacktPubl ishing/Learning-Elasticsearch`. We also have other code bundles from our rich catalog of books and videos available at `https://github.com/PacktPublishing/`. Check them out!

Errata

Although we have taken every care to ensure the accuracy of our content, mistakes do happen. If you find a mistake in one of our books—maybe a mistake in the text or the code—we would be grateful if you could report this to us. By doing so, you can save other readers from frustration and help us improve subsequent versions of this book. If you find any errata, please report them by visiting `http://www.packtpub.com/submit-errata`, selecting your book, clicking on the Errata Submission Form link, and entering the details of your errata. Once your errata are verified, your submission will be accepted and the errata will be uploaded to our website or added to any list of existing errata under the Errata section of that title.

To view the previously submitted errata, go to `https://www.packtpub.com/books/conten t/support`and enter the name of the book in the search field. The required information will appear under the Errata section.

Piracy

Piracy of copyrighted material on the Internet is an ongoing problem across all media. At Packt, we take the protection of our copyright and licenses very seriously. If you come across any illegal copies of our works in any form on the Internet, please provide us with the location address or website name immediately so that we can pursue a remedy.

Please contact us at `copyright@packtpub.com` with a link to the suspected pirated material.

We appreciate your help in protecting our authors and our ability to bring you valuable content.

Questions

If you have a problem with any aspect of this book, you can contact us at `questions@packtpub.com`, and we will do our best to address the problem.

1
Introduction to Elasticsearch

In this chapter, we will focus on the basic concepts of **Elasticsearch**. We will start by explaining the building blocks and then discuss how to create, modify and query in Elasticsearch. Getting started with Elasticsearch is very easy; most operations come with default settings. The default settings can be overridden when you need more advanced features.

I first started using Elasticsearch in 2012 as a backend search engine to power our Analytics dashboards. It has been more than five years, and I never looked for any other technologies for our search needs. Elasticsearch is much more than just a search engine; it supports complex aggregations, geo filters, and the list goes on. Best of all, you can run all your queries at a **speed** you have never seen before. To understand how this magic happens, we will briefly discuss how Elasticsearch works internally and then discuss how to talk to Elasticsearch. Knowing how it works internally will help you understand its strengths and limitations. Elasticsearch, like any other open source technology, is very rapidly evolving, but the core fundamentals that power Elasticsearch don't change. By the end of this chapter, we will have covered the following:

- Basic concepts of Elasticsearch
- How to interact with Elasticsearch
- How to create, read, update, and delete
- How does search work
- Availability and horizontal scalability
- Failure handling
- Strengths and limitations

Basic concepts of Elasticsearch

Elasticsearch is a highly scalable open source search engine. Although it started as a text search engine, it is evolving as an analytical engine, which can support not only search but also complex aggregations. Its distributed nature and ease of use makes it very easy to get started and scale as you have more data.

One might ask what makes Elasticsearch different from any other document stores out there. Elasticsearch is a **search engine** and not just a key-value store. It's also a very **powerful analytical engine**; all the queries that you would usually run in a batch or offline mode can be executed in real time. Support for features such as autocomplete, geo-location based filters, multilevel aggregations, coupled with its user friendliness resulted in industry-wide acceptance. That being said, I always believe it is important to have the right tool for the right job. Towards the end of the chapter, we will discuss it's strengths and limitations.

In this section, we will go through the basic concepts and terminology of Elasticsearch. We will start by explaining how to insert, update, and perform a search. If you are familiar with SQL language, the following table shows the equivalent terms in Elasticsearch:

Database	Table	Row	Column
Index	Type	Document	Field

Document

Your data in Elasticsearch is stored as **JSON (Javascript Object Notation)** documents. Most NoSQL data stores use JSON to store their data as JSON format is very concise, flexible, and readily understood by humans. A document in Elasticsearch is very similar to a row when compared to a relational database. Let's say we have a `User` table with the following information:

Id	Name	Age	Gender	Email
1	Luke	100	M	luke@gmail.com
2	Leia	100	F	leia@gmail.com

The users in the preceding user table, when represented in JSON format, will look like the following:

```
{
    "id": 1,
```

```
    "name": "Luke",
    "age": 100,
    "gender": "M",
    "email": "luke@gmail.com"
  }

{
    "id": 2,
    "name": "Leia",
    "age": 100,
    "gender": "F",
    "email": "leia@gmail.com"
  }
```

A row contains columns; similarly, a document contains fields. Elasticsearch documents are very **flexible** and support storing **nested** objects. For example, an existing user document can be easily extended to include the address information. To capture similar information using a table structure, you need to create a new address table and manage the relations using a foreign key. The user document with the address is shown here:

```
{
    "id": 1,
    "name": "Luke",
    "age": 100,
    "gender": "M",
    "email": "luke@gmail.com",
    "address": {
      "street": "123 High Lane",
      "city": "Big City",
      "state": "Small State",
      "zip": 12345
    }
}
```

Reading similar information without the JSON structure would also be difficult as the information would have to be read from multiple tables. Elasticsearch allows you to store the entire JSON as it is. For a database table, the schema has to be defined before you can use the table. Elasticsearch is built to handle **unstructured data** and can automatically determine the data types for the fields in the document. You can index new documents or add new fields without adding or changing the schema. This process is also known as **dynamic mapping**. We will discuss how this works and how to define schema in Chapter 3, *Modeling Your Data and Document Relations*.

Index

An index is similar to a database. The term index should not be confused with a database index, as someone familiar with traditional SQL might assume. Your data is stored in one or more indexes just like you would store it in one or more databases. The word indexing means **inserting/updating** the documents into an Elasticsearch index. The name of the index must be unique and typed in all lowercase letters. For example, in an e-commerce world, you would have an index for the items--one for orders, one for customer information, and so on.

Type

A type is similar to a database table, an index can have one or more types. Type is a logical separation of different kinds of data. For example, if you are building a blog application, you would have a type defined for articles in the blog and a type defined for comments in the blog. Let's say we have two types--articles and comments.

The following is the document that belongs to the article type:

```
{
    "articleid": 1,
    "name": "Introduction to Elasticsearch"
}
```

The following is the document that belongs to the comment type:

```
{
    "commentid": "AVmKvtPwWuEuqke_aRsm",
    "articleid": 1,
    "comment": "Its Awesome !!"
}
```

We can also define **relations** between different types. For example, a parent/child relation can be defined between articles and comments. An article (parent) can have one or more comments (children). We will discuss relations further in `Chapter 3`, *Modeling Your Data and Document Relations*.

Cluster and node

In a traditional database system, we usually have only one server serving all the requests. Elasticsearch is a **distributed system**, meaning it is made up of one or more nodes (servers) that act as a **single application**, which enables it to scale and handle load beyond what a single server can handle. Each node (server) has part of the data. You can start running Elasticsearch with just one node and add more nodes, or, in other words, **scale the cluster** when you have more data. A cluster with three nodes is shown in the following diagram:

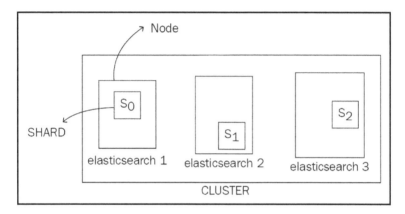

In the preceding diagram, the cluster has three nodes with the names **elasticsearch1, elasticsearch2, elasticsearch3**. These three nodes work together to handle all the indexing and query requests on the data. Each cluster is identified by a unique name, which defaults to elasticsearch. It is often common to have multiple clusters, one for each environment, such as staging, pre-production, production.

Just like a cluster, each node is identified by a unique name. Elasticsearch will automatically assign a unique name to each node if the name is not specified in the configuration. Depending on your application needs, you can add and remove nodes (servers) on the fly. Adding and removing nodes is seamlessly handled by Elasticsearch.

We will discuss how to set up an Elasticsearch cluster in Chapter 2, *Setting Up Elasticsearch and Kibana*.

Shard

An index is a collection of one or more shards. All the data that belongs to an index is distributed across multiple shards. By spreading the data that belongs to an index to multiple shards, Elasticsearch can store information beyond what a single server can store. Elasticsearch uses **Apache Lucene** internally to index and query the data. A shard is nothing but an Apache Lucene instance. We will discuss Apache Lucene and why Elasticsearch uses Lucene in the *How search works* section later.

I know we introduced a lot of new terms in this section. For now, just remember that all data that belongs to an index is spread across one or more shards. We will discuss how shards work in the *Scalability and Availability* section towards the end of this chapter.

Interacting with Elasticsearch

The primary way of interacting with Elasticsearch is via **REST API**. Elasticsearch provides JSON-based REST API over HTTP. By default, Elasticsearch REST API runs on port 9200. Anything from creating an index to shutting down a node is a simple REST call. The APIs are broadly classified into the following:

- **Document APIs**: CRUD (**Create Retrieve Update Delete**) operations on documents
- **Search APIs**: For all the search operations
- **Indices APIs**: For managing indices (creating an index, deleting an index, and so on)
- **Cat APIs**: Instead of JSON, the data is returned in tabular form
- **Cluster APIs**: For managing the cluster

We have a chapter dedicated to each one of them to discuss more in detail. For example, indexing documents in `Chapter 4`, *Indexing and Updating Your Data* and search in `Chapter 6`, *All About Search* and so on. In this section, we will go through some basic CRUD using the Document APIs. This section is simply a brief introduction on how to manipulate data using Document APIs. To use Elasticsearch in your application, clients in all major languages, such as Java, Python, are also provided. The majority of the clients acts as a wrapper around the REST API.

To better explain the CRUD operations, imagine we are building an e-commerce site. And we want to use Elasticsearch to power its search functionality. We will use an index named `chapter1` and store all the products in the type called `product`. Each product we want to index is represented by a JSON document. We will start by creating a new product document, and then we will retrieve a product by its identifier, followed by updating a product's category and deleting a product using its identifier.

Creating a document

A new document can be added using the Document API's. For the e-commerce example, to add a new product, we execute the following command. The body of the request is the product document we want to index.

```
PUT http://localhost:9200/chapter1/product/1
{
    "title": "Learning Elasticsearch",
    "author": "Abhishek Andhavarapu",
    "category": "books"
}
```

Let's inspect the request:

INDEX	chapter1
TYPE	product
IDENTIFIER	1
DOCUMENT	JSON
HTTP METHOD	PUT

The document's properties, such as title, author, the category, are also known as `fields`, which are similar to SQL columns.

 Elasticsearch will automatically create the index `chapter1` and type `product` if they don't exist already. It will create the index with the default settings.

When we execute the preceding request, Elasticsearch responds with a JSON response, shown as follows:

```
{
    "_index": "chapter1",
    "_type": "product",
    "_id": "1",
    "_version": 1,
    "_shards": {
      "total": 1,
      "successful": 1,
      "failed": 0
    },
    "created": true
}
```

In the response, you can see that Elasticsearch created the document and the version of the document is 1. Since you are creating the document using the HTTP PUT method, you are required to specify the document identifier. If you don't specify the identifier, Elasticsearch will respond with the following error message:

```
No handler found for uri [/chapter1/product/] and method [PUT]
```

If you don't have a unique identifier, you can let Elasticsearch assign an identifier for you, but you should use the POST HTTP method. For example, if you are indexing log messages, you will not have a unique identifier for each log message, and you can let Elasticsearch assign the identifier for you.

 In general, we use the HTTP POST method for creating an object. The HTTP PUT method can also be used for object creation, where the client provides the unique identifier instead of the server assigning the identifier.

We can index a document without specifying a unique identifier as shown here:

```
POST http://localhost:9200/chapter1/product/
{
  "title": "Learning Elasticsearch",
  "author": "Abhishek Andhavarapu",
  "category": "books"
}
```

In the above request, URL doesn't contain the unique identifier and we are using the HTTP POST method. Let's inspect the request:

INDEX	chapter1
TYPE	product
DOCUMENT	JSON
HTTP METHOD	POST

The response from Elasticsearch is shown as follows:

```
{
    "_index": "chapter1",
    "_type": "product",
    "_id": "AVmKvtPwWuEuqke_aRsm",
    "_version": 1,
    "_shards": {
      "total": 1,
      "successful": 1,
      "failed": 0
    },
    "created": true
}
```

You can see from the response that Elasticsearch assigned the unique identifier AVmKvtPwWuEuqke_aRsm to the document and created flag is set to true. If a document with the same unique identifier already exists, Elasticsearch replaces the existing document and increments the document version. If you have to run the same PUT request from the beginning of the section, the response from Elasticsearch would be this:

```
{
    "_index": "chapter1",
    "_type": "product",
    "_id": "1",
    "_version": 2,
    "_shards": {
      "total": 1,
      "successful": 1,
      "failed": 0
    },
    "created": false
}
```

In the response, you can see that the created flag is false since the document with id: 1 already exists. Also, observe that the version is now 2.

Retrieving an existing document

To retrieve an existing document, we need the index, type and a unique identifier of the document. Let's try to retrieve the document we just indexed. To retrieve a document we need to use HTTP GET method as shown below:

```
GET http://localhost:9200/chapter1/product/1
```

Let's inspect the request:

INDEX	chapter1
TYPE	product
IDENTIFIER	1
HTTP METHOD	GET

Response from Elasticsearch as shown below contains the product document we indexed in the previous section:

```
{
    "_index": "chapter1",
    "_type": "product",
    "_id": "1",
    "_version": 2,
    "found": true,
    "_source": {
      "title": "Learning Elasticsearch",
      "author": "Abhishek Andhavarapu",
      "category": "books"
    }
}
```

The actual JSON document will be stored in the _source field. Also note the version in the response; every time the document is updated, the version is increased.

Updating an existing document

Updating a document in Elasticsearch is more complicated than in a traditional SQL database. Internally, Elasticsearch retrieves the old document, applies the changes, and re-inserts the document as a new document. The update operation is very expensive. There are different ways of updating a document. We will talk about updating a partial document here and in more detail in the *Updating your data* section in Chapter 4, *Indexing and Updating Your Data*.

Updating a partial document

We already indexed the document with the unique identifier 1, and now we need to update the category of the product from just `books` to `technical books`. We can update the document as shown here:

```
POST http://localhost:9200/chapter1/product/1/_update
{
  "doc": {
    "category": "technical books"
  }
}
```

The body of the request is the field of the document we want to update and the unique identifier is passed in the URL.

 Please note the _update endpoint at the end of the URL.

The response from Elasticsearch is shown here:

```
{
    "_index": "chapter1",
    "_type": "product",
    "_id": "1",
    "_version": 3,
    "_shards": {
      "total": 1,
      "successful": 1,
      "failed": 0
    }
}
```

As you can see in the response, the operation is successful, and the version of the document is now 3. More complicated update operations are possible using scripts and upserts.

Deleting an existing document

For creating and retrieving a document, we used the POST and GET methods. For deleting an existing document, we need to use the HTTP DELETE method and pass the unique identifier of the document in the URL as shown here:

```
DELETE http://localhost:9200/chapter1/product/1
```

Let's inspect the request:

INDEX	chapter1
TYPE	product
IDENTIFIER	1
HTTP METHOD	DELETE

The response from Elasticsearch is shown here:

```
{
    "found": true,
    "_index": "chapter1",
    "_type": "product",
    "_id": "1",
    "_version": 4,
    "_shards": {
      "total": 1,
      "successful": 1,
      "failed": 0
    }
}
```

In the response, you can see that Elasticsearch was able to find the document with the unique identifier 1 and was successful in deleting the document.

How does search work?

In the previous section, we discussed how to create, update, and delete documents. In this section, we will briefly discuss how search works internally and explain the basic query APIs. Mostly, I want to talk about the **inverted index** and **Apache Lucene**. All the data in Elasticsearch is internally stored in Apache Lucene as an inverted index. Although data is stored in Apache Lucene, Elasticsearch is what makes it distributed and provides the easy-to-use APIs. We will discuss Search API in detail in Chapter 6, *All About Search*.

Importance of information retrieval

As the computation power is increasing and cost of storage is decreasing, the amount of day-to-day data we deal with is growing exponentially. But without a way to retrieve the information and to be able to query it, the information we collect doesn't help.

Information retrieval systems are very important to make sense of the data. Imagine how hard it would be to find some information on the Internet without Google or other search engines out there. Information is not knowledge without information retrieval systems.

Simple search query

Let's say we have a `User` table as shown here:

Id	Name	Age	Gender	Email
1	Luke	100	M	luke@gmail.com
2	Leia	100	F	leia@gmail.com

Now, we want to query for all the users with the name `Luke`. A SQL query to achieve this would be something like this:

```
select * from user where name like '%luke%'
```

To do a similar task in Elasticsearch, you can use the `search` API and execute the following command:

```
GET http://127.0.0.1:9200/chapter1/user/_search?q=name:luke
```

Let's inspect the request:

INDEX	chapter1
TYPE	user
FIELD	name

Just like you would get all the rows in the `User` table as a result of the SQL query, the response to the Elasticsearch query would be JSON documents:

```
{
    "id": 1,
    "name": "Luke",
    "age": 100,
    "gender": "M",
    "email": "luke@gmail.com"
}
```

Querying using the URL parameters can be used for simple queries as shown above. For more practical queries, you should pass the query represented as **JSON** in the request body. The same query passed in the request body is shown here:

```
POST http://127.0.0.1:9200/chapter1/user/_search
{
    "query": {
      "term": {
        "name": "luke"
      }
    }
}
```

The Search API is very flexible and supports different kinds of filters, sort, pagination, and aggregations.

Inverted index

Before we talk more about search, I want to talk about the inverted index. Knowing about inverted index will help you understand the limitations and strengths of Elasticsearch compared with the traditional database systems out there. Inverted index at the core is how Elasticsearch is different from other NoSQL stores, such as MongoDB, Cassandra, and so on.

We can compare an inverted index to an old library catalog card system. When you need some information/book in a library, you will use the card catalog, usually at the entrance of the library, to find the book. An inverted index is similar to the card catalog. Imagine that you were to build a system like Google to search for the web pages mentioning your search keywords. We have three web pages with *Yoda* quotes from *Star Wars*, and you are searching for all the documents with the word `fear`.

Document1: *Fear leads to anger*

Document2: *Anger leads to hate*

Document3: *Hate leads to suffering*

In a library, without a card catalog to find the book you need, you would have to go to every shelf row by row, look at each book title, and see whether it's the book you need. Computer-based information retrieval systems do the same.

Without the inverted index, the application has to go through each web page and check whether the word exists in the web page. An inverted index is similar to the following table. It is like a map with the term as a key and list of the documents the term appears in as value.

Term	Document
Fear	1
Anger	1,2
Hate	2,3
Suffering	3
Leads	1,2,3

Once we construct an index, as shown in this table, to find all the documents with the term `fear` is now just a lookup. Just like when a library gets a new book, the book is added to the card catalog, we keep building an inverted index as we encounter a new web page. The preceding inverted index takes care of simple use cases, such as searching for the single term. But in reality, we query for much more complicated things, and we don't use the exact words. Now let's say we encountered a document containing the following:

Yosemite national park may be closed for the weekend due to forecast of substantial rainfall

We want to visit Yosemite National Park, and we are looking for the weather forecast in the park. But when we query for it in the human language, we might query something like `weather in yosemite` or `rain in yosemite`. With the current approach, we will not be able to answer this query as there are no common terms between the query and the document, as shown:

Document	Query
rainfall	rain

To be able to answer queries like this and to improve the search quality, we employ various techniques such as **stemming, synonyms** discussed in the following sections.

Stemming

Stemming is the process of reducing a derived word into its root word. For example, rain, raining, rained, rainfall has the common root word "rain". When a document is indexed, the root word is stored in the index instead of the actual word. Without stemming, we end up storing rain, raining, rained in the index, and search relevance would be very low. The query terms also go through the stemming process, and the root words are looked up in the index. Stemming increases the likelihood of the user finding what he is looking for. When we query for `rain in yosemite`, even though the document originally had rainfall, the inverted index will contain term **rain**.

We can configure stemming in Elasticsearch using Analyzers. We will discuss how to set up and configure analyzers in `Chapter 3`, *Modeling Your Data and Document Relations*.

Synonyms

Similar to rain and raining, weekend and sunday mean the same thing. The document might not contain Sunday, but if the information retrieval system can also search for synonyms, it will significantly improve the search quality. Human language deals with a lot of things, such as tense, gender, numbers. Stemming and synonyms will not only improve the search quality but also reduce the index size by removing the differences between similar words.

More examples:

Pen, Pen[s] -> Pen

Eat, Eating -> Eat

Phrase search

As a user, we almost always search for phrases rather than single words. The inverted index in the previous section would work great for individual terms but not for phrases. Continuing the previous example, if we want to query all the documents with a phrase `anger leads to` in the inverted index, the previous index would not be sufficient. The inverted index for terms anger and leads is shown below:

Term	Document
Anger	1,2
Leads	1,2,3

From the preceding table, the words `anger` and `leads` exist both in `document1` and `document2`. To support phrase search along with the document, we also need to record the position of the word in the document. The inverted index with word position is shown here:

Term	Document
Fear	1:1
Anger	1:3, 2:1
Hate	2:3, 3:1
Suffering	3:3
Leads	1:2, 2:2, 3:2

Now, since we have the information regarding the position of the word, we can search if a document has the terms in the same order as the query.

Term	Document
anger	1:3, 2:1
leads	1:2, 2:2

Since `document2` has `anger` as the first word and `leads` as the second word, the same order as the query, `document2` would be a better match than `document1`. With the inverted index, any query on the documents is just a simple lookup. This is just an introduction to inverted index; in real life, it's much more complicated, but the fundamentals remain the same. When the documents are indexed into Elasticsearch, documents are processed into the inverted index.

Apache Lucene

Apache Lucene is one of the most matured implementations of the inverted index. Lucene is an open source full-text search library. It's very high performing, entirely written in Java. Any application that requires text search can use Lucene. It allows adding full-text search capabilities to any application. Elasticsearch uses Apache Lucene to manage and create its inverted index. To learn more about Apache Lucene, please visit `http://lucene.apache.org/core/`.

We will talk about how distributed search works in Elasticsearch in the next section.

The term index is used both by Apache Lucene (inverted index) and Elasticsearch index. For the remainder of the book, unless specified the term **index** refers to an **Elasticsearch index**.

Scalability and availability

Let's say you want to index a billion documents; having just a single machine might be very challenging. Partitioning data across multiple machines allows Elasticsearch to scale beyond what a single machine do and support high throughput operations. Your data is split into small parts called *shards*. When you create a index, you need to tell Elasticsearch the number of shards you want for the index and Elasticsearch handles the rest for you. As you have more data, you can scale horizontally by adding more machines. We will go in to more details in the sections below.

There are type of shards in Elasticsearch - *primary* and *replica*. The data you index is written to both primary and replica shards. Replica is the exact copy of the primary. In case of the node containing the primary shard goes down, the replica takes over. This process is completely transparent and managed by Elasticsearch. We will discuss this in detail in the *Failure Handling* section below. Since primary and replicas are the exact copies, a search query can be answered by either the primary or the replica shard. This significantly increases the number of simultaneous requests Elasticsearch can handle at any point in time.

As the index is distributed across multiple shards, a query against an index is executed in parallel across all the shards. The results from each shard are then gathered and sent back to the client. Executing the query in parallel greatly improves the search performance.

In the next section, we will discuss the relation between node, index and shard.

Relation between node, index, and shard

Shard is often the most confusing topic when I talk about Elasticsearch at conferences or to someone who has never worked on Elasticsearch. In this section, I want to focus on the relation between node, index, and shard. We will use a cluster with three nodes and create the same index with multiple shard configuration, and we will talk through the differences.

Three shards with zero replicas

We will start with an index called esintroduction with three shards and zero replicas. The distribution of the shards in a three node cluster is as follows:

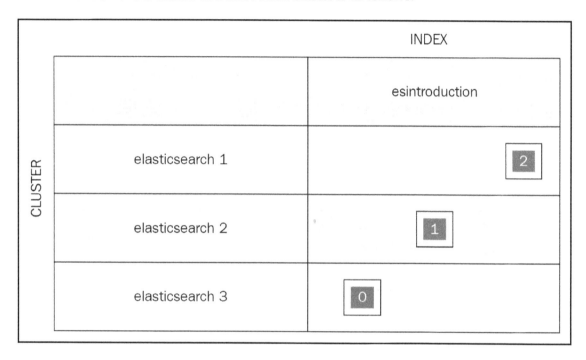

In the above screenshot, shards are represented by the green squares. We will talk about replicas towards the end of this discussion. Since we have three nodes(servers) and three shards, the shards are evenly distributed across all three nodes. Each node will contain one shard. As you index your documents into the esintroduction index, data is spread across the three shards.

Six shards with zero replicas

Now, let's recreate the same esintroduction index with six shards and zero replicas. Since we have three nodes (servers) and six shards, each node will now contain two shards. The esintroduction index is split between six shards across three nodes.

The distribution of shards for an index with six shards is as follows:

The esintroduction index is spread across three nodes, meaning these three nodes will handle the index/query requests for the index. If these three nodes are not able to keep up with the indexing/search load, we can scale the esintroduction index by adding more nodes. Since the index has six shards, you could add three more nodes, and Elasticsearch automatically rearranges the shards across all six nodes. Now, index/query requests for the esintroduction index will be handled by six nodes instead of three nodes. If this is not clear, do not worry, we will discuss more about this as we progress in the book.

Six shards with one replica

Let's now recreate the same esintroduction index with six shards and one replica, meaning the index will have 6 primary shards and 6 replica shards, a total of 12 shards. Since we have three nodes (servers) and twelve shards, each node will now contain four shards. The esintroduction index is split between six shards across three nodes. The green squares represent shards in the following figure.

The solid border represents primary shards, and replicas are the dotted squares:

As we discussed before, the index is distributed into multiple shards across multiple nodes. In a distributed environment, a node/server can go down due to various reasons, such as disk failure, network issue, and so on. To ensure availability, each shard, by default, is replicated to a node other than where the primary shard exists. If the node containing the primary shard goes down, the shard replica is promoted to primary, and the data is not lost, and you can continue to operate on the index. In the preceding figure, the esintroduction index has six shards split across the three nodes. The primary of shard 2 belongs to node elasticsearch 1, and the replica of the shard 2 belongs to node elasticsearch 3. In the case of the elasticsearch 1 node going down, the replica in elasticsearch 3 is promoted to primary. This switch is completely transparent and handled by Elasticsearch.

Distributed search

One of the reasons queries executed on Elasticsearch are so fast is because they are **distributed**. Multiple shards act as one index. A search query on an index is executed in parallel across all the shards.

Let's take an example: in the following figure, we have a cluster with two nodes: Node1, Node2 and an index named chapter1 with two shards: **S0**, **S1** with one replica:

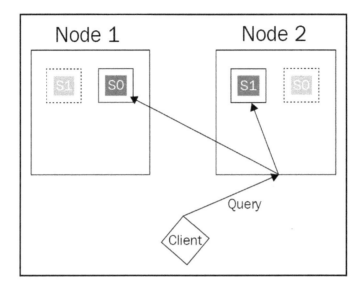

Assuming the chapter1 index has 100 documents, S1 would have 50 documents, and S0 would have 50 documents. And you want to query for all the documents that contain the word Elasticsearch. The query is executed on S0 and S1 in **parallel**. The results are gathered back from both the shards and sent back to the client. Imagine, you have to query across million of documents, using Elasticsearch the search can be distibuted. For the application I'm currently working on, a query on more than 100 million documents comes back within 50 milliseconds; which is simply not possible if the search is not distributed.

Failure handling

Elasticsearch **handles failures automatically**. This section describes how the failures are handled internally. Let's say we have an index with two shards and one replica. In the following diagram, the shards represented in solid line are primary shards, and the shards in the dotted line are replicas:

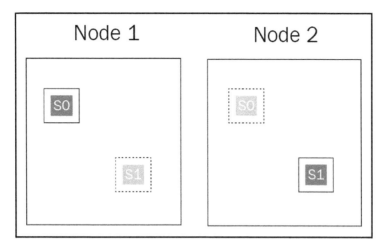

As shown in preceding diagram, we initially have a cluster with two nodes. Since the index has two shards and one replica, shards are distributed across the two nodes. To ensure availability, primary and replica shards never exist in the same node. If the node containing both primary and replica shards goes down, the data cannot be recovered. In the preceding diagram, you can see that the primary shard S0 belongs to Node 1 and the replica shard S0 to the Node 2.

Next, just like we discussed in the *Relation between Node, Index and Shard* section, we will add two new nodes to the existing cluster, as shown here:

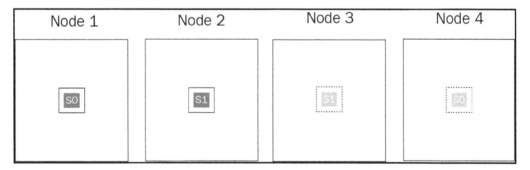

The cluster now contains four nodes, and the shards are automatically allocated to the new nodes. Each node in the cluster will now contain either a primary or replica shard. Now, let's say Node2, which contains the primary shard S1, goes down as shown here:

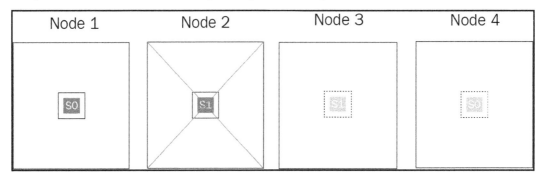

Since the node that holds the primary shard went down, the replica of S1, which lives in Node3, is promoted to primary. To ensure the replication factor of 1, a copy of the shard S1 is made on Node1. This process is known as **rebalancing** of the cluster.

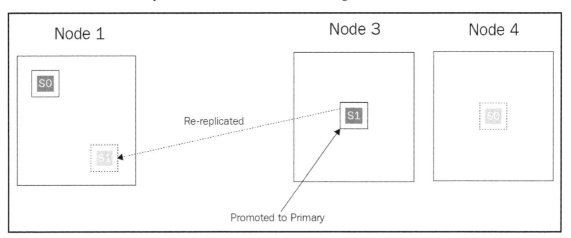

Depending on the application, the number of shards can be configured while creating the index. The process of rebalancing the shards to other nodes is entirely transparent to the user and handled automatically by Elasticsearch.

Strengths and limitations of Elasticsearch

The strengths of Elasticsearch are as follows:

- Very flexible Query API:
    - It supports JSON-based REST API.
    - Clients are available for all major languages, such as Java, Python, PHP, and so on.
    - It supports filtering, sort, pagination, and aggregations in the same query.
- Supports auto/dynamic mapping:
    - In the traditional SQL world, you should predefine the table schema before you can add data. Elasticsearch handles **unstructured data** automatically, meaning you can index JSON documents without predefining the schema. It will try to figure out the field mappings automatically.
    - Adding/removing the new/existing fields is also handled automatically.
- Highly scalable:
    - **Clustering, replication of data, automatic failover** are supported out of the box and are completely transparent to the user. For more details, refer to the *Availability and Horizontal Scalability* section.
- Multi-language support:
    - We discussed how stemming works and why it is important to remove the difference between the different forms of root words. This process is completely different for different languages. Elasticsearch supports many languages out of the box.
- Aggregations:
    - Aggregations are one of the reasons why Elasticsearch is like nothing out there.
    - It comes with very a **powerful analytics engine**, which can help you slice and dice your data.
    - It supports **nested aggregations**. For example, you can group users first by the city they live in and then by their gender and then calculate the average age of each bucket.

- Performance:
    - Due to the inverted index and the distributed nature, it is **extremely high performing**. The queries you traditionally run using a batch processing engine, such as Hadoop, can now be executed in **real time.**
- Intelligent filter caching:
    - The most recently used queries are cached. When the data is modified, the cache is invalidated automatically.

The limitations of Elasticsearch are as follows:

- Not real time - eventual consistency (**near real time**):
    - The data you index is only available for search after 1 sec. A process known as **refresh** wakes up every 1 sec by default and makes the data searchable.
- Doesn't support SQL like **joins** but provides parent-child and nested to handle relations.
- Doesn't support transactions and rollbacks: Transactions in a distributed system are expensive. It offers version-based control to make sure the update is happening on the latest version of the document.
- Updates are expensive. An update on the existing document deletes the document and re-inserts it as a new document.
- Elasticsearch might lose data due to the following reasons:
    - Network partitions.
    - Multiple nodes going down at the same time.
    - Elasticsearch has come a long way in improving resiliency. The current status can be tracked at `https://www.elastic.co/guide/en/elasticsearch/resiliency/current/index.html`.

We will discuss all these concepts in detail in the further chapters.

Summary

In this chapter, you learned the basic concepts of Elasticsearch. Elasticsearch REST APIs make most operations simple and straightforward. We discussed how to index, update, and delete documents. You also learned how distributed search works and how failures are handled automatically. At the end of the chapter, we discussed various strengths and limitations of Elasticsearch.

In the next chapter, we will discuss how to set up Elasticsearch and Kibana. Installing Elasticsearch is very easy as it's designed to run out of the box. Throughout this book, several examples have been used to better explain various concepts. Once you have Elasticsearch up and running, you can try the queries for yourself.

2

Setting Up Elasticsearch and Kibana

In this chapter, we will discuss how to set up **Elasticsearch** and **Kibana**. We will first install Elasticsearch as a single-node cluster and then install Kibana. Running Elasticsearch is very easy as it can be started without any configuration; it is designed to run out of the box. Once we have Elasticsearch up and running, we will go through various APIs that are available to gauge the health of the cluster. By the end of this chapter, we will have covered the following:

- Installing Elasticsearch
- Installing Kibana
- Kibana Dev Tools
- HTTP clients
- Monitoring cluster health

Installing Elasticsearch

In this section, we will install Elasticsearch on a local machine as a single-node cluster. Once we have the cluster up and running, we will learn how to use cluster APIs to check the health of the nodes. We have a *Windows* section for Windows users, a *Mac OS X* section for Mac users, and a *Debian/RPM* section for users who want to install using the Debian (deb)/RPM package.

If you are a Linux/Unix user, you can either install using the Debian/RPM package or you can follow instructions in the *Mac OS X* section.

Installing Java

Elasticsearch is a Java-based application. Before we can run Elasticsearch, we need to make sure that we have Java installed. You need a **Java Runtime Environment(JRE)**. Elasticsearch recommends **Oracle Java Development Kit** (**JDK**) 1.8.0_73 or higher. You can check the Java version installed on your computer by running the following command in the command prompt or terminal:

```
java -version
```

If you don't have Java installed or if you have an older version, please follow the instructions in the following link:

```
http://docs.oracle.com/javase/8/docs/technotes/guides/install/install_overvie
w.html
```

If you are a Windows or Mac user, you can skip to the Windows or Mac OS X section for detailed instructions.

At the time of writing, the latest Java version is 1.8.0_121, which can be downloaded from `http://www.oracle.com/technetwork/java/javase/downloads/jdk8-downloads-2133151.html`.

Please accept the license agreement and download the JDK in the choice of your package format. Once you have Java installed, please verify the Java version using the `java -version` command.

Windows

First, let's check the Java version using command prompt by executing the `java -version` command. If you either have an older Java version or don't have Java installed, go to the following Oracle site, and download the JDK in the `.exe` format. Accept the license agreement before you can download the `.exe` file:

```
http://www.oracle.com/technetwork/java/javase/downloads/jdk8-downloads-
2133151.html
```

Once you install Java using the `.exe` file, verify that the `JAVA_HOME` environment variable is set by executing the following command in the command prompt:

```
echo %JAVA_HOME%
```

If `JAVA_HOME` is not set or is pointing to the directory with an older Java version, you can update your `JAVA_HOME` system variable by following the given steps:

1. Right-click on *My Computer*, and select *Properties*.
2. Click on *Advanced system Settings* to open *System Properties*.
3. In *System Properties*, go to *Advanced Tab*, and click on *Environment Variables*.
4. Edit/add `JAVA_HOME` to `C:\Program Files\Java\jdk1.8.0_121` or the location where you installed the JDK.
5. Close the command prompt, and open it again to reload the environment variables.
6. Verify that `JAVA_HOME` is set by running `java -version`.

Once we have verified Java version, let's download the latest version of Elasticsearch in the `zip` package format from `https://www.elastic.co/downloads/elasticsearch`.

The `Elasticsearch 5.1.2 zip` package can be downloaded from this:

```
https://artifacts.elastic.co/downloads/elasticsearch/elasticsearch-5.1.2.zip
```

Once you have downloaded the ZIP file, unzip the ZIP package to your choice of location.

Starting and stopping Elasticsearch

You can start Elasticsearch using the binary scripts in the *bin* folder. To start Elasticsearch instance, execute the following commands:

```
cd c:\elasticsearch-5.1.2
bin\elasticsearch.bat
```

If Elasticsearch is started successfully, you will see the `started` message at the end of the messages in the console shown as follows:

```
[2017-01-26T20:20:35,919][INFO ][o.e.h.HttpServer] [elasticsearch1]
publish_address {127.0.0.1:9200}, bound_addresses {[fe80::1]:9200},
{[::1]:9200}, {127.0.0.1:9200}
[2017-01-26T20:20:35,919][INFO ][o.e.n.Node] [elasticsearch1] started
```

As you can see the from the preceding log message, Elasticsearch is running at `http://127.0.0.1:9200`. We just started Elasticsearch as a single-node cluster.

Since you started Elasticsearch using the command prompt, to stop Elasticsearch, you can just terminate the process by pressing *Ctrl* + *C*. If you stop Elasticsearch successfully, you should see a message in the console similar to the one shown as follows:

```
[2017-01-26T20:22:34,092][INFO ][o.e.n.Node] [elasticsearch1] stopping ...
[2017-01-26T20:22:34,104][INFO ][o.e.n.Node] [elasticsearch1] stopped
[2017-01-26T20:22:34,104][INFO ][o.e.n.Node] [elasticsearch1] closing ...
[2017-01-26T20:22:34,110][INFO ][o.e.n.Node] [elasticsearch1] closed
```

You can see from the console log that Elasticsearch has been stopped.

Mac OS X

First, let's verify the Java version by executing the `java -version` command in your terminal. If you either have an older Java version or don't have Java installed, go to the following Oracle site and download the JDK in the `.dmg` format. Accept the license agreement before you can download the `dmg` file:

```
http://www.oracle.com/technetwork/java/javase/downloads/jdk8-downloads-2133151.html
```

Once you install Java using the `dmg` file, verify that `JAVA_HOME` is set by executing the following command in a terminal:

```
echo $JAVA_HOME
```

If `JAVA_HOME` is not set or is pointing to the directory with an older Java version, you can update your `JAVA_HOME` system variable by following these steps:

1. Open your terminal, and open your `.bash_profile` file by executing `vi ~/.bash_profile`.
2. You can edit the file by pressing the letter *i*.
3. In the file, set the `JAVA_HOME` environment variable by adding the following to the end of the file:

   ```
   export JAVA_HOME=/Library/Java/JavaVirtualMachines/jdk1.8.0_121.jdk/Contents/Home
   export PATH=$JAVA_HOME/bin:$PATH
   ```

4. Save and exit by pressing the *ESC* key and entering `:wq`.
5. Close and reopen your terminal to update the environment variables.
6. Verify `JAVA_HOME` by executing `echo $JAVA_HOME`.

Once we have confirmed the Java version, let's download the latest version of Elasticsearch in the `tar.gz` format by running the following command in your terminal:

```
curl -L -O
https://artifacts.elastic.co/downloads/elasticsearch/elasticsearch-5.1.2.ta
r.gz
tar -xvf elasticsearch-5.1.2.tar.gz
```

Once you have downloaded the ZIP file, unzip the tar package to your choice of location.

Starting and stopping Elasticsearch

You can start Elasticsearch using the binary scripts in the *bin* folder. To start Elasticsearch instance, execute the following commands:

```
cd elasticearch-5.1.2
./bin/elasticsearch
```

If Elasticsearch is started successfully, you will see the `started` message at the end of the messages in the console as shown here:

```
[2017-01-26T20:20:35,919][INFO ][o.e.h.HttpServer] [elasticsearch1]
publish_address {127.0.0.1:9200}, bound_addresses {[fe80::1]:9200},
{[::1]:9200}, {127.0.0.1:9200}
[2017-01-26T20:20:35,919][INFO ][o.e.n.Node] [elasticsearch1] started
```

As you can see from the preceding log message, we have Elasticsearch running at `http://127.0.0.1:9200`. We just started Elasticsearch as a single-node cluster.

Since you started Elasticsearch using the command prompt. To stop, you can just terminate the process by pressing `Ctrl + C`. If you stop Elasticsearch successfully, you should see a message in the console similar to what shown as follows:

```
[2017-01-26T20:22:34,092][INFO ][o.e.n.Node] [elasticsearch1] stopping ...
[2017-01-26T20:22:34,104][INFO ][o.e.n.Node] [elasticsearch1] stopped
[2017-01-26T20:22:34,104][INFO ][o.e.n.Node] [elasticsearch1] closing ...
[2017-01-26T20:22:34,110][INFO ][o.e.n.Node] [elasticsearch1] closed
```

You can see from the preceding console log that Elasticsearch has been successfully stopped.

DEB and RPM packages

You can also install Elasticsearch using the Debian or **RPM (Red Hat Package Manager)** package. When installing using DEB or RPM packages, Elasticsearch will be installed to `/usr/share/elasticsearch`. Please note that the directory structure is different when you install using Debian or RPM package compared to the zip/tar file.

Debian package

For a Debian-based operating system, such as Ubuntu, you can download the Debian package directly from the Elasticsearch website using the following link:

```
https://artifacts.elastic.co/downloads/elasticsearch/elasticsearch-5.1.2.deb
```

After you download the package, you can install Elasticsearch using the following command:

```
sudo dpkg -i elasticsearch-5.1.2.deb
```

When using the Debian package, Elasticsearch will be installed as a service. You can start and stop Elasticsearch using a service command as shown in the following *Starting and Stopping Elasticsearch* section.

RPM package

For RPM-based operating systems, such as Centos and Red Hat, you can download the RPM package directly from the Elasticsearch website using the following link:

```
https://artifacts.elastic.co/downloads/elasticsearch/elasticsearch-5.1.2.rpm
```

After you download the package, you can install Elasticsearch using the following command:

```
sudo rpm --install elasticsearch-5.1.2.rpm
```

When using the RPM package, Elasticsearch will be installed as a service. You can start and stop Elasticsearch using the `service` command as shown in the following *Starting and Stopping Elasticsearch* section.

Starting and stoping Elasticsearch

If you install Elasticsearch using a Debian or RPM package, you can start/stop Elasticsearch using the `service` command.

You can start Elasticsearch using the `service` command shown as follows:

```
sudo -i service elasticsearch start
```

You can stop Elasticsearch using the `service` command shown as follows:

```
sudo -i service elasticsearch stop
```

You can check the `log` file, shown as follows, to make sure Elasticsearch is started/stopped successfully. If Elasticsearch is started, you should see a log message saying `started`, and if it is stopped successfully, you should see a log message saying `stopped`:

```
tail -100 /var/log/elasticsearch/elasticsearch.log
```

If you want to start Elasticsearch automatically on a system startup, you can configure `SysV init` or `systemd` depending on your operating system.

Sample configuration files

If you are just starting with Elasticsearch, the following are the sample `elasticsearch.yml` files for a cluster with one or more nodes. The configuration is specific to a single node and has to be configured for all the nodes in the cluster. If you install Elasticsearch using `zip` or `.tar.gz`, the `elasticsearch.yml` file is located in the config directory in the main `elasticsearch-5.1.2` folder. If you install Elasticsearch using DEB/RPM, it is located by default in the `/etc/elasticsearch` folder. We will go into more details in `Chapter 9`, *Production and Beyond*.

If you are starting with just one node, you need to set the cluster name, node name, and the IP address that the Elasticsearch should bind to. If no IP address is provided, it will bind to the localhost:

```
cluster.name: es-dev
node.name: elasticsearch1
network.host: 0.0.0.0
```

If you are starting with two or more nodes in the cluster, along with the aforementioned properties, you also have to specify the IP address of other nodes in the cluster so that they can discover each other.

The following is the configuration for `node1`:

```
cluster.name: es-dev
node.name: elasticsearch1
network.host: 0.0.0.0
discovery.zen.ping.unicast.hosts: ["node1_ip_address:9300",
"node2_ip_address:9300"]
```

The following is the configuration for `node2`:

```
cluster.name: es-dev
node.name: elasticsearch2
network.host: 0.0.0.0
discovery.zen.ping.unicast.hosts: ["node1_ip_address:9300",
"node2_ip_address:9300"]
```

 Note that the cluster name should be the same for all the nodes in the cluster. Internally, the nodes communicate with each other using the transport protocol, and the port number for the transport protocol is 9300.

Verifying Elasticsearch is running

In `Chapter 1`, *Introduction to Elasticsearch*, we described the `RESTful` API that Elasticsearch provides. By default, Elasticsearch runs on the `9200` HTTP port. Once Elasticsearch is running, you can verify Elasticsearch by executing the `http://127.0.0.1:9200` URL in your favorite browser. You should see a JSON response similar to the following:

```
{
    "name": "A_TmR2p",
    "cluster_name": "elasticsearch",
    "cluster_uuid": "Mp7tziykSjymFwBYozM4RA",
    "version": {
      "number": "5.1.2",
      "build_hash": "c8c4c16",
      "build_date": "2017-01-11T20:18:39.146Z",
      "build_snapshot": false,
      "lucene_version": "6.3.0"
    },
    "tagline": "You Know, for Search"
}
```

You can see from the JSON response that the node name is `A_TmR2p`, cluster name is `elasticsearch`, along with a few other details. By default, Elasticsearch assigns a random name (`A_TmR2p`) to the node on startup.

Installing Kibana

In this section, we will install Kibana. Kibana is a web interface to visualize and analyze the data in Elasticsearch. Kibana also provides developer tools, which is very handy for running Elasticsearch queries. The queries used in the book can be executed using Kibana developer tools. You need Elasticsearch up and running before you can start using Kibana. Make sure the Kibana version matches the Elasticsearch version. At the time of writing, the latest Elasticsearch version is 5.1.2.

Mac OS X

You can download Kibana for Mac OS X from the following Elasticsearch website:

```
curl -L -O
https://artifacts.elastic.co/downloads/kibana/kibana-5.1.2-darwin-x86_64.ta
r.gz
tar -xvf kibana-5.1.2-darwin-x86_64.tar.gz
```

Once you have downloaded the ZIP file, unzip the tar package to your choice of location.

Starting and stopping Kibana

You can start Kibana using the binary scripts in the *bin* folder. If Elasticsearch is not running on the 127.0.0.1:9200 port, you have to change the Kibana configuration settings. Open the configuration as shown next:

```
cd kibana-5.1.2-darwin-x86_64
sudo vi config/kibana.yml
```

In the configuration file, find the elasticsearch.url setting and replace the value with the IP address and port of where Elasticsearch is running. To start Kibana, execute the following commands:

```
./bin/kibana
```

If Kibana is started successfully, you will see Ready at the end of the messages in the console as shown next:

```
[21:56:30.709] [info][listening] Server running at http://localhost:5601
[21:56:30.710] [info][status][ui settings] Status changed from
uninitialized to yellow - Elasticsearch plugin is yellow
[21:56:35.717] [info][status][plugin:elasticsearch@5.1.2] Status changed
from yellow to yellow - No existing Kibana index found
```

```
[21:56:36.177] [info][status][plugin:elasticsearch@5.1.2] Status changed
from yellow to green - Kibana index ready
[21:56:36.177] [info][status][ui settings] Status changed from yellow to
green - Ready
```

As you can see the from the above log message, we have Kibana running at `http://127.0.0.1:5601`. Since you started Kibana using the command prompt. To stop Kibana, you can just terminate the process by pressing *Ctrl* + *C*. You can also start Kibana and detach it from your session by running:

```
./bin/kibana & disown
```

The output of this command is the process id as shown below:

```
[1] 2455
```

To stop Kibana, you can use the process id to stop it. You can use `kill -9` command as shown below:

```
kill -9 2455
```

Windows

You can download Kibana for Windows from Elasticsearch website shown below:

```
https://artifacts.elastic.co/downloads/kibana/kibana-5.1.2-windows-x86.zip
```

Once you have downloaded the ZIP file, unzip the ZIP package to your choice of location.

Starting and stopping Kibana

You can start Kibana using the binary scripts in the *bin* folder. If Elasticsearch is not running on port `9200`, you have to change the Kibana configuration settings. Open the configuration file (`config\kibana.yml`) using your favorite text editor.

In the configuration file, find `elasticsearch.url` setting and replace the value with IP address and port where Elasticsearch is running. To start Kibana, execute the following commands:

```
cd c:\kibana-5.1.2-windows-x86
bin\kibana.bat
```

If Kibana is started successfully, you will see `Ready` at the end of the messages in the console as shown below:

```
[21:56:30.709] [info][listening] Server running at http://localhost:5601
[21:56:30.710] [info][status][ui settings] Status changed from
uninitialized to yellow - Elasticsearch plugin is yellow
[21:56:35.717] [info][status][plugin:elasticsearch@5.1.2] Status changed
from yellow to yellow - No existing Kibana index found
[21:56:36.177] [info][status][plugin:elasticsearch@5.1.2] Status changed
from yellow to green - Kibana index ready
[21:56:36.177] [info][status][ui settings] Status changed from yellow to
green - Ready
```

As you can see from the preceding log message, we have Kibana running at `http://127.0.0.1:5601`. Since you started Kibana using the command prompt, to stop Kibana, you can just terminate the process by pressing *Ctrl + C*.

Query format used in this book (Kibana Console)

The query format used in this book is based on **Kibana Console**. When using other HTTP clients such as cURL or Postman, the Elasticsearch endpoint (like `http://127.0.0.1:900`) should be passed in the URL, when using Kibana Console it is automatically inferred from Kibana settings. Using Kibana Console while in development or for debugging is strongly recommended. You can access Kibana Console by going to Dev Tools tab in the navigation bar on the left.

The Kibana Console look like the following:

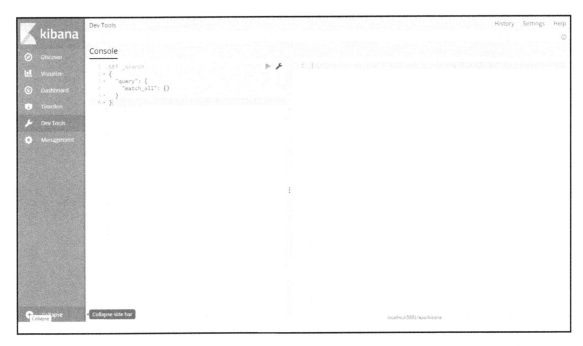

Kibana Console has a very simple UI and is divided into request and response windows. The request window makes it very easy to work with JSON requests and supports auto-completion and auto indentation. The response window makes it very easy to follow the JSON response as you can expand or minimize parts of the JSON response. You can also copy any `curl` command in its entirety from this book or anywhere else into the request window.

In the preceding screenshot, the HTTP method, the Search API endpoint, and query are specified in the request. This minimalistic design, support for autocompleting the query, and JSON formatting make it very easy to interact with Elasticsearch. It also saves the queries in the request window so that you can run them later.

> If running a Kibana instance is not an option, you can also use **Sense**. Sense and Kibana Console offer the exact functionality. Sense is moved to Kibana as Kibana Console. Sense is a Chrome plugin built by Elastic. You can download Sense plugin for Chrome from
> `https://chrome.google.com/webstore/detail/sense-beta/lhjgkmllcaa`
> `dmopgmanpapmpjgmfcfig?hl=en`.
> You don't need Kibana to use Sense. But you need to specify the Elasticsearch server address at the top.

If using Kibana or Sense is not an option, in the next section we will discuss alternatives.

Using cURL or Postman

The primary way of interacting with Elasticsearch is using the REST API over HTTP. If Kibana or Sense is not an option for you, you can use any of the popular HTTP clients, such as **cURL** or **Postman**. Curl is a command line-based client available on most operating systems. Postman is an UI-based HTTP client available for major operating systems. You can get postman from the following link:

```
https://www.getpostman.com/
```

To execute the queries in this book using other HTTP clients, you have to specify the Elasticsearch server address (such as `http://127.0.0.1:9200`) in front of the API endpoint to execute the query. Let's take an example query found in this book:

```
POST es-index/_search
{
  "query": {
    "match_all": {}
  }
}
```

To execute the preceding query in cURL, you should add the `curl` command and the `-d` flag and wrap the query in single quotes. The `HTTP POST` method should be used as `-XPOST`. The preceding query would look like the following:

```
curl -XPOST http://127.0.0.1:9200/es-index/_search -d '{
  "query": {
    "match_all": {}
  }
}'
```

To run the preceding query using Postman, you need to specify the HTTP method as POST, the URL as `http://127.0.0.1:9200/es-index/_search`, and the request should be passed in the body as shown next:

```
{
  "query": {
    "match_all": {}
  }
}
```

The choice of HTTP client doesn't affect the query or performance in any way.

Health of the cluster

Elasticsearch provides various APIs for operational management of clusters and nodes. One of the important APIs is cluster API. In the previous section, we started a single-node cluster. We can check the health of the cluster using the cluster API as follows:

```
http://127.0.0.1:9200/_cluster/health?pretty
```

The pretty flag at the end of the URL makes the JSON response more readable. The response from the cluster API is shown next:

```
{
    "cluster_name": "es-dev",
    "status": "green",
    "timed_out": false,
    "number_of_nodes": 1,
    "number_of_data_nodes": 1,
    "active_primary_shards": 0,
    "active_shards": 0,
    "relocating_shards": 0,
    "initializing_shards": 0,
    "unassigned_shards": 0,
    "delayed_unassigned_shards": 0,
    "number_of_pending_tasks": 0,
    "number_of_in_flight_fetch": 0,
    "task_max_waiting_in_queue_millis": 0,
    "active_shards_percent_as_number": 100
}
```

You can tell from the JSON response that the current status of the cluster is **green** (the cluster status can be green, yellow, or red). In Chapter 1, *Introduction to Elasticsearch*, in the *Relation between Node, Index and Shard* section, we discussed shards and how they are allocated to the nodes. The cluster status is mainly the indication of shards being correctly allocated in the cluster.

The following table describes what each status means:

Status	Description
Red	Red means some shards couldn't be allocated in the cluster. We discussed in `Chapter 1`, *Introduction to Elasticsearch*, data that belongs to an index is spread across multiple shards. Let's say one of the nodes containing the shards of the index is down and the shard couldn't be allocated to any node in the cluster. This can happen due to shard corruption or nodes running out of disk space and many other reasons. In this case, a query against the index comes back with incomplete results as all the shards are not available.
Yellow	Yellow means the primary shard is allocated, but the replicas couldn't be allocated. In this case, any queries against the index still come back with the right results, but if the node containing the primary shard goes down, your data is lost.
Green	Green means everything is great. Primary and replica shards are allocated correctly, and you are ready to go.

Next, from the response, you can tell the number of nodes is one and the number of the data nodes is also one. In the *Types of nodes* section of `Chapter 9`, *Production and beyond*, we will describe different types of nodes. In a single-node cluster, the same node acts as master, data, and ingest nodes. The response also includes the status regarding the shards and the overall cluster.

Summary

In this chapter, we learned how to install and configure Elasticsearch. We also learned how to install Kibana. We discussed the various HTTP clients we can use to talk to Elasticsearch. A lot of examples have been used throughout the book to better explain various concepts. With Elasticsearch and Kibana up and running, you can now try out the queries in the examples.

In the next chapter, we will talk about how to model data and manage relations in Elasticsearch.

3
Modeling Your Data and Document Relations

In the previous chapter, we learned how to set up and configure Elasticsearch. Once the cluster is up and running, you can start indexing your data. Elasticsearch will automatically figure out the schema of the documents when you index, which works great for getting started. But for all practical purposes, you have to tell Elasticsearch the schema of your data to avoid any surprises. Modeling your data is one of the most important steps before using Elasticsearch. In this chapter, you'll learn how to model your data and handle relations between different document types. In this chapter, we will cover the following:

- Configure mappings
- Dynamic mapping
- Core data types
- Complex data types
- Geo location
- Modeling relations in Elasticsearch

Mapping

Mapping is the process of defining the schema or the structure of the documents. It describes the properties of the fields in the document. The properties of the field include the data type (for example, string, integer, and so on) and the metadata. In the previous chapters, we discussed how the documents are converted into the inverted index when we index them. During indexing, the mappings of the fields define how the fields are indexed and stored in the inverted index.

Just like you would define table schema in SQL, it is important to set the mappings of the index before you index any data. As we discussed before, a type in Elasticsearch is like an SQL table, which groups documents of similar nature (you would define one type for users, one for orders). Each type has its mapping defined. Having different mappings could also be a motivation to define a new type.

> Apache Lucene, which stores your data under covers, has no concept of types. The type information is stored in metadata and handled by Elasticsearch.

Before we talk about the different data types Elasticsearch supports, let's take a look at a document and how to define its mapping. Let's say we want to index the user documents, shown as follows:

```
{
    "id": 1,
    "name": "User1",
    "age": "55",
    "gender": "M",
    "email": "user1@gmail.com",
    "last_modified_date": "2017-01-03"
}

{
    "id": 2,
    "name": "User2",
    "age": "40",
    "gender": "F",
    "email": "user2@gmail.com",
    "last_modified_date": "2016-12-02"
}
```

Next, we want to query all the users who are older than 50. If we index these documents as is, we will not be able to run the query as the age field will be indexed as text by default, and you can't perform range-based queries on a text field. Similarly, for the date field, you have to tell Elasticsearch how the date is formatted. For example, for the last modified date field 2017-01-03, Elasticsearch will not be able to say whether the month is 01 or 03. We have to specify the format. The date format can be specified when the mapping is defined. In the next section, we will discuss dynamic mapping.

Dynamic mapping

When you index a document without specifying the mapping, Elasticsearch will automatically determine the data types for the fields in the document. To understand how dynamic mapping works, let's try indexing a person document as shown next:

```
PUT chapter3/person/1
{
  "name": "john",
  "age": 100,
  "date_of_birth": "1970/01/01"
}
```

Now, let's check the mapping of the person type, which is set automatically:

```
GET chapter3/person/_mapping
```

The response of get mapping is shown next:

```
{
  "chapter3": {
    "mappings": {
      "person": {
        "properties": {
          "age": {
            "type": "integer"
          },
          "date_of_birth": {
            "type": "date",
            "format": "yyyy/MM/dd HH:mm:ss||yyyy/MM/dd||epoch_millis"
          },
          "name": {
            "type": "keyword"
          }
        }
      }
    }
  }
}
```

You can see from the preceding response that Elasticsearch determined the data type of the age field as long, the date_of_birth field as date, and the name field as text. When a new field is encountered, it tries to determine whether the field is boolean, long, text, or date.

Mapping numbers and boolean data fields are straightforward, but to map date fields, the string value is first checked to see whether it matches any known date patterns.

By default, the string value is checked against the three formats shown as follows:

```
"strict_date_optional_time", "yyyy/MM/dd HH:mm:ss Z", "yyyy/MM/dd Z"
```

Although Elasticsearch can determine the data type, you should set the mapping to all known fields to avoid any surprises. By default, for any fields that are not in the mapping, data type is determined based on the first encountered value of the field. To avoid unexpected mapping, you can turn off dynamic mapping, as shown next:

```
PUT chapter3
{
 "mappings": {
    "news": {
       "dynamic" : false,
       "properties": {
          "desc": {
             "type": "text"
          }
        }
      }
    }
}
```

The dynamic setting accepts three different values:

- **true**: By default, new fields are automatically added to the mapping
- **false**: Fields not in the mapping are ignored
- **strict**: An exception is thrown if you try to index a document with an unknown field

Sometimes automatic date detection can cause problems. That data type is determined based on the first encounter of the field value. If the first string value accidentally matches the default date format, the data type of the field can be set to date instead of text. When indexing the next document, a mapping error is thrown as you are trying to index a string into the date field. To avoid this, you can turn off automatic date detection, as shown next:

```
PUT chapter3/_mapping/news
  {
    "date_detection": false,
    "properties": {
      "source": {
        "type": "text"
      }
    }
  }
```

Create index with mapping

To define or add a mapping, we have to use the Mapping API. Mapping for a type, like anything else, is represented in JSON.

Mapping APIs will let you do the following:

- Create a new index with mappings
- Add a new type to an existing index
- Add a new field to an existing type

First, let's create an index named `chapter3` and define the mapping for the `user` type. The mapping for the`user` type is defined as a JSON document as shown next.

 Note that the HTTP method used for the request is PUT.

```
#Delete existing index if any
DELETE chapter3

PUT chapter3
  {
    "mappings": {
      "user": {
        "properties": {
          "age": {
            "type": "integer"
          },
          "email": {
            "type": "keyword"
          },
          "gender": {
            "type": "keyword"
          },
          "id": {
            "type": "integer"
          },
          "last_modified_date": {
            "type": "date",
            "format": "yyyy-MM-dd"
          },
          "name": {
            "type": "keyword"
          }
```

```
          }
        }
      }
    }
```

If the index is successfully created, you should see a response, as shown here:

```
{
   "acknowledged": true
}
```

Since the mapping is set, when you index the document, the age field will be indexed as an integer, and you can execute range queries. In the preceding mapping, also note how we defined the format of the date as yyyy-MM-dd, telling Elasticsearch how to parse the date field.

Adding a new type/field

In the previous section, we discussed how to create an index with mapping. In this section, we will discuss how to add a new type and new fields. Let's add a new type called history to keep track of user-login history.

Please note _mapping at the end of the URL. You can add a type named history to the chapter3 index, as shown next:

```
PUT chapter3/_mapping/history
{
   "properties": {
     "username": {
       "type": "keyword"
     },
     "login_date": {
       "type": "date",
       "format": "yyyy-MM-dd"
     }
   }
}
```

You should see an acknowledged true message if the type is successfully added. Next, let's try adding a new field to the type history we just added. Along with the username and login_date, we also want to record the location or the IP address from where the user logged in. To store IP addresses, Elasticsearch has a special IP data type. We can add the ip_address field to the history type, as shown here:

```
PUT chapter3/_mapping/history
```

```
{
  "properties": {
    "id_address": {
      "type": "ip"
    }
  }
}
```

By setting the `ip_address` field as IP data type, we can execute range and aggregation queries on the IP address. We will discuss the IP data type in the following sections.

Getting the existing mapping

Mapping API is also used to retrieve existing mapping. You can check the mappings of an existing index or type as shown next:

```
GET chapter3/_mapping
```

 Note that the HTTP method used for the request is GET.

The response shown next contains the mapping of all the types in the `chapter3` index:

```
{
  "chapter3": {
    "mappings": {
      "history": {
        "properties": {
          "id_address": {
            "type": "ip"
          },
          "login_date": {
            "type": "date",
            "format": "yyyy-MM-dd"
          },
          "username": {
            "type": "keyword"
          }
        }
      },
      "user": {
        "properties": {
          "age": {
            "type": "integer"
```

```
        },
        "email": {
          "type": "keyword"
        },
        "gender": {
          "type": "keyword"
        },
        "id": {
          "type": "integer"
        },
        "last_modified_date": {
          "type": "date",
          "format": "yyyy-MM-dd"
        },
        "name": {
          "type": "keyword"
        }
      }
    }
   }
  }
}
```

You can also get the mapping of a single type as shown next:

```
GET chapter3/user/_mapping
```

Mapping conflicts

Mapping of the existing fields cannot be changed. As the documents are indexed, they are stored in the inverted index according to the data type. If you try to update the mapping of an existing field, you will get a mapping exception, as shown next:

```
{
   "error": {
     "root_cause": [
        {
          "type": "merge_mapping_exception",
          "reason": "Merge failed with failures {[mapper [username] of
different type, current_type [string], merged_type [integer]]}"
        }
     ],
     "type": "merge_mapping_exception",
     "reason": "Merge failed with failures {[mapper [username] of different
type, current_type [string], merged_type [integer]]}"
   },
```

```
    "status": 400
  }
```

You can always add new fields or use multi-fields to index the same field using multiple data types, but you cannot update an existing mapping. We will discuss multi-fields in *Mapping the same field with different mappings* section below. If you want to change the mapping, you have to re-create the index or use Reindex API. We will discuss Reindex API in `Chapter 5`, *Organizing Your data and Bulk Data Ingestion*. If you don't care about the already indexed data, you can work around by adding a new field with the correct data type.

Data type

In the traditional SQL world, a column data type can only be a simple data type, such as integer, boolean, and so on. Since data in Elasticsearch is represented as JSON, it supports data types that are complex and nested.

The different data types supported are as follows:

- Core data types:
    - Text
    - Keyword
    - Date
    - Numeric
    - Boolean
    - Binary
- Complex data types:
    - Array
    - Object (JSON object)
    - Nested
- Geo data types:
    - Geo-point
    - Geo-shape
- Specialized data types:
    - IP

Before we go through each data type, let's talk about the metafields each document contains.

Metafields

Each document we index has the following meta fields, also known as **identity** meta fields as they are used to identify a document uniquely:

- `_index`: This is the name of the index the document belongs to.
- `_uid`: This is the combination of `_type` and `_id`.
- `_type`: This is the mapping type the document belongs to.
- `_id`: This is the unique identifier of the document.

In the next section, we will discuss how to deal with null values.

How to handle null values

When Elasticsearch encounters a JSON null value in the document, it skips the field as it cannot be indexed or searched. But if you want to search for all documents containing a null value, you can tell Elasticsearch to replace the null value with a default value.

For example, we have a login history document with the `username`, `date`, and `login_status` fields as shown next:

```
{
  "username" : "user1",
  "login_date" : "2017-01-31T00:00:00",
  "login_status" : "successful"
}
```

And sometimes the `login_status` is sent as null by default. If the `login_status` field is null, the `login_status` field is skipped. But we want to store the `login_status` field as `UNKNOWN` whenever the `login_status` field is null. We can do so by specifying the null value for `login_status` in the mapping, as shown next:

```
PUT chapter3/_mapping/history
  {
    "properties": {
      "username": {
        "type": "keyword"
      },
      "login_date": {
        "type": "date",
        "format": "yyyy-MM-dd"
      },
      "login_status": {
```

```
      "type": "keyword",
      "null_value": "UNKNOWN"
    }
  }
}
```

While indexing, if the `login_status` field value of the history document is null, it will be indexed as UNKNOWN, and we can query for all the login history documents with the `login_status` field as UNKNOWN, as shown next:

```
GET chapter3/history/_search?q=login_status:UNKNOWN
```

Please note that the `null_value` should be of the same data type as the field. An integer field cannot have a null value that is a string.

Storing the original document

In `Chapter 1`, *Introduction to Elasticsearch*, we learned how data is stored internally in the inverted index. Along with the inverted index, the original JSON document is also stored as the _source field. The _source field is used to show the original JSON document in the result. By default, the source of the document is stored. The _source field is used not only to return the original document but also for scripting updates and reindexing the data. If you don't foresee using the _source field, you can disable it to save the disk space. You can disable the _source field in the mapping, as shown next:

```
PUT chapter3/_mapping/order
  {
    "_source": {
      "enabled": false
    },
    "properties": {
      "buyer": {
        "type": "keyword"
      },
      "seller": {
        "type": "keyword"
      },
      "itemtitle": {
        "type": "text"
      }
    }
  }
```

You can disable the _source field if you only want the document ID in the response and don't plan to update or reindex the data.

Searching all the fields in the document

Elasticsearch lets you search for a value across all the fields in the document. If you are exploring the data or you don't care about which field contains the search input, you can use the _all field. To make this possible, when you index a document, all the field values in the document are combined into one big string, separated by a space and indexed as the _all field. For example, we are indexing e-commerce order documents, and order documents contain buyer, seller, and item_title fields. An example order document is shown next:

```
PUT chapter3/order/1
  {
    "buyer": "john",
    "seller": "jake",
    "item_title": "iphone",
    "order_date": "2017-02-08"
  }
```

When the preceding document is indexed along with the document fields, Elasticsearch indexes all the field values into one big string ("john jake iphone 2017-02-08") as the _all field. The query for all the orders that contain item_title as iphone is shown next:

```
GET chapter3/order/_search?q=item_title:iphone
```

In the preceding query, we queried for all the documents that contain item_title as iphone. But if we want to search for all the fields in the document, we can query the _all field. By default, if no field is specified, Elasticsearch will query the _all field. We can query the _all field, as shown next:

```
GET chapter3/order/_search?q=iphone
```

When indexing the _all field, all the fields in the document are combined into one big string irrespective of their mapping type. In the preceding document, even though order_date is a date field, it is treated as a string when the _all field is indexed.

By default, the _all field is enabled. If you don't plan to use the _all field, it can be disabled in the mapping as shown next. Disabling it will reduce the size of the index on disk:

```
PUT chapter3/_mapping/order
```

```
{
  "_all": {
    "enabled": false
  },
  "properties": {
    "buyer": {
      "type": "keyword"
    },
    "seller": {
      "type": "keyword"
    },
    "item_title": {
      "type": "text"
    }
  }
}
```

You cannot disable the _all field for an existing type. To disable the _all field, you have to recreate the index and set the mapping. Elasticsearch also supports excluding individual fields from the _all field instead of disabling it for the entire type. You can exclude individual fields from the _all field on the fly. For example, if we want the buyer and seller fields to be excluded from the _all field, we can set the include_in_all flag to false, as shown next:

```
PUT chapter3/_mapping/order
{
  "properties": {
    "buyer": {
      "type": "keyword",
      "include_in_all": false
    },
    "seller": {
      "type": "keyword",
      "include_in_all": false
    },
    "item_title": {
      "type": "text"
    }
  }
}
```

In the next section, we will discuss analyzers and why mapping is essential to get the correct search results.

Difference between full-text search and exact match

In this section, we will describe analyzers and why they are necessary for text search. Let's say we have a document containing the following information:

```
{
    "date": "2017/02/01",
    "desc": "It will be raining in yosemite this weekend"
}
```

If we want to search for the documents that contain word `yosemite`, we could run an SQL query as shown here:

```
select * from news where desc like '%yosemite%'
```

This functionality is very limited and is never sufficient for real-world text-search queries. For example, if a user is looking for the weather forecast in Yosemite, he/she would query for the same in human language using something such as `rain in yosemite`. Since SQL can only match the exact words, and the document doesn't contain the word `rain`, the query will not come back with any results.

Elasticsearch is a full-text search engine and is built to handle these kinds of queries. Before the documents are indexed into Elasticsearch, the fields in the document are analyzed. Analyzing the data breaks the text phrases into individual terms, and depending on the analyzer we use, the words are reduced to their root forms. The following example will make it more clear. Elasticsearch provides the **Analyze API** to inspect how it analyzes the text internally. Let's see what happens when we analyze the document about yosemite, which contains the text `It will be raining in yosemite this weekend`:

```
GET
_analyze?analyzer=english&text=It+will+be+raining+in+yosemite+this+weekend
```

The response of the analyze API is a list of tokens as shown next:

```
{
    "tokens": [
        {
            "token": "rain",
            "start_offset": 11,
            "end_offset": 18,
            "type": "<ALPHANUM>",
            "position": 3
        },
        {
```

```
      "token": "yosemit",
      "start_offset": 22,
      "end_offset": 30,
      "type": "<ALPHANUM>",
      "position": 5
    },
    {

      "token": "weekend",
      "start_offset": 36,
      "end_offset": 43,
      "type": "<ALPHANUM>",
      "position": 7
    }
  ]
}
```

The text is broken down into three tokens: rain, yosemit, and weekend, and since we used the English language analyzer, the terms are also reduced to their root forms (raining became rain). The tokens you see in the preceding response are then stored in the inverted index. In the response, along with the token, position and offset information are also stored to support phrase search.

Similar to how the text fields in the document are analyzed during indexing, the text in the query is also analyzed. Let's take an example: when the user queries rain in yosemite it goes through a similar analysis process. We can use the _analyze API to look at how Elasticsearch break downs the search input as shown next:

```
GET _analyze?analyzer=english&text=rain+in+yosemite
```

The response of the analysis is shown here:

```
{
  "tokens": [
    {
      "token": "rain",
      "start_offset": 0,
      "end_offset": 4,
      "type": "<ALPHANUM>",
      "position": 0
    },
    {
      "token": "yosemit",
      "start_offset": 8,
      "end_offset": 16,
      "type": "<ALPHANUM>",
      "position": 2
    }
```

```
      ]
   }
```

You can see from the preceding response that the `rain in yosemite` query is broken down into the `"rain"` and `"yosemit"`. Using the tokens, Elasticsearch tries to find the documents in the inverted index. By default, the same analyzer is used for indexing and querying.

If no analyzer is specified in the mapping, all the text fields are analyzed using a standard analyzer, which splits the text on space and removes the casing and so on. If you want a language specific analyzer as shown in preceding example, we can specify the analyzer in the mapping. We can configure the analyzer of the `desc` field to use an English language analyzer, as shown next:

```
PUT chapter3/_mapping/weather
  {
    "properties": {
      "desc": {
        "type": "text",
        "analyzer": "english"
      }
    }
  }
```

Elasticsearch supports lots of analyzers out of the box. The default is the standard analyzer. You can check how each analyzer works using the Analyze API. For the complete list of all the analyzers Elasticsearch supports, please visit the following link:

```
https://www.elastic.co/guide/en/elasticsearch/reference/current/analysis-ana
lyzers.html
```

Core data types

In this section, we will discuss the core data types supported by Elasticsearch. You can set the mapping using the Mapping API.

Text

Starting Elasticsearch 5.0, the `string` data type is deprecated and replaced by the `text` and `keyword` data types. If you want to perform a full-text search as we discussed in the previous section, you should use `text` data type. If you only want an exact match, you should use `keyword` data type. We will discuss `keyword` data type in the next section.

Let's take the same example we used in `Chapter 1`, *Introduction to Elasticsearch*. We have a document containing the following fields:

```
{
    "date": "2017-01-01",
    "description": "Yosemite national park may be closed for the weekend due
to forecast of substantial rainfall"
}
```

For the description field in the preceding document, we should use text data type. Text fields are analyzed, and depending on what analyzer you use, it also takes care of removing stop words, such as `"a"` or `"the"`. You can set the mapping of the field description to text and the analyzer to English, as shown next:

```
PUT chapter3/_mapping/news
{
    "properties": {
        "description": {
            "type": "text",
            "analyzer": "english"
        }
    }
}
```

Text mapping also accepts several optional parameters. Most of these properties are to make the search more accurate. I will briefly describe these parameters in this section and talk about important parameters in more detail in `Chapter 6`, *All about search*. The following parameters are accepted:

- **analyzer**: This denotes the analyzer that should be used while indexing and searching.
- **boost**: Boost helps in ordering the search results. When one or more documents have the same relevancy score, boosting a field helps the ordering of the results. By default, all fields in the document are equally important. The default value is `1.0`. You can set the boost on a field, for example `price`, to `2.0`. When two or more products have the same relevancy score, the ordering of the products will be based on the price.
- **fielddata**: Fielddata is an in-memory data structure used to support sorting and aggregation for text fields. The default value is false.
- **fields**: For example, you have an item title that can be in English or German. Multifields will let you index the title field using an English analyzer and a German analyzer so that you search on both the fields during query time.

- **include_in_all**: This property is about whether to include this field in the `_all` field. The `_all` field helps you search for all the fields in the documents without specifying a field.
- **index**: This is used if you want the field to be searchable.
- **index_options**: When adding the field to the inverted index, this property specifies whether any additional information needs to be stored. It accepts docs, freqs, positions, and offsets and defaults to positions.
- **norms**: This is used when scoring the results to determine whether the length of the field should be taken into account.
- **position_increment_gap**: This property can be set to better support phase queries. Defaults to 100
- **store**: This determines whether the field should be stored in the `_source` field.
- **search_analyzer**: By default, the same analyzer that is used for indexing is used for searching. You can the change the `search_analyzer` using this property
- **search_quote_analyzer**: If you are searching for a phrase and want the phrase to be analyzed differently, this property can be set. This defaults to the search_analyzer
- **similarity**: The results of a search query are scored based on the similarity algorithm specified in this property. Defaults to BM25. We will discuss BM25 in detail in `Chapter 6`, *All about search.*
- **term_vector**: When a field is broken into individual terms, this property controls whether the term vectors need to be stored.

Some of the aforementioned properties could be very advanced. We will describe the important properties in the next sections.

Keyword

In the previous section, we discussed the `text` data type, which is used for free text search. Keyword data type should be used if you want the exact match. For example name, e-mail, city, and so on.

You can set the mapping of the name field to the keyword, as shown next:

```
PUT chapter3/_mapping/user
  {
    "properties": {
      "email": {
        "type": "keyword"
      }
```

```
        }
    }
```

The keyword data type is used for fields that need sorting or aggregations.

Date

The date data type is used to represent date fields in Elasticsearch. In JSON, the date fields are passed as a string. To parse the date correctly, you should tell Elasticsearch how the date string is formatted. If no format is specified, Elasticsearch tries to parse the date field using the `yyyy-MM-dd'T'HH:mm:ssz` format, also known as `strict_date_optional_time`, which requires date and optional time.

An example document is shown as follows:

```
{
    "creation_date": "2017-01-01",
    "desc": "Yosemite national park may be closed for the weekend due to
forecast of substantial rainfall"
}
```

You can tell Elasticsearch how `creation_date` is formatted in the mapping, as shown next:

```
PUT chapter3/_mapping/news
{
    "properties": {
        "creation_date": {
            "type": "date",
            "format": "yyyy-MM-dd"
        }
    }
}
```

If you are expecting the date in multiple formats, you can specify multiple formats separated by || in the format field. It will try each format until it finds a successful one. You can set multiple date formats in the mapping, as shown here:

```
PUT chapter3/_mapping/news
{
    "properties": {
        "creation_date": {
            "type": "date",
            "format": "YYYY-mm-dd||YYYY-mm-dd HH:mm:ss"
        }
    }
}
```

If no time zone is specified in the date, dates are stored in the **UTC** (**Universal Time Coordinated**) format. Internally, the date field is stored as a long number, which represents the number of milliseconds elapsed since Jan 1, 1970 (epoch).

Numeric

To represent numeric data type, Elasticsearch provides the following types:

- **long**: This is used to represent a long value (signed 64-bit integer)
- **integer**: This is used to represent an integer (signed 32-bit integer)
- **short**: This is used to represent a shot (signed 16-bit integer)
- **byte**: This is used to represent a byte (signed 8-bit integer)
- **double**: This is used to represent a double value (double precision float)
- **float**: This is used to represent a float value (single precision float)
- **half_float**: This is used to represent a half float value (half precision float)
- **scaled_float**: This is used to represent a float value with scaling factor

You can pick the data type that suits your need best as Elasticsearch optimizes the internal storage irrespective of the type you choose. Worth mentioning is the `scaled_float` data type. Since it's more expensive to store float than integers, Elasticsearch tries to optimize this by storing the float as an integer. It converts the float into an integer by multiplying the float value with the scaling factor. Let's take an example document as shown here:

```
{
  "date": "2017-01-01",
  "city": "San Jose"
  "temperature" : "71.50"
}
```

Since temperature can only have two decimal points, you can store the `temperature` field as `scaled_float` and set the scaling factor to `100`. You can set the mapping of the `temperature` field, as shown here:

```
PUT chapter3/_mapping/weather
{
  "properties": {
    "temperature": {
      "type": "scaled_float",
      "scaling_factor": "100"
    }
  }
}
```

Internally, temperature is stored as `71.50 * 100`, which is `7150`. How Elasticsearch stores the value internally is entirely transparent to the user. The higher the scaling factor, the more storage is used to store the float value.

Boolean

The boolean data type is used to represent boolean fields (true or false). Boolean mapping can be set as follows:

```
PUT chapter3/_mapping/boolean
{
   "properties": {
     "boolean_field": {
       "type": "boolean"
     }
   }
}
```

Binary

The binary data type is used to store a `Base64` encoded string. Binary data type fields are not indexed and only stored by default. You can set binary mapping as shown here:

```
PUT chapter3/_mapping/binary
{
   "properties": {
     "binary_field": {
       "type": "binary"
     }
   }
}
```

Binary data types can be used to blob data such as images, large objects compressed, and so on.

Complex data types

In the previous section, we talked about simple data types. In this section, we will talk about how to set mapping for arrays, objects, and nested objects.

Array

There is no special data type for an array. A field can contain one or more fields of the same data type. Let's look at an example where we have two documents, as shown next:

Document 1:

```
{ "keyword_field" : "keyword1" }
```

Document 2:

```
{
    "keyword_field" : ["keyword2", "keyword3"]
}
```

The mapping for `keyword_field` is defined as shown next:

```
{
    "properties": {
      "keyword_field": {
        "type": "keyword"
      }
    }
}
```

No special handling is required for arrays.

Object

Elasticsearch documents are JSON objects. A field in the document can be a simple integer or an entire object. For example, the person document as shown next contains name, which is a simple text field, and address, which is an object. And an address can also have inner objects. The person object is shown here:

```
{
   "id": 1,
   "name": "User1",
   "address": {
     "street": "123 High Lane",
     "city": "Big City"
   }
}
```

Unlike a simple data type, when an object is stored into inverted index, it is broken down into key-value pairs. The person document is stored as shown here:

```
{
    "id": 1,
    "name": "User1",
    "address.street": "123 High Lane",
    "address.city": "Big City"
}
```

Since the object is stored as key-value pairs, it gets tricky when you have an array of objects. Let's see what happens when the person has multiple addresses. The person document is represented as shown next:

```
{
  "id": 1,
  "name": "User1",
  "address": [
    {
       "street": "123 High Lane",
       "city": "Big City"
    },
    {
       "street" : "436 Low Lane",
       "city": "Small City"
    }
  ]
}
```

The preceding document is stored internally as follows:

```
{
    "id" : 1,
    "name" : "User1",
    "address.street" : ["123 High Lane", "436 Low Lane"]
    "address.city" : ["Big City", "Small City"]
}
```

When the address objects are stored in the inverted index, the relation between parts of the same address is lost. For example, if you query for all documents that contain street as `123 High Lane` and `Small City`, by looking at the original document, there should be no results. But the query comes back with the document we just indexed as a result. The relation between the `street` and `city` is lost due to how the document is stored. If your application needs the relation intact, you should use nested data type, which we will discuss in the next section.

You can set the object mapping type as shown next:

```
{
    "properties": {
      "id": {
        "type": "integer"
      },
      "name": {
        "type": "keyword"
      },
      "address": {
        "properties": {
          "street": {
            "type": "keyword"
          },
          "city": {
            "type": "keyword"
          }
        }
      }
    }
}
```

Please note that there is no special mapping for an array of addresses (object).

Nested

As we discussed in the previous section, when we have an array of objects, the array is flattened due to which the object relations don't exist anymore. To solve this, Elasticsearch provides nested datatype. When you use nested datatype, each object in the array is indexed as a new document internally. Since the objects are handled internally as separate documents, you have to use a special type of query to query nested documents. We will discuss nested queries and sorting in the *Handling document relations using nested* section of `Chapter 7`, *More than a search engine*.

The mapping for the address field can be set as nested, as shown next:

```
{
    "properties": {
      "id": {
        "type": "integer"
      },
      "name": {
        "type": "keyword"
      },
```

```
        "address_nested": {
          "type": "nested",
          "properties": {
            "street": {
              "type": "keyword"
            },
            "city": {
              "type": "keyword"
            }
          }
        }
      }
    }
  }
}
```

Please note how we explicitly set the type as nested for the `address_nested` field.

Geo data type

In the previous sections, we discussed the simple and complex data types Elasticsearch supports. In this section, how to store location-based data. Elasticsearch makes it very easy to work with location-based queries, such as querying within a radius, aggregations based on location, sorting by location, and so on. With the rapid growth of mobile, location is one of the key factors driving the search results. To run location-based queries, you have to set the field data type to geo.

Elasticsearch supports two data types to store location-based data:

- `geo-point`: This is used to store the longitude and latitude of a location.
- `geo-shape`: This is used to store geo shapes, such as circles and polygons.

In this section, we will only discuss how to set the mapping for the `geo-point` data type. The `geo-shape` data type is for storing geo shapes. To know more about geo-shape, please visit the following link:

`https://www.elastic.co/guide/en/elasticsearch/reference/current/geo-shape.html`

In the *Geo and Spatial Filtering* section of `chapter 7`, *More than a search engine*, we will discuss how to execute location based queries. Using geo queries is not very different from other queries, except for a few parameters.

Geo-point data type

We can set the geo-point data mapping for the `geo_location` field, as shown next:

```
PUT chapter3/_mapping/address
  {
    "properties": {
      "geo_location": {
        "type": "geo_point"
      }
    }
  }
```

In the following example, we will index an address document with geolocation:

```
PUT chapter3/address/1
{
  "street": "123 High Lane",
  "city": "Big City",
  "geo_location": {
    "lat": 37.3,
    "lon": 121.8
  }
}
```

Please make sure the mapping type for `geo_location` is set before you index the address document otherwise the `geo_location` field will be stored as an object with `lat` and `lon` as strings. If all goes well, you should see a response as follows:

```
{
  "_index": "chapter3",
  "_type": "address",
  "_id": "1",
  "_version": 1,
  "result": "created",
  "_shards": {
    "total": 1,
    "successful": 1,
    "failed": 0
  },
  "created": true
}
```

Note that the `geo_location` field value in the document can also be represented as:

- string in the format of `"lat,lon"` (`"geo_location"` : `"37.3,121.8"`)
- array with the format `[lon, lat]` (`"geo_location"` : `[121.8,37.3]`)
- geo hash (`"geo_location"` : `"wwws5wk01xyw"`)

Specialized data type

Elasticsearch supports the following specialized data types:

- **IP**: This is used to store IP address
- **Completion**: This is used to support the auto-complete feature
- **Percolator**: This is used to support reverse search

We will discuss IP data type in the next section. Completion and percolator are best explained with examples, and we will discuss them in detail in `Chapter 7`, *More than a search engine*.

IP

In the previous section, we discussed `geo` data type, which is used to store location-based data. In this section, we will discuss `IP` data type, which is used to store IP addresses. Both **IPv4** and **IPv6** addresses are supported. For example, we have a login history document, and we want to store the IP address of the client in the history. We can add an `ip_address` field to history mapping, as shown next:

```
PUT chapter3/_mapping/history
{
  "properties": {
    "ip_address": {
      "type": "ip"
    }
  }
}
```

You can index the history document with an IP address, as shown here:

```
{
    "username" : "user1",
    "ip_address" : "10.123.24.33",
    "login_status" : "SUCCESSFUL"
}
```

Mapping the same field with different mappings

Sometimes you want to index the same field with different mappings. For example, you want to index the title field both as text and as keyword. You can use the keyword field for an exact match and the text field for text search. You can do this by defining two fields, one with keyword mapping and other with text mapping, as shown next:

```
{
    "properties": {
      "title_text": {
        "type": "text"
      },
      "title_keyword": {
        "type": "keyword"
      }
    }
}
```

You can index the document as follows:

```
{
  "title_text"    : "Learning Elasticsearch",
  "title_keyword" : "Learning Elasticsearch"
}
```

While indexing, the same value is used for both the `title_text` and `title_keyword` fields. The document source will now have two fields with the same value. To avoid data duplication, while indexing and storing the document source, Elasticsearch provides **fields mapping**.

Using fields mapping, the same field can be indexed as both text and keyword. As shown in the mapping below, `title` will be indexed as text and `title.exact` will be indexed as keyword which can be used for exact match, sorting and so on.

The multi-fields mappings for title field is shown here:

```
{
    "properties": {
      "title": {
        "type": "text",
        "fields": {
          "exact": {
            "type": "keyword"
          }
        }
      }
    }
}
```

You can index the document as follows:

```
{
  "title" : "Learning Elasticsearch"
}
```

With the multi fields mapping set, during indexing, Elasticsearch will internally index the title field both as text and keyword. The keyword field can be accessible via `title.exact`.

Handling relations between different document types

In the relational world, data is often divided into multiple tables and is linked using foreign keys. To get the data, a join is used to combine data from one or more tables. But in the NoSQL world, data is usually denormalized and stored as one big document. However, it is often advantageous to store these documents separately. Data in Elasticsearch is immutable. An update to an existing document means fetching the old document, applying the change, and re-indexing it as a new document. The update is an expensive operation. If possible, we have to keep the updates to a minimum.

For example, a blog article can have one or more comments, and an order can have one or more line items. If we can separate the article and comment documents, we don't have to update the article when there is a new comment. Elasticsearch provides two ways to handle the relations between the documents. The first one is parent-child, and the second is nested. Both have their pros and cons. First, let's discuss the parent-child document relation.

Note that Apache Lucene, the underlying data store, only stores data as flat documents. Elasticsearch adds the abstraction above Lucene to handle relationships between the documents.

Parent-child document relation

For parent-child document relations, the relationship between two different document types is set by specifying the parent ID while indexing the child documents. Parent and child document types are separate documents, both accessible using their IDs. We index both the documents like any other regular documents, but when indexing the child document, the parent ID is required. It is a one-to-many relationship. A parent document can have multiple child documents, but a child document can only have one parent document.

You should consider using parent-child document relations in the following cases:

- Updates to parent and child documents are independent. For example, a new comment can be added without updating the parent article
- The child documents are updated more than the parent documents

Let's set the mappings for a blog application, you have article type, which is the parent, and comment type, which is the child. The parent-child mapping between article and comment can be set as shown next:

```
PUT blog
{
  "mappings": {
    "article": { #Parent
      "properties": {
        "title": {
          "type": "text"
        },
        "category": {
          "type": "keyword"
        }
      }
    },
    "comment": { #Child
      "_parent": {
        "type": "article"
      },
      "properties": {
        "comment": {
```

```
        "type": "text"
      },
      "userid": {
        "type": "keyword"
      }
    }
  }
}
```

Once the mapping is set, documents can be indexed as follows:

```
#Parent
PUT blog/article/1
{
  "title" : "Hello world !!",
  "category" : "Introduction"
}

#Children
PUT blog/comment/10?parent=1
{
  "comment" : "This world is awesome",
  "userid" : "user1"
}
```

The article document (parent) is indexed like a regular document, but when indexing the comment document (child), the ID of the article (parent) is specified.

Elasticsearch provides has_child/has_parent to support querying parent-child. For example, we can query all the articles that contain comments from a particular user, as shown next:

```
POST blog/article/_search
  {
    "query": {
      "has_child": {
        "type": "comment",
        "query": {
          "term": {
            "userid": "user1"
          }
        }
      }
    }
  }
```

Don't worry if the preceding query doesn't make sense. We will discuss parent-child queries in detail in the *Handling document relations using parent-child* section in `Chapter 7`, *More than a search engine*. Although the parent-child document relation seems very promising, queries are very expensive as the Elasticsearch has to maintain the mapping between parent and child documents in memory.

How are parent-child documents stored internally?

A child document is stored in the same shard as the parent document. By storing both the documents on the same shard, Elasticsearch can avoid extra trips to fetch the data. When indexing the child document, it uses the parent ID to find the shard where the parent document exists. What makes parent-child queries expensive is managing the mapping between parent and child documents. Elasticsearch stores the join information in what it calls **global-ordinals**, which are lazily built the first time the query is executed.

Nested

We discussed how to set the mappings for nested documents in the nested data type section before. When documents are stored as nested documents, they are stored as hidden documents and are managed by Elasticsearch. But the disadvantage is that to update the parent or the nested document, the entire document needs to be updated. For example, we have the user document as shown here:

```
{
  "id": 1,
  "name": "User1",
  "address": [ #Nested
     {
        "street": "123 High Lane",
        "city": "Big City"
     },
     {
        "street" : "436 Low Lane",
        "city": "Small City"
     }
  ]
}
```

To update parent document fields like `name` or to update the nested document fields like `street` the entire user document needs to updated. Nested documents like address cannot be accessed independently as they are hidden.

Because of how nested documents are stored, queries on nested documents are much faster when compared to parent-child. But, if you have to update child documents more frequently than the parent document or vice versa, as the parent/child documents can be updated independently, parent-child may be a better fit depending on the application needs.

Elasticsearch supports querying nested documents using nested queries. We will talk about nested queries in the *Handling document relations using nested* section in `Chapter 7`, *More than a search engine*.

Routing

We discussed before that an index contains one or more shards. During indexing, the document ID is used to determine which shard the document belongs to, using a simple formula as follows:

```
hash(document_id) % no_of_shards
```

To retrieve a document using the document ID, the same formula is used to determine the shard the document belongs to, and the document is retrieved:

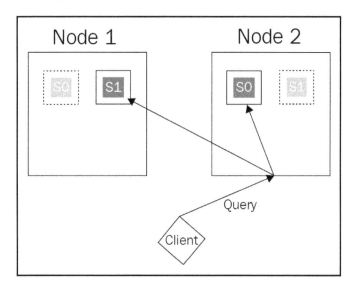

When executing a search query, the node that receives the request is known as the **coordinating node**. The coordinating node (Node2) sends the query to all the shards of the index, aggregates the results, and sends them back to the client.

By default, a query has to be executed on all the shards of the index. But if you have a way to group similar data together, routing can be used to send the requests to a single shard instead of all the shards in the index.

For example, you want to use Elasticsearch to power the order history of an e-commerce site, the user should be able to query for his/her orders. We can use routing to store all the orders that belong to the a user in the same shard. When querying for the orders that belong to a user, Elasticsearch will use the routing value (user ID) to determine the shard and execute the query only on a single shard. Without routing, the query needs to be executed on all the shards.

 Potential downfalls of using routing are hot spots. If some users in the system are much bigger than others, there is a possibility that all the big users can end up in the same shard. This leads to uneven distribution of data and underutilization of resources and can potentially bring down the entire cluster.

At the time of indexing, you should specify the ID on which the document should be routed. Instead of using the document ID, the routing value is used to determine the shard. For example, if all the orders are indexed using the user ID as the routing value, when querying for orders placed by `user1`, the query needs to executed only on one shard.

The order mapping with routing can be configured as follows:

```
PUT chapter3/_mapping/order
{
  "_routing": {
    "required": true
  },
  "properties": {
    "order_id": {
      "type": "text"
    },
    "user_id": {
      "type": "keyword"
    },
    "order_total": {
      "type": "integer"
    }
  }
}
```

Once the mapping is set, we can index the document and set the routing as follows:

```
PUT chapter3/order/1?routing=user1
  {
    "order_id": "23y86",
    "user_id": "user1",
    "order_total": 15
  }
```

Note how we set the routing in the URL when we are indexing the order. If the routing value is not specified, a routing exception is thrown. We can get the order document we just indexed as shown here:

```
GET chapter3/order/1?routing=user1
```

Since the routing value is used to determine the shard the document lives in, we have to specify the routing value to retrieve the document using its ID.

Summary

In this chapter, you learned about various simple and complex data types Elasticsearch supports. You also learned how to handle unstructured data using dynamic mappings. We discussed how full-text search works and the difference between exact match and full-text search. We discussed how to manage document relations. We also covered routing and how it works.

In the next chapter, we will discuss how to index and update your data.

4
Indexing and Updating Your Data

In the previous chapter, we discussed how to model your data. In this chapter, we will discuss how to index and update your data. We will start by discussing how to index and what happens when you index a document. Elasticsearch is a **near real-time** system, meaning the data you index is available for search only after a small delay. We will discuss the reason for this delay and how we can control the delay. This chapter will also show you various ways to update your data and we will discuss what happens when you update a document and why updates are expensive.

In this chapter, we will cover the following:

- Indexing your data
- Updating your data
- Using Kibana to discover
- Using Elasticsearch in your application
- How Elasticsearch handles concurrency
- How primary and replica shards interact

Indexing your data

Document are indexed using the index API. We can index a new person document into the `chapter4` index as shown here:

```
PUT chapter4/person/1
{
  "id": 1,
```

```
      "name": "user1",
      "age": "55",
      "gender": "M",
      "email": "user1@gmail.com",
      "last_modified_date": "2017-02-15"
  }
```

The document we just indexed is uniquely identified by the index, type and identifier. You can either specify your identifier or let Elasticsearch pick one for you. If you want to specify an identifier, you have to use the PUT HTTP method. If you use the POST HTTP method, a unique identifier is automatically assigned to the document. The response to the preceding command is shown as follows:

```
  {
    "_index": "chapter4",
    "_type": "person",
    "_id": "1",
    "_version": 1,
    "result": "created",
    "_shards": {
      "total": 2,
      "successful": 1,
      "failed": 0
    },
    "created": true
  }
```

An index operation creates the document if the document doesn't exist already. If a document with same ID already exists, the contents of the document are replaced with the request and the version is incremented. You will see a response as shown next:

```
  {
    "_index": "chapter4",
    "_type": "person",
    "_id": "1",
    "_version": 2,
    "result": "updated",
    "_shards": {
      "total": 2,
      "successful": 1,
      "failed": 0
    },
    "created": false
  }
```

You can see from the response that result is updated and created is set to false. You can also tell Elasticsearch to only create by specifying the op type, as shown here:

```
PUT chapter4/person/1?op_type=create
{
  "id": 1,
  "name": "user1",
  "age": "55",
  "gender": "M",
  "email": "user1@gmail.com",
  "last_modified_date": "2017-02-15"
}
```

If the document with the same ID already exists, the operation is rejected, and you will see that a document already exists error in the response. The response is shown as follows:

```
{
   "error": {
     "root_cause": [
        {
           "type": "version_conflict_engine_exception",
           "reason": "[person][1]: version conflict, document already exists
(current version [2])",
           "index_uuid": "9rcbu7LZR42te04D_G9r-g",
           "shard": "0",
           "index": "chapter4"
        }
     ],
     "type": "version_conflict_engine_exception",
     "reason": "[person][1]: version conflict, document already exists
(current version [2])",
     "index_uuid": "9rcbu7LZR42te04D_G9r-g",
     "shard": "0",
     "index": "chapter4"
   },
   "status": 409
 }
```

The response is sent with a `409 Conflict` HTTP response code.

Indexing errors

Different kinds of errors can happen during indexing. In this section, we will list the most common errors and how to handle them.

Node/shards errors

Node/shards errors can occur if the node is not available or the shard is not allocated to a node. Index and query responses contain a shards section, which will tell us the number of the shards on which the operation is successful. Even though the operation is not successful on all the shards, Elasticsearch will respond with **partial** results. For example, if you are executing a query on an index with two shards and one of the shards is not available, the query response comes back with the results from just one shard. It is important to watch for the number of shards the operation is successful from the response.

Let's index a person document as shown here:

```
PUT chapter4/person/2
  {
    "id": 2,
    "name": "user2",
    "age": "55",
    "gender": "M",
    "email": "user2@gmail.com",
    "last_modified_date": "2017-02-18"
  }
```

The response to the preceding query is shown as follows:

```
  {
    "_index": "chapter4",
    "_type": "person",
    "_id": "2",
    "_version": 1,
    "result": "created",
    "_shards": {
      "total": 2,
      "successful": 1,
      "failed": 0
    },
    "created": true
  }
```

You can see from the response that the total number of shards is 2, and the indexing is only successful on 1 shard. In the preceding example, our cluster has only one node. When an index is created, by default, it is created with one replica. The primary shard and the replica of a shard cannot be allocated on the same node. As the cluster has only one node, the replica shard couldn't be assigned to a node in the cluster, and the indexing operation is successful only on the primary shard.

Serialization/mapping errors

These kinds of errors happen due to JSON serialization issues or if you are trying to index an integer into a string field. For example, you are trying to index a person document, and the mapping for the age field is set to an integer. If you try to index one as the age field as shown next, you will see a mapping error:

```
PUT chapter4/person/3
{
  "id": 3,
  "name": "user3",
  "age": "one",
  "gender": "M",
  "email": "user3@gmail.com",
  "last_modified_date": "2017-02-18"
}
```

The response to the preceding request is shown next:

```
{
    "error": {
      "root_cause": [
        {
          "type": "mapper_parsing_exception",
          "reason": "failed to parse [age]"
        }
      ],
      "type": "mapper_parsing_exception",
      "reason": "failed to parse [age]",
      "caused_by": {
        "type": "number_format_exception",
        "reason": "For input string: \"one\""
      }
    },
    "status": 400
}
```

Thread pool rejection error

Elasticsearch has a thread pool for index, search, bulk, refresh and so on. If the thread pool for indexing is full, Elasticsearch will reject the indexing operation. If you get this error occasionally, you can add application logic to retry the index operation. If you are getting this error frequently, you should consider getting better hardware or increase the thread pool size.

The thread pool size is based on the number of CPU processors available in the node. Elasticsearch doesn't recommend changing the default thread pool size unless you know what you are doing.

Managing an index

We discussed in Chapter 3, *Modeling your data and document relations*, how we could index a document without creating the index or setting the mapping first. Elasticsearch automatically creates the index with the default settings and uses dynamic mapping to figure out the mapping. In the previous section, we indexed a document into the chapter4 index. Let's inspect the default settings:

```
GET chapter4/_settings
```

You will see a response as follows:

```
{
    "chapter4": {
      "settings": {
        "index": {
          "creation_date": "1493529955647",
          "number_of_shards": "5",
          "number_of_replicas": "1",
          "uuid": "gvScXYjKQVmS6HsYub_Rbg",
          "version": {
            "created": "5010299"
          },
          "provided_name": "chapter4"
        }
      }
    }
}
```

You can see from the preceding response that the index has been created with the default settings of 5 shards and 1 replica meaning 5 primary shards and 5 replica shards. If you need to change the default settings, you have to delete the existing index and recreate the index. Let's delete the chapter4 index so that we can recreate it. You can delete the chapter4 index as shown next:

```
DELETE chapter4
```

Note that the HTTP method is DELETE. This single command deletes the index, which cannot be undone. Please double check the index name before running the delete command.

Let's recreate the chapter4 index with 3 shards and 1 replicas:

```
PUT chapter4
{
  "settings": {
    "index": {
      "number_of_shards": "3",
      "number_of_replicas": "1"
    }
  }
}
```

Now, let's verify the index settings:

```
GET chapter4/_settings
```

You will see the response as follows:

```
{
    "chapter4": {
      "settings": {
        "index": {
          "creation_date": "1493530055030",
          "number_of_shards": "3",
          "number_of_replicas": "1",
          "uuid": "1eBr7XoMTgyzryJRl4wG8g",
          "version": {
            "created": "5010299"
          },
          "provided_name": "chapter4"
        }
      }
    }
}
```

Once the index is created, the number of shards in the index cannot be changed. If you want to increase or decrease the number of shards you have to create a new index with new settings and re-index the data. Starting Elasticsearch 5.0, you can use the reindex API to recreate an index with different index configurations. We will discuss the reindex API in detail in Chapter 5, *Organizing Your Data and Bulk Data Ingestion*.

Unlike the number of shards, the number of replicas can be increased or decreased on the fly as follows:

```
PUT chapter4/_settings
{
  "index": {
    "number_of_replicas": 2
  }
}
```

You should see an acknowledged response as follows:

```
{"acknowledged":true}
```

As shown in the preceding response, Elasticsearch accepted the request and will start working on replicating the shards in the background. We created the index with the required shard configuration. Next, let's set mappings for the `chapter4` index, `product` type as shown here:

```
PUT chapter4/_mapping/product
{
    "properties": {
      "id": {
        "type": "integer"
      },
      "name": {
        "type": "text"
      },
      "age": {
        "type": "integer"
      },
      "gender": {
        "type": "keyword"
      },
      "email": {
        "type": "keyword"
      },
      "last_modified_date": {
        "type": "date"
      }
    }
  }
```

We can also set both the `settings` and `mappings` while creating the index as shown next:

```
PUT /chapter4
{
    "settings": {
```

```
        "index": {
          "number_of_shards": "3",
          "number_of_replicas": "1"
        }
      },
      "mappings": {
        "product": {
          "properties": {
            "id": {
              "type": "integer"
            },
            "name": {
              "type": "text"
            },
            "age": {
              "type": "integer"
            },
            "gender": {
              "type": "keyword"
            },
            "email": {
              "type": "keyword"
            },
            "last_modified_date": {
              "type": "date"
            }
          }
        }
      }
    }
```

Now we can index the documents, and there shouldn't be any surprises.

What happens when you index a document?

In this section, we will discuss what happens internally when you index a document. An Elasticsearch index is nothing but a collection of shards. Each shard, as we discussed before, is an Apache Lucene index. To be able to search for the documents, the fields in the documents are analyzed and stored in an inverted index. Unlike SQL databases, Elasticsearch is a near real-time search engine, meaning the documents you index are only available after a small delay. The default is 1 sec. By the end of this section, it will be clear why there is a delay and how we can control the delay.

First, let's recreate the `chapter4` index with 2 shards and 1 replica:

```
DELETE chapter4

PUT chapter4
{
  "settings": {
    "index": {
      "number_of_shards": "2",
      "number_of_replicas": "1"
    }
  }
}
```

Let's index a document into the `chapter4` index we just created:

```
PUT chapter4/person/2
{
    "id": 2,
    "name": "user2",
    "age": "55",
    "gender": "M",
    "email": "user2@gmail.com",
    "last_modified_date": "2017-02-18"
}
```

Since an index can have one more shard, Elasticsearch first determines the shard the document belongs to using the `hash(document_id) % number_of_shards` formula. When retrieving the document by its `id`, the same formula is used to determine the shard and fetch the document.

Just like an Elasticsearch index is made up of multiple shards, a shard (Lucene index) is made up of multiple segments (s1, s2, s3) as shown next. The following diagram represents the internals of a shard:

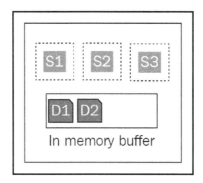

When you index a document into the Lucene index (shard), the document is first written to an in-memory buffer. A process known as `refresh` wakes up on a schedule and reads the documents from the in-memory buffer and creates a new `segment`. In the preceding diagram, the next time the Lucene index is refreshed, a new `S4` segment is created, which contains documents `D1` and `D2`.

Each Lucene segment is an independent index that can be searched. As new documents are added, the refresh process reads the documents from the in-memory buffer and creates new segments. The segment contains the inverted index and other information required for searching the documents. When a new segment is created, it is first written to the file system cache and committed to the physical disk when certain conditions are met.

 File system cache is a system memory where a file read from the physical disk is cached. The next read operation reads the file directly from memory. File system cache is a cache between processes and the physical disk. Any writes to the file are written to cache and not the physical disk. At regular intervals, the data in the file system cache is written to the disk. In this way, the operating system optimizes the cost of reading and witting from the physical disk.

By default, the refresh interval is `1` second, due to which the documents indexed are only available for search after `1` second. If you need a document to be searchable immediately after you index, you can set `refresh` to `true`, as shown next:

```
PUT chapter4/person/3?refresh=true
{
    "id": 3,
    "name": "User3",
    "age": "55",
    "gender": "M",
    "email": "user3@gmail.com",
    "last_modified_date": "2017-02-15"
}
```

The preceding command will index and refresh so that the document is visible for search immediately. You can also manually refresh the entire `chapter4` index as shown next:

```
POST chapter4/_refresh
```

You can refresh all indexes as follows:

```
POST /_refresh
```

Refresh is a costly operation, and depending on whether you need real-time search, you can increase or decrease the refresh interval. If your data doesn't have to be searchable immediately after you index, you should consider increasing the refresh interval. For example, we set the refresh interval to `30s`, the data indexed into the `chapter4` index is only searchable after 30 seconds. We can increase the refresh interval for the `chapter4` index to `30` seconds as shown next :

```
PUT chapter4/_settings
{
  "index": {
    "refresh_interval": "30s"
  }
}
```

During bulk indexing, you can disable refresh temporarily to increase the indexing performance. Refresh can be disabled by setting `refresh_interval` to `-1`. After the indexing is done, you can set the `refresh_interval` back to what it was before.

Updating your data

In this section, we will discuss different ways of updating existing documents. Internally, an update is always a delete and re-index. You can update using the entire document (replacing the original document), or update a single field or add a new field, or update a field using scripts, such as incrementing a counter.

Update using an entire document

When you index a document with the existing document ID, it will replace the current document with the new document. As shown next, we can update the document ID `1` using the entire document:

```
PUT chapter4/person/1
{
  "id": 1,
  "name": "name update 1",
  "age": 55,
  "gender": "M",
  "email": "user1@gmail.com",
  "last_modified_date": "2017-02-15"
}
```

The response is as follows:

```
{
    "_index": "chapter4",
    "_type": "person",
    "_id": "1",
    "_version": 2,
    "result": "updated",
    "_shards": {
      "total": 2,
      "successful": 1,
      "failed": 0
    },
    "created": false
}
```

You can see from the response that the result of the operation is updated, version is 2, and created is false.

Partial updates

In the previous section, we discussed how to update using the entire document. In this section, we will discuss how to update only one or two fields in the document. Elasticsearch provides the update API to update an existing document partially. The update API first retrieves the old document, then uses the _source of the existing documents to apply the changes, deletes the old document, and indexes the document as a new document. The fields to be updated are specified in the doc field of the request.

 For partial updates to work, _source needs to enabled.

Let's say we want to update just the name of the person and not worry about any other field in the document. We will use the update API to update the existing document as shown next:

```
POST chapter4/person/1/_update
{
  "doc": {
    "name": "name udpate 2"
  }
}
```

The response is as follows:

```
{
  "_index": "chapter4",
  "_type": "person",
  "_id": "1",
  "_version": 3,
  "result": "updated",
  "_shards": {
  "total": 2,
  "successful": 1,
  "failed": 0
  }
}
```

You can see from the response that the result of the operation is updated, version is 3.

Scripted updates

Scripted updates will come in handy when you want to update a document based on a condition. Without a way to script, you have to first retrieve the document, check the conditions on the document, apply the changes, and re-index the document. Partial updates retrieve the document internally from the shard, recursively apply the changes, and re-index the documents avoiding the network round trips.

Scripted updates can also be used to increment a counter. The application doesn't have to worry about the current value. We can increment the age field in the person document using script as shown next:

```
POST chapter4/person/1/_update
{
   "script": "ctx._source.age+=1"
}
```

Elasticsearch supports many scripting languages to execute inline scripts, the default scripting language is Painless. Let's say we want to classify a document we indexed before into adults and teenagers. We can use an inline script as shown next to check the person's age and add a new field called person_type. The following command will update a person document based on a script:

```
POST chapter4/person/1/_update
  {
     "script": {
       "inline": "if (ctx._source.age > params.age) { ctx._source.person_type
= 'adult' } else { ctx._source.person_type = 'teenager' }",
```

```
        "params": {
          "age": 19
        }
    }
}
```

Now, let's retrieve the person document with ID 2. The response is as follows:

```
{
    "id": 2,
    "name": "name update 1",
    "age": "55",
    "gender": "M",
    "email": "user2@gmail.com",
    "last_modified_date": "2017-02-18",
    "person_type": "adult"
}
```

You can see from the response that a new `person_type` field is added to the document.

Upsert

We discussed in the previous section that if you want to update only a few fields in the document, you can do so by specifying the fields in the doc field of the request. When partially updating a document, if the document doesn't already exist, the update will fail. If you want to create a new document, if the document doesn't exist, you can set the `doc_as_upsert` flag to true. Setting the upsert to true will create a new document with the fields in the doc field. Let's take an example:

```
POST chapter4/person/3/_update
{
    "doc": {
      "name": "user3"
    },
    "doc_as_upsert": true
}
```

In the preceding example, since the person document with ID 3 doesn't exist, a new document with fields in the doc is created. Now, let's retrieve the person document with ID 3. The response is as follows:

```
{
    "_index": "chapter4",
    "_type": "person",
    "_id": "3",
```

```
      "_version": 1,
      "found": true,
      "_source": {
         "name": "user3"
      }
   }
```

You can see from the response that the new document only contains the name field.

NOOP

We updated the name of the person document ID 2 to `name update 2` in the previous section, as shown here:

```
POST chapter4/person/2/_update
{
   "doc": {
      "name": "name update 2"
   }
}
```

If you try to run the update again, the operation is ignored as there is no change. The response will contain the result as `noop`, as shown here:

```
{
   "_index": "chapter4",
   "_type": "person",
   "_id": "2",
   "_version": 1,
   "result": "noop",
   "_shards": {
      "total": 0,
      "successful": 0,
      "failed": 0
   }
}
```

You can disable this behavior by setting the detect_noop to false:

```
POST chapter4/person/2/_update
{
   "doc" : {
      "name" : "name update 2"
   },
   "detect_noop" : "false"
}
```

With `detect_noop` set to `false`, it will update the document no matter what. The response is as follows:

```
{
    "_index": "chapter4",
    "_type": "person",
    "_id": "2",
    "_version": 2,
    "result": "updated",
    "_shards": {
      "total": 2,
      "successful": 1,
      "failed": 0
    }
}
```

What happens when you update a document?

In the previous section, we discussed what happens when you index a document. In this section, we will discuss how document updates are handled and why an update is an expensive operation.

As discussed before, when a document is indexed, it's stored in a segment. By design, a segment once created cannot be changed. Being immutable offers several advantages. For example, once the segment file is read into the file system cache, it can live there forever as it doesn't change, and Lucene doesn't have to worry about locking the file for any changes. But if a segment cannot be modified, how can we update an existing document? To perform an update, first the existing document is soft deleted, and the updated document is indexed as a new document.

 As the data in the segments cannot be changed, delete operation is a soft delete. The ID of the document is recorded into a file that tracks the list of deleted documents.

Merging segments

By default, the refresh process creates a new segment every second. This will result in the creation of lots of segments. As a search on the shard has to go through all the segments in the shard, having lots of segments will slow down the search performance.

Segments also need lots of resources, such as file handlers, CPU, disk space, and memory. Since segments are immutable, any updates and deletes are only soft deleted due to which we will eventually run out of disk space. To decrease the number of segments, Lucene merges the segments of similar size into a bigger segment. While merging the segments, the documents that are marked as deleted are not copied to the merged segment. Until the segments merge, the document is not physically removed from the disk:

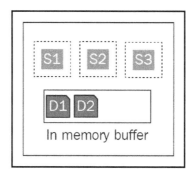

While the old segments are merged into a bigger segment, search requests are still served from the old segments. Once the merge is complete, new segments can serve the search requests and old segments are removed from the disk. The more the updates, the more frequently segments are merged. Merging involves CPU, memory, and I/O resources due to which updates are expensive.

Using Kibana to discover

Kibana UI makes it very easy to explore and visualize your data. You can add filters based on the fields in the document in click of a button and inspect the document source. For each field, you can see the top five values and their field value statistics. In this section, we will discuss how to explore using Kibana. Open Kibana by going to `http://localhost:5601/`.

Before you can use an index in Kibana, you have to tell Kibana to use an index name or an index pattern. To do this, perform the following steps:

1. Go to the Management tab on the left.
2. Select Index Patterns
3. In the Index Patterns page, select the **+Add New** button.

4. Input the index name as `chapter4`, and select the time-field name as `last_modified_date`.
5. Click on **Create**.

Now go to the Discover tab on the left navigation bar, and you should see a screen as shown here:

Since we configured the time-field name as `last_modified_date`, a histogram with the distribution of the documents is shown. You can also add filters for the fields in the document. To filter the documents that contain gender `equal` to M, perform the following steps:

- Click on gender in the field list on the left. The top five values for the field are displayed.
- Click on the **Positive Filter** icon (magnifying glass with the + symbol).
- The documents are now filtered, and gender M is highlighted in the source of the document.

Kibana, by default, adds a date time filter for the last 15 minutes. In the preceding example, since `last_modified_date` is set as the time field, it adds the filter for `last_modified_date > now-15m` to all the requests. If you cannot see any documents, that is because of the date time filter. You can change the time range by clicking on the clock icon in the top right corner.

You should see a screen similar to this:

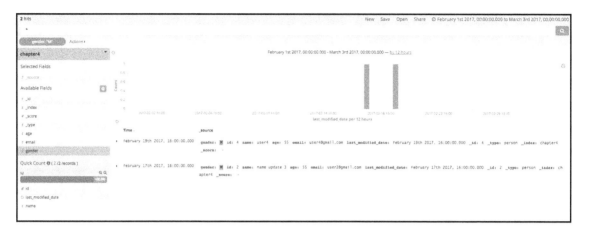

You can change the time range by selecting the clock icon in the top right corner. You can also sort the documents by the values in the field by clicking on the field name in the documents table header.

Using Elasticsearch in your application

Until this chapter, we used HTTP clients, such as Kibana or Postman, to talk to Elasticsearch. In this section, we will discuss how to integrate Elasticsearch into your application.

You can talk to Elasticsearch in two ways:

- **Rest API**: You can use any HTTP clients, such as Apache HTTP client or Jersey to interact with the REST API. If your application is Java based, you should consider using the Elasticsearch Java REST Client. We will discuss this in more detail in the *Java REST Client* section.
- **Native Client**: Elasticsearch has a native client for almost all major languages, such as Java, .NET, PHP, and so on. There are also many community-supported clients. For more details about the officially supported clients, please visit `https ://www.elastic.co/guide/en/elasticsearch/client/index.html`.

For Java, along with the REST client, Elasticsearch also supports transport and node clients. Transport and node clients use the TCP protocol for communications, other clients use HTTP to communicate with the cluster.

Official clients provide more than just a way to interact with Elasticsearch. They also offer the following:

- Round robins the requests between all the nodes in the cluster.
- Automatic node discovery (sniffing).
- Automatic failover in case of node failure.
- Connection pooling/persistence. Opening a new TCP connection for every request is very expensive, and the connection polling significantly improves the performance.
- Trace-level logging. When the trace level is turned on, every request and response is logged, which is great for debugging purposes.

Java

As you know Elasticsearch is a Java-based application, and along with the REST client, it also supports two native clients (Transport and Node). Like anything else, there are pros/cons while choosing one over the other. The easiest to get started with is the transport client as it would come with the request/response builders. We will discuss further details in the following sections.

The following are the choices for a Java-based application:

- Transport client
- Node client
- Rest client
- Third party clients

Transport client

The transport client connects to Elasticsearch using the transport protocol, a binary protocol used internally for communication between the nodes. The transport client handles serialization of the data with very little or almost no overhead. When using the transport client, it is recommended to have both the client and the server on the same Elasticsearch and JVM versions. Along with handling the request/response, it also takes care of discovering the cluster state and load balancing the requests between all the nodes in the cluster.

Dependencies

You can add the transport client to your application using Maven or Gradle:

```
<dependency>
    <groupId>org.elasticsearch.client</groupId>
    <artifactId>transport</artifactId>
    <version>5.1.2</version>
</dependency>
```

As shown in this code snippet, you can include the latest version of Elasticsearch transport client dependency in your pom.xml file.

The Gradle version is as follows:

```
dependencies {
    compile group: 'org.elasticsearch.client', name: 'transport', version:
'5.1.2'
}
```

You also need to add log4j2 dependencies:

```
<dependency>
    <groupId>org.apache.logging.log4j</groupId>
    <artifactId>log4j-api</artifactId>
    <version>2.7</version>
</dependency>
<dependency>
    <groupId>org.apache.logging.log4j</groupId>
    <artifactId>log4j-core</artifactId>
    <version>2.7</version>
</dependency>
```

Initializing the client

Once you have added the transport client dependency, you can initialize the client as shown here:

```
TransportAddress node1 =
new InetSocketTransportAddress(InetAddress.getByName("node1"), 9300);

TransportAddress node2 =
new InetSocketTransportAddress(InetAddress.getByName("node2"), 9300);

Settings setting = Settings.builder().put("cluster.name",
"elasticsearch").build();

TransportClient client = new PreBuiltTransportClient(settings);
```

```
//Add the known nodes to the client
client.addTransportAddress(node1);
client.addTransportAddress(node2);
```

To initialize the client, you need the following:

- Cluster name
- IP address of the nodes in the clusters
- Port numbers if Elasticsearch is not running on the defaults ports (Note that the port used is 9300 instead of 9200)

Sniffing

In the preceding example, we initialized the client with node1 and node2. By default, the transport client will round robin the requests between the nodes provided during the client initialization. The transport client can also be configured to automatically get the list of other nodes in the cluster. If nodes are added/removed from the cluster, transport client can automatically discover the cluster state. Periodically, it will refresh the list of available nodes and exclude the faulty nodes. When initializing the client, this can be enabled by setting the client.transport.sniff to true.

When sniffing is enabled, the client calls the cluster state API on a schedule to get the cluster state. The cluster state is refreshed automatically every 5 sec by default. Sniffing will make sure your application can still run despite node failures. You can enable client sniffing as shown next:

```
TransportAddress node1 =
new InetSocketTransportAddress(InetAddress.getByName("node1"), 9300);

TransportAddress node2 =
new InetSocketTransportAddress(InetAddress.getByName("node2"), 9300);

Settings setting = Settings.builder()
.put("cluster.name", "elasticsearch")
.put("client.transport.sniff", true)
.build();

TransportClient client = new PreBuiltTransportClient(settings);

//Add the known nodes to the client
client.addTransportAddress(node1);
client.addTransportAddress(node2);
```

The disadvantages of using the transport client are as follows:

- Being an internal protocol, you need to use the same Elasticsearch version on both the client and the server.
- You might also have to deal with any dependency version mismatches between Elasticsearch dependencies, such as log4j, Jackson, Joda, and your application.
- The transport client comes with the entire Elasticsearch dependencies, such as Apache Lucene, and so on.

The advantages of using the transport client are as follows:

- It uses TCP to communicate with the cluster. TCP being a low-level protocol than HTTP, the performance is better when using TCP.
- It comes with the complete request and response builders. No client serialization/deserialization of request/response is required.
- It offers connection pooling/persistence. Creating a new TCP connection for every request is very expensive.

Node client

Similar to transport client, node client is a native client that uses a binary protocol to communicate with Elasticsearch. The difference is when using a node client, the node client is added as one of the nodes to the cluster. And since the client is part of the cluster, it can route the request to the correct nodes directly, saving a few network hopes. Since the node client acts as one of the nodes in the cluster, other nodes ping the node client. This is a problem if you have a large cluster. Unless your performance benchmarks says the node client is better, it is recommended to use the transport or REST client.

REST client

Using transport client means you need to have all the Elasticsearch dependencies in your application and deal with any library version conflicts between Elasticsearch and your application. Starting Elasticsearch 5.0, a new REST client is introduced to solve this problem. The REST client uses the Apache HTTP client internally. The REST client, apart from calling the Elasticsearch REST API, also takes care of discovering other nodes in the cluster, failure handling, and a lot more.

You can add the REST client dependency to your application using Maven or Gradle. The following is an example of using Maven:

```
<dependency>
    <groupId>org.elasticsearch.client</groupId>
    <artifactId>rest</artifactId>
    <version>5.1.2</version>
</dependency>
```

You can include the latest version of Elasticsearch REST client dependency in your `pom.xml` file.

The following is an example of using Gradle:

```
dependencies {
    compile group: 'org.elasticsearch.client', name: 'rest', version:
    '5.1.2'
}
```

You can initialize the REST client using the RestClient Builder as shown here:

```
RestClient client = RestClient.builder(
    new HttpHost("host1", 9200, "http"),
    new HttpHost("host2", 9200, "http"))
    .build();
```

Note that the port number is `9200` since the REST client uses HTTP to communicate with the cluster.

Sniffing is one of the important features Elasticsearch clients offer. When sniffing is enabled, other nodes in the cluster are automatically discovered. Please refer to the *Sniffing* section for more details. It is provided as a library and can be included in your application as a Maven dependency:

```
<dependency>
    <groupId>org.elasticsearch.client</groupId>
    <artifactId>sniffer</artifactId>
    <version>5.1.2</version>
</dependency>
```

You can configure to run sniffing every 1 minute as shown here:

```
Sniffer sniffer =
Sniffer.builder(restClient).setSniffIntervalMills(60000).build();
```

When sniffing is enabled, it automatically gets the list of available nodes in the cluster and round robins the requests to all available data nodes. The REST client is very lightweight; it doesn't come with Elasticsearch dependencies and doesn't support request/response builders. The application using the REST client has to build the JSON request and handle the serialization/deserialization of request/response.

Third party clients

You can also use third-party HTTP clients, such as `Jest`, which support request/response builders and support node discovery as new nodes are added or existing nodes are removed. For more details, refer to the Jest GitHub page here:

```
https://github.com/searchbox-io/Jest/tree/master/jest
```

Indexing using Java client

Once the client is initialized, we will use the index API to index a JSON document. In this example, we will be using the transport client to index the document. To index, we have to use the `prepareIndex` method. All the operations using the client are asynchronous and will return a future:

```
Future<IndexResponse> future =
        client.prepareIndex("chapter4", "person", 1").setSource(document);
```

To make the operation synchronous, we can call the GET method as shown here:

```
IndexResponse response = client.prepareIndex("chapter4", "person",
"1").setSource(document).get();
```

The following are the details of the preceding example:

- **Index**: chapter4
- **Type**: person
- **Document ID**: 1

The document to be indexed is set using the preceding `setSource` method. The easiest and most practical way to generate JSON is to use a third-party library, such as Jackson or Gson. You can add Jackson to your application using Maven dependency as shown next:

```
<dependency>
  <groupId>com.fasterxml.jackson.core</groupId>
  <artifactId>jackson-databind</artifactId>
  <version>2.8.0</version>
```

```
</dependency>
```

The following is the Java POJO class representing the person document we want to index:

```
public class Person {
 private int id;
 private String name;
 private int age;
 private String gender;
 private String email;
 private String lastModifiedDate;

 .. getters and setters
}
```

We will use `Jackson ObjectMapper` to serialize the person object to JSON, as shown here:

```
ObjectMapper mapper = new ObjectMapper();

//Convert the object to bytes
byte[] document = mapper.writeValueAsBytes(personObj);

// Index : chapter4
// Type : person
// Doc Id : 1
IndexResponse response = client.prepareIndex("chapter4", "person",
"1").setSource(document).get();
```

The document to be indexed can be passed to `setSource` as the following:

- String
- Bytes array
- Map

We can also pass a Java Map to `setSource`, which will be converted to JSON during indexing:

```
Map<String, Object> document = new HashMap<String, Object>();
document.put("id", 1);
document.put("name", "user1");
document.put("age", 55);
document.put("gender", "M");
document.put("email", "user1@gmail.com");
document.put("last_modified_date", new Date());

IndexResponse response = client.prepareIndex("chapter4", "person",
"1").setSource(document).get();
```

We can also use the Elasticsearch helper `XContentBuilder` to build the JSON document as shown next:

```
import static org.elasticsearch.common.xcontent.XContentFactory.*;

XContentBuilder builder = jsonBuilder()
    .startObject()
        .field("id", "1")
        .field("name", "user1")
        .field("age", "55")
        .field("gender", "M")
        .field("email", "user1@gmail.com")
        .field("last_modified_date", new Date())
    .endObject();

String document = builder.string();

IndexResponse response = client.prepareIndex("chapter4", "person",
"1").setSource(document).get();
```

You can check the `IndexResponse` to make sure there are no failures. As shown next, we can check the ID of the document in the index response to verify that the document is successfully indexed:

```
if(response.getId() != null) {
    // success
}
```

We discussed the different types of indexing errors that can happen in the *Indexing Errors* section.

Concurrency

We discussed before that an update operation has to first retrieve the old document, apply the changes, and re-index the document. Between retrieving the old document and re-indexing the document, if some other operation updates the document, you would potentially overwrite the change. To solve this problem, Elasticsearch increments the version of the document on each operation.

If the version of the document has been changed between the document retrieval and re-indexing, the index operation fails. Let's take an example:

```
POST chapter4/person/2/_update
{
    "doc" : {
```

```
      "name" : "name update 3"
    }
  }
```

The response to the preceding operation is as follows:

```
{
  "_index": "chapter4",
  "_type": "person",
  "_id": "2",
  "_version": 4,
  "result": "updated",
  "_shards": {
    "total": 2,
    "successful": 2,
    "failed": 0
  }
}
```

You can see from the preceding response that the version of the document is 4after the update operation. For the next update, we can specify the version:

```
PUT chapter4/person/2?version=4
{
  "id": 2,
  "name": "name update 1",
  "age": "55",
  "gender": "M",
  "email": "user2@gmail.com",
  "last_modified_date" : "2017-02-18"
}
```

The operation only succeeds if the current version of the document is 4. You can see from the following response that the document has been updated and the version of the document is now 5:

```
{
  "_index": "chapter4",
  "_type": "person",
  "_id": "2",
  "_version": 5,
  "result": "updated",
  "_shards": {
    "total": 2,
    "successful": 2,
    "failed": 0
  }
}
```

If you try running the same update with version 4, you would see a response `409 HTTP response code`, as shown here:

```
{
  "error": {
   "root_cause": [
     {
        "type": "version_conflict_engine_exception",
        "reason": "[person][2]: version conflict, current version [5] is different than the      one provided [4]",
        "index_uuid": "9rcbu7LZR42te04D_G9r-g",
        "shard": "0",
        "index": "chapter4"
     }
    ],
    "type": "version_conflict_engine_exception",
    "reason": "[person][2]: version conflict, current version [5] is different than the one provided [4]",
    "index_uuid": "9rcbu7LZR42te04D_G9r-g",
    "shard": "0",
    "index": "chapter4"
   },
   "status": 409
}
```

To avoid failure due to a conflict, you can ask Elasticsearch to retry. The number of times it has to retry before the operation fails can be specified via the `retry_on_conflict` URL parameter, as shown next:

```
POST chapter4/person/2/_update?retry_on_conflict=3
{
   "doc": {
     "name": "name update 2"
   }
}
```

In a version conflict, Elasticsearch will try for 3 times before it fails the operation.

Translog

In the *What happens when you index a document* section, we discussed that when you index a document, the refresh process creates a new segment. Since writing the segment to the disk on every refresh is very expensive, the segment is only written to in-memory file system cache. When certain conditions are met, a process known as Lucene commit writes all the files (segments) in the memory to a physical disk.

If a node crashes before the files in memory are persisted to the physical disk, the data in the file system cache is lost, and any uncommitted changes are also lost. But Lucene commit is very expensive and cannot be done after every operation. To solve this problem, Elasticsearch introduced transaction log, which is a write-ahead log:

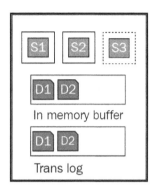

During an index or delete operation, the document is written to both the memory buffer and the transaction log. The index/delete operation is only acknowledged after the data in the translog is persisted to disk. If the system crashes before the segments are persisted to the disk, they are replayed from the translog on the server restart. When the translog becomes too big and certain other conditions are met, a new translog is created automatically. This process is known as the flush.

Async versus sync

By default, the index operation is only acknowledged after the translog is committed to disk in the primary and replica shards. If you are performing a bulk index and don't mind losing a few seconds of data in case of a failure, you can set the translog to committed on an interval rather than on every index operation. Changing the translog to async greatly improves the index performance.

CRUD from translog

We discussed in the previous section that the data you index is only available for search after one second. That's because the refresh process runs once a second and makes the data searchable by writing it to the inverted index. But when you retrieve a document by its ID, you will always get the latest data.

When you retrieve a document by its ID, Elasticsearch will check the translog to see if the translog contains the latest data that is not committed to the inverted index yet.

Although documents are searchable only after the refresh process runs, when a document is retrieved using its ID, you will always get the latest data.

Primary and Replica shards

As you know the data in an index is split across one or more shards. By splitting your data across multiple shards, Elasticsearch can scale beyond what a single machine can do. Elasticsearch is a distributed system, and system failures are bound to happen. Since each shard is an independent Lucene index that can live on any node in the cluster, Elasticsearch provides a way to maintain a copy of the primary shard in a different node of the cluster. In case the node containing the primary shard fails, the replica shard (copy), which exists in a different node, is promoted to primary. For more information, please refer to the *Failure Handling* section in Chapter 1, *Introduction to Elasticsearch*.

In this section, we will talk about how the data between primary and replica is synchronized:

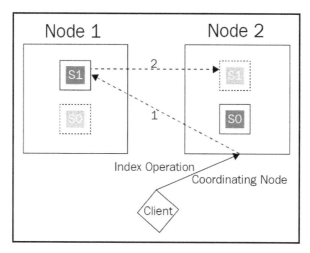

Let's say we have a cluster of two nodes as shown in the preceding figure. The shards represented by the solid lines are primary shards, and the shards represented by the dotted lines are replicas. We are indexing a document into the chapter4 index and the person type, as shown here:

```
PUT http://node2:9200/chapter4/person/4
{
```

```
"id": 4,
"name": "user4",
"age": "55",
"gender": "M",
"email": "user4@gmail.com",
"last_modified_date" : "2017-02-20"
}
```

To execute the preceding indexing operation, the following will happen:

1. The request can be sent to any node in the cluster, and the node receiving the request is called the coordinating node.
2. The coordinating node uses the document ID or routing value to determine the shard on which the operation needs to be executed. In this example, let's say the preceding document with ID 1 belongs to S1.
3. Internally, the request is forwarded to the primary shard S1 in Node 1.
4. The primary shard executes the operation locally and sends the request to all the replicas in parallel.
5. Once all the replicas respond back to primary, an acknowledgment is sent back to the client.

Now let's look at the response in the following operation:

```
{
  "_index": "chapter4",
  "_type": "person",
  "_id": "4",
  "_version": 1,
  "result": "created",
  "_shards": {
    "total": 2,
    "successful": 2,
    "failed": 0
  },
  "created": true
}
```

You can see from the preceding response the result of the operation is created. Let's look at the _shards sections of the response. You can see that the total number of shards are 2 (primary and replica), and both are successful.

Primary preference

A query can be answered by a primary or a replica shard as they are exact copies. Query requests are usually round robin between primary and replica shards. Since the request is first executed on the primary shard and then forwarded to the replicas, there may be a time when the data from the primary is different from the replica. If your application always needs the latest data, you can use the preference property to control which shard the request is executed on.

Let's consider the following example:

```
POST chapter4/person/_search?preference=_primary
{
  "query": {
    "match": {
      "name": "user1"
    }
  }
}
```

The preceding request will be executed only on the primary shards. The other option is `_primary_first`. The request is executed first on primary, and if the primary is not available, it is executed on the replica shard:

```
POST chapter4/person/_search?preference=_primary_first
{
  "query": {
    "match": {
      "name": "user1"
    }
  }
}
```

We will talk more about the other preferences Elasticsearch supports in `Chapter 6`, *All about search*.

More replicas for query throughput

Replicas not only help with the failover but also increase the query throughput. A replica is the exact copy of the primary and is hosted in different node of the cluster. The queries are usually randomized between primary and replica shards.

If your application is read heavy, you should consider increasing the number of replicas.

If some of the shards are not available or don't respond back in time, Elasticsearch responds back with a partial result and is indicated in the _shards section of the response. You should always check the _shards to make sure the response has complete results.

Increasing/decreasing the number of replicas

We can increase and decrease the number of replicas of an index on the fly. Consider changing the number of replicas to 0 before any bulk indexing operations, and you can change the number of replicas back to the original value once done:

```
PUT chapter4/_settings
{
  "index" : {
    "number_of_replicas" : 0
  }
}
```

You should see a response similar to this:

```
{"acknowledged":true}
```

Summary

In this chapter, you learned how to index and update your data. We discussed the various Elasticsearch clients available and how to use them. We discussed what happens internally when you index or update. You also learned about refresh interval and why there is a delay between indexing your data and it being available for search. We also covered how Elasticsearch deals with concurrency, and how data is synchronized between primary and replica shards.

In the next chapter, will discuss the various bulk APIs Elasticsearch has to offer and how to organize your data.

5

Organizing Your Data and Bulk Data Ingestion

In this chapter, you'll learn how to manage indices in Elasticsearch. Until this chapter, you learned about operating on a single document. In this chapter, you'll learn about the various APIs Elasticsearch has to offer to support bulk operations. They can be very effective when its comes to rebuilding the entire index or batching requests together in a single call. Due to how the data in stored internally in Elasticsearch, the number of shards or the mapping of the fields cannot be changed after the index creation. You'll learn about Reindex API, which can rebuild the index with the correct settings. Using Elasticsearch for time-based data is a very common usage pattern. We will discuss different ways to manage time-based indices. By the end of this chapter, we will have covered the following:

- Multi Get API
- Update by Query API
- Delete by Query API
- Reindex API
- Dealing with time-based indexes
- Shrink API

Bulk operations

In this section, we will discuss various bulk operations Elasticsearch supports. Batching multiple requests together saves network round trips, and the requests in the batch can be executed in parallel. Elasticsearch has a dedicated thread pool for bulk operations, and the number of requests it can process in parallel depends on the number of the CPU processors in the node.

The following are the different bulk operations supported:

- **Bulk API**: This can be used to batch multiple index and delete operations and execute them using a single API call.
- **Multi Get API**: This can be used to retrieve documents using document IDs.
- **Update by query**: This can be used to update a set of documents that match a query.
- **Delete by query**: This can be used to delete the documents that match a query.

Bulk API

Bulk API is ideal for indexing or deleting large sets of data. Create, index, update, and delete operations are supported. For each request along with the document source, metadata information, such as index name, type, unique identifier, and routing, should be provided. Each bulk request is separated by a new line. A bulk request can have a mixture of create, index, update, and delete requests. The node receiving the bulk request (also known as coordinating node) groups the requests by the shard they belong to and executes them in parallel. The thread pools that execute single and bulk requests are independent.

Let's say we are adding shirts to the e-commerce inventory. We can use the bulk API to add the product documents to the index as follows:

```
POST /_bulk
{ "create" : { "_index" : "chapter5", "_type" : "product", "_id" : "1"}}
{ "product_name" : "Long Sleeve Shirt - White", "unit_price" : "30" }
{ "index" : { "_index" : "chapter5", "_type" : "product", "_id" : "2"}}
{ "product_name" : "Button down Shirt", "unit_price" : "40" }
{ "create" : { "_index" : "chapter5", "_type" : "product", "_id" : "3"}}
{ "product_name" : "Non-Iron Solid Shirt", "unit_price" : "40" }
```

 The `create` operation will fail if the document already exists. Instead, you can also use the `index` operation, which will replace the document source with the request if the document with the same ID already exists. During the `index` operation, if the `_id` is not specified, a unique identifier is generated automatically.

Next, along with the `product_name` and `unit_price` fields, we want to add the `shiping_price` field to the document. We can use either use `index` operation and specify the entire source or use `update` with the partial document. In the following example, we will use an `update` operation to add the new field.

Since we are operating on the same index and type, we can also specify the index and type in the URL instead of the metadata, as shown next:

```
POST chapter5/product/_bulk
{ "update" : { "_id" : "1", "_retry_on_conflict" : 2 }}
{ "doc" : { "shipping_price" : 7.0 } }
{ "update" : { "_id" : "2", "_retry_on_conflict" : 2}}
{ "doc" : { "shipping_price" : 6.5 } }
{ "update" : { "_id" : "3", "_retry_on_conflict" : 2}}
{ "doc" : { "shipping_price" : 5.0 } }
```

Update operation has to first retrieve the original document and then apply the changes. Between retrieving the document and updating it, if another process makes changes to the document, we can use the _retry_on_conflict parameter to specify the number of times the operation has to be retried before it fails the request. The response of the preceding query is shown next:

```
{
    "took": 10,
    "errors": false,
    "items": [
      {
        "update": {
          "_index": "chapter5",
          "_type": "product",
          "_id": "1",
          "_version": 2,
          "result": "updated",
          "_shards": {
            "total": 2,
            "successful": 1,
            "failed": 0
          },
          "status": 200
        }
      },
      {
        "update": {
          "_index": "chapter5",
          "_type": "product",
          "_id": "2",
          "_version": 2,
          "result": "updated",
          "_shards": {
            "total": 2,
            "successful": 1,
            "failed": 0
```

```
      },
      "status": 200
    }
  },
  {
    "update": {
      "_index": "chapter5",
      "_type": "product",
      "_id": "3",
      "_version": 2,
      "result": "updated",
      "_shards": {
        "total": 2,
        "successful": 1,
        "failed": 0
      },
      "status": 200
    }
  }
 ]
}
```

Next, if we want to delete the product documents, we can use the bulk query as follows:

```
POST chapter5/product/_bulk
{ "delete" : { "_id" : "1" } }
{ "update" : { "_id" : "4", "_retry_on_conflict" : 2 }}
{ "doc" : { "unit_price" : 39.99 } }
```

Each query in the bulk request is executed **independently**, and one operation does not affect the other. In the preceding query, we tried to update a document (ID: 4) that doesn't exist. The delete operation is successful and update operation error is shown in the response. The errors flag at the beginning of the bulk response is also set to true, indicating they are errors while executing the bulk request. The response of the preceding query is as follows:

```
{
  "took": 2,
  "errors": true,
  "items": [
    {
      "delete": {
        "found": true,
        "_index": "chapter5",
        "_type": "product",
        "_id": "1",
        "_version": 4,
        "result": "deleted",
```

```
      "_shards": {
        "total": 2,
        "successful": 1,
        "failed": 0
      },
      "status": 200
    }
  },
  {
    "update": {
      "_index": "chapter5",
      "_type": "product",
      "_id": "4",
      "status": 404,
      "error": {
        "type": "document_missing_exception",
        "reason": "[product][4]: document missing",
        "index_uuid": "K8unwaIZQTyGwUb4tFN3sQ",
        "shard": "2",
        "index": "chapter5"
      }
    }
  }
  ]
}
```

The number of requests in a batch depends on various factors, such as the document size, hardware, and so on. Since the entire bulk request has to be loaded into memory before executing the request, depending on the number of requests, memory can be an issue and can take a lot longer to transfer the data over the network. You should experiment bulk with different batch sizes to find the sweet spot.

If you are indexing data that is not required to be searchable immediately, consider turning off the refresh interval or increasing the refresh interval. This will reduce the strain on the system and increase the index throughput. You can temporarily disable the refresh as shown next:

```
PUT /chapter5/_settings
  {
    "index": {
      "refresh_interval": "-1"
    }
  }
```

The bulk request indexes the data first in primary and then replicas. During bulk indexing, you can also consider removing the replicas and enable them once the indexing is complete. Only remove replicas if you are indexing the data for the first time or for an inactive index, as removing replica might affect the query throughput.

Multi Get API

Multi Get API is used to retrieve multiple documents using a single request. A simple request to get the documents based on the unique identifier is shown here:

```
POST chapter5/product/_mget
{
  "ids" : ["2", "3"]
}
```

The response of the preceding query is as follows:

```
{
  "docs": [
    {
      "_index": "chapter5",
      "_type": "product",
      "_id": "2",
      "_version": 2,
      "found": true,
      "_source": {
        "product_name": "Button down Shirt",
        "unit_price": "40",
        "shipping_price": 6.5
      }
    },
    {
      "_index": "chapter5",
      "_type": "product",
      "_id": "3",
      "_version": 2,
      "found": true,
      "_source": {
        "product_name": "Non-Iron Solid Shirt",
        "unit_price": "40",
        "shipping_price": 5
      }
    }
  ]
}
```

To retrieve documents from different index/types, metadata information can be specified as follows:

```
POST _mget
  {
    "docs": [
      {
        "_index": "chapter5",
        "_type": "product",
        "_id": "2"
      },
      {
        "_index": "chapter5",
        "_type": "product",
        "_id": "3"
      }
    ]
  }
```

By default, the complete source of the document is returned. You can use the _source field to include/exclude the fields of the document in the response, as shown next:

```
POST _mget
  {
    "docs": [
      {
        "_index": "chapter5",
        "_type": "product",
        "_id": "2",
        "_source": [
          "product_name"
        ]
      },
      {
        "_index": "chapter5",
        "_type": "product",
        "_id": "3",
        "_source": {
          "exclude": "unit_price"
        }
      }
    ]
  }
```

The response to the preceding request is as follows:

```
{
    "docs": [
        {
            "_index": "chapter5",
            "_type": "product",
            "_id": "2",
            "_version": 2,
            "found": true,
            "_source": {
                "product_name": "Button down Shirt"
            }
        },
        {
            "_index": "chapter5",
            "_type": "product",
            "_id": "3",
            "_version": 2,
            "found": true,
            "_source": {
                "shipping_price": 5,
                "product_name": "Non-Iron Solid Shirt"
            }
        }
    ]
}
```

Update by query

Update by Query API is used to update all documents that match a particular query. Depending on the number of documents in the index, this can be a very resource-demanding operation and can slow the existing search or index operations. We will discuss the different ways to control the number of requests per second and how to parallel this operation.

For example, for the products we indexed using the bulk API in the previous section, we want to add a new `price_with_tax` field, which contains the price plus tax. We will use update by query and scripting for the calculation. Assuming `10%` is the tax, we will use the unit price to determine the price with tax. We will be use the default scripting language Painless for this operation. The following query is using `match_all` to match all the documents, but you can specify a query if you want to limit the documents you want to update.

The `_update_by_query` API is shown here:

```
POST chapter5/_update_by_query
{
  "script": {
    "inline": "ctx._source.price_with_tax = ctx._source.unit_price * 1.1",
    "lang": "painless"
  },
  "query": {
    "match_all": {}
  }
}
```

The response to the preceding query is as follows:

```
{
    "took": 9,
    "timed_out": false,
    "total": 2,
    "updated": 2,
    "deleted": 0,
    "batches": 1,
    "version_conflicts": 0,
    "noops": 0,
    "retries": {
      "bulk": 0,
      "search": 0
    },
    "throttled_millis": 0,
    "requests_per_second": -1,
    "throttled_until_millis": 0,
    "failures": []
}
```

Update by query works by taking a snapshot of the existing index and performing the update on each document. In the preceding response, you can see that `version_conflicts:0` and we don't have conflicts. Version conflicts happen if the document is updated between taking the snapshot and updating it. By default, if a conflict occurs, the operation fails and the updates performed so far will remain. If you want the operation to continue despite version conflicts, you can specify that when running the request as shown here:

```
POST chapter5/_update_by_query?conflicts=proceed
{
  "script": {
    "inline": "ctx._source.price_with_tax = ctx._source.unit_price * 1.1",
    "lang": "painless"
```

```
    },
    "query": {
      "match_all": {}
    }
  }
```

The `update` operation will not be failed if there is a conflict, and any conflicts that occur during the update are specified in the response. In the preceding response, you can see that the number of batches (`batches:1`) is 1. If the index you are trying to update is quite large, instead of waiting for the response to come back, you can ask Elasticsearch to respond with a task ID. You can then use the task API to track the progress or cancel the task. To make Elasticsearch respond with task ID, you need to set the `wait_for_completion` to `false` as a query parameter as shown below:

```
POST chapter5/_update_by_query?wait_for_completion=false
{
  "script": {
    "inline": "ctx._source.price_with_tax = ctx._source.unit_price * 1.1",
    "lang": "painless"
  },
  "query": {
    "match_all": {}
  }
}
```

The response to the preceding query is shown here. It contains the task ID:

```
{
  "task": "xZjyFE19Q0yGxehcys6ydg:307842"
}
```

You can track the status of the task using the task ID, as follows:

```
GET /_tasks/xZjyFE19Q0yGxehcys6ydg:307842
```

The status response is shown here:

```
{
  "completed": true,
  "task": {
    "node": "xZjyFE19Q0yGxehcys6ydg",
    "id": 307842,
    "type": "transport",
    "action": "indices:data/write/update/byquery",
    "status": {
      "total": 2,
      "updated": 2,
      "created": 0,
```

```
      "deleted": 0,
      "batches": 1,
      "version_conflicts": 0,
      "noops": 0,
      "retries": {
        "bulk": 0,
        "search": 0
      },
      "throttled_millis": 0,
      "requests_per_second": -1,
      "throttled_until_millis": 0
    },
    "description": "",
    "start_time_in_millis": 1491805218867,
    "running_time_in_nanos": 5283799,
    "cancellable": true
  },
  "response": {
    "took": 5,
    "timed_out": false,
    "total": 2,
    "updated": 2,
    "created": 0,
    "deleted": 0,
    "batches": 1,
    "version_conflicts": 0,
    "noops": 0,
    "retries": {
      "bulk": 0,
      "search": 0
    },
    "throttled_millis": 0,
    "requests_per_second": -1,
    "throttled_until_millis": 0,
    "failures": []
  }
}
```

You can see in the preceding response that the task is completed, but you can also cancel the task using the cancel task API as shown here:

```
POST /_tasks/xZjyFE19Q0yGxehcys6ydg:307842/_cancel
```

Delete by query

Delete by Query API is very similar to update by query but can be used to delete the documents that match the query. It works by taking a snapshot of the index and deleting the documents. Between taking the snapshot and executing the delete query, if the documents are modified, the operation fails due to the version conflict. To proceed on failures, `conflicts=proceed` can be specified as a URL parameter, and any failures that occur are reported in the response. For example, to delete all the documents that contain the word `shirt`, the query is as follows:

```
POST chapter5/_delete_by_query?conflicts=proceed
{
  "query": {
    "match": {
      "product_name": "shirt"
    }
  }
}
```

The response to the preceding query is shown here:

```
{
  "took": 5,
  "timed_out": false,
  "total": 2,
  "deleted": 2,
  "batches": 1,
  "version_conflicts": 0,
  "noops": 0,
  "retries": {
    "bulk": 0,
    "search": 0
  },
  "throttled_millis": 0,
  "requests_per_second": -1,
  "throttled_until_millis": 0,
  "failures": []
}
```

You can set `wait_for_completion=false` as a URL parameter to get the task ID as a response to the query and track the progress of the query using the task API.

Reindex API

Before Elasticsearch 5.0, to change the index settings, or change the mapping of an index, you have a create a new index and reindex the data. Reindexing a large index is usually lot of work, which involves reading the data from the source like a SQL database, transforming the data into Elasticsearch documents and loading the data into Elasticsearch. For large applications, batch processing engines such as Hadoop are used to reindex the data. Depending on how big the index is or how complicated the ETL (Extract, Transform, Load) process is, reindex can be very expensive. To solve this, Reindex API was introduced. The original JSON document used for indexing is stored in the _source field which can be used by the Reindex API to reindex the documents. The Reindex API can be used for the following:

- To change the mapping/settings of an existing index
- To combine documents from multiple indexes in one index
- To copy only missing documents
- To copy a subset of documents from one index to other
- To copy top N documents based on sort value
- To copy only a subset of fields from the source index to destination index

Just like _update_by_query and _delete_by_query, reindex works by taking a snapshot of the existing index. You can set wait_for_completion=false in the URL to get the task ID as a response to the query and track the progress of the query using the Task API as shown next:

```
GET /_tasks/xZjyFE1970BGxehcys6ydg:309742
```

Change mappings/settings

Reindex API can be used to change the index settings like increasing/decreasing the number of shards, disabling the _all field and so on. It can also be used to change the mapping of an existing field, for example, you want to change the mapping of an keyword field to date.

The Shrink API can also be used to decrease the number of shards. To decrease the number of shards, Shrink API is relatively much cheaper than the reindex operation. Please refer to the *Shrink API* section for more details.

To change the index setting/mappings of the existing index, first create the destination index with the desired settings and use the Reindex API as shown next:

```
POST _reindex
  {
    "source": {
      "index": "source_index"
    },
    "dest": {
      "index": "dest_index"
    }
  }
```

Combining documents from one or more indices

You can combine the documents from one or more indices into one big index, as shown next:

```
POST _reindex
  {
    "source": {
      "index": [
        "source_index_1",
        "source_index_2"
      ]
    },
    "dest": {
      "index": "dest_index"
    }
  }
```

Copying only missing documents

You can copy only missing documents from one index to another by setting the `op_type` to **create**. Any existing documents with the same identifier will get a conflict. By setting conflicts to proceed in the request, reindex will ignore the existing documents, as shown next:

```
POST _reindex
  {
    "conflicts": "proceed",
    "source": {
      "index": "source_index"
    },
```

```
    "dest": {
      "index": "dest_index",
      "op_type": "create"
    }
  }
```

Copying a subset of documents into a new index

You can use Reindex API to copy only the documents that match a query. Suppose you have a index which contains application logs and you want to copy only the error logs into a new index. You can use reindex as shown next:

```
POST _reindex
  {
    "source": {
      "index": "source_index_1",
      "type": "log",
      "query": {
        "term": {
          "level": "ERROR"
        }
      }
    },
    "dest": {
      "index": "dest_index"
    }
  }
```

Copying top N documents

You can use Reindex API to copy top N documents based on a field. Suppose you want to copy only the last 1,000 logs based on the timestamp field to a new index. You can use the Reindex API as shown here:

```
POST _reindex
  {
    "size": 1000,
    "source": {
      "index": "source_index",
      "sort": {
        "timestamp": "desc"
      }
    },
    "dest": {
```

```
      "index": "dest_index"
    }
  }
```

Copying the subset of fields into new index

You can copy a subset of fields in the document as shown here:

```
POST _reindex
{
  "source": {
    "index": [
      "source_index_1"
    ],
    "_source": [
      "field1",
      "field2"
    ]
  },
  "dest": {
    "index": "dest_index"
  }
}
```

Depending on how big the source index is, reindex can be an expensive operation. It is recommended to disable all the replicas on the destination index and enable them once the reindex is complete.

Ingest Node

Traditionally, **Logstash** is used to preprocess your data before indexing into Elasticsearch. Using Logstash, you can define pipelines to extract, transform, and index your data into Elasticsearch.

In Elasticsearch 5.0, the ingest node has been introduced. Using the ingest node, pipelines to modify the documents before indexing can be defined. A pipeline is a series of processors, each processor working on one or more fields in the document. The most commonly used Logstash filters are available as processors. For example, using a `grok` filter to extract data from an Apache log file into a document, extracting fields from JSON, changing the date format, calculating geo-distance from a location, and so on. The possibilities are endless. Elasticsearch supports many processors out of the box. You can also develop your own processors using any JVM-supported languages.

By default, all nodes in the cluster can act as ingest nodes. Depending on the amount of processing required, you can use new or existing nodes in the cluster as dedicated ingest nodes. To add or remove a pipeline, `_ingest` API is provided. Ingest API also supports simulating the pipeline against a given document to debug and test the pipeline. The basic structure of a pipeline is shown next:

```
PUT _ingest/pipeline/<pipeline-name>
  {
    "pipeline": {
      "description": "pipeline-description",
      "processors": []
    }
  }
```

The processors as shown above accept a list of processors, which are executed serially. To better explain Ingest API, let us take an e-commerce site example. When a user views a product/item, a message is logged in the format shown next. By the end of this section, we will define a pipeline to transform the log message into a JSON document and index the document into Elasticsearch. We will also use aggregations to find the most viewed items:

```
{
  "message": "127.0.0.1 2017-04-11T09:02:34.234+07:00 USA 1 Web"
}
```

Let's define a pipeline to parse the log message using the `grok` processor.

 Grok is nothing but a collection of regular expressions to parse unstructured data like logs into structured data. The syntax of a grok pattern is `%{SYNTAX:SEMANTIC}`, the syntax is the name of the pattern and semantic is the name of the field. For example, in `%{IP:client}` the IP is the pattern and client is the name of the field in the JSON document. A list of pre-defined patterns can be found at `https://github.com/logstash-plugins/logstash-patterns-core/tree/master/patterns`

We can use the following `grok` pattern to transform the above shown log message into a JSON document :

```
"%{IP:client} %{TIMESTAMP_ISO8601:timestamp} %{WORD:country}
%{NUMBER:itemId}
%{WORD:platform}"
```

Before creating the pipeline, we can test the pipeline using the **_simulate** endpoint as shown next:

```
POST _ingest/pipeline/_simulate
{
   "pipeline": {
      "description": "Item View Pipeline",
      "processors": [
         {
            "grok": {
               "field": "log",
               "patterns": [
                  "%{IP:client} %{TIMESTAMP_ISO8601:timestamp} %{WORD:country}
%{NUMBER:itemId} %{WORD:platform}"
               ]
            }
         }
      ]
   },
   "docs": [
      {
         "_source": {
            "log": "127.0.0.1 2017-04-11T09:02:34.234+07:00 USA 1 Web"
         }
      }
   ]
}
```

The response to the preceding query is shown here:

```
{
   "docs": [
      {
         "doc": {
            "_id": "_id",
            "_index": "_index",
            "_type": "_type",
            "_source": {
               "country": "USA",
               "itemId": "1",
               "log": "127.0.0.1 2017-04-11T09:02:34.234+07:00 USA 1 Web",
               "client": "127.0.0.1",
               "platform": "Web",
               "timestamp": "2017-04-11T09:02:34.234+07:00"
            },
            "_ingest": {
               "timestamp": "2017-04-12T06:51:37.005+0000"
            }
```

```
      }
    }
  ]
}
```

You can see from the preceding response that the log message is transformed into a JSON document using the grok processor. Along with the fields, the original log message is also stored as the log field in the document. Next, we can add a processor to remove the log field from the document, as shown here:

```
POST _ingest/pipeline/_simulate
  {
    "pipeline": {
      "description": "Item View Pipeline",
      "processors": [
        {
          "grok": {
            "field": "log",
            "patterns": [
              "%{IP:client} %{TIMESTAMP_ISO8601:timestamp} %{WORD:country}
%{NUMBER:itemId} %{WORD:platform}"
            ]
          }
        },
        {
          "remove": {
            "field": "log"
          }
        }
      ]
    },
    "docs": [
      {
        "_source": {
          "log": "127.0.0.1 2017-04-11T09:02:34.234+07:00 USA 1 Web"
        }
      }
    ]
  }
```

The response to the preceding query is as follows:

```
{
  "docs": [
    {
      "doc": {
        "_id": "_id",
        "_index": "_index",
```

```
            "_type": "_type",
            "_source": {
              "country": "USA",
              "itemId": "1",
              "client": "127.0.0.1",
              "platform": "Web",
              "timestamp": "2017-04-11T09:02:34.234+07:00"
            },
            "_ingest": {
              "timestamp": "2017-04-12T06:54:09.406+0000"
            }
          }
        }
      ]
  }
```

The resulting document looks a lot better than the raw log message. Next, we want to store the document in a month-based index. All the messages that are logged in the same month belong to the same index. Grouping the logs based a time interval makes it very easy to clean or delete old logs. We will use the `date_index_name` processor, which takes a date field as input and outputs the index name to which the document belongs:

```
POST _ingest/pipeline/_simulate
  {
    "pipeline": {
      "description": "Item View Pipeline",
      "processors": [
        {
          "grok": {
            "field": "log",
            "patterns": [
              "%{IP:client} %{TIMESTAMP_ISO8601:timestamp} %{WORD:country}
%{NUMBER:itemId} %{WORD:platform}"
            ]
          }
        },
        {
          "remove": {
            "field": "log"
          }
        },
        {
          "date_index_name": {
            "field": "timestamp",
            "index_name_prefix": "viewitem-",
            "date_rounding": "M",
            "index_name_format": "yyyy-MM"
```

```
            }
          }
        ]
      },
      "docs": [
        {
          "_source": {
            "log": "127.0.0.1 2017-04-11T09:02:34.234+07:00 USA 1 Web"
          }
        }
      ]
    }
```

In the preceding query, we used the `date_index_name` processor to figure out the index the document belongs to. The `index_name_prefix` is the prefix value added to the `index_name_format`. In the preceding query, the index name will be `viewitem_2017_04`. The `date_rounding` rounds the date field to the date math field specified. The following `date_rounding` options are supported:

Time unit	Description
y	year
M	month
w	week
d	day
h	hour
m	minute
s	second

The response to the preceding query is shown here:

```
{
    "docs": [
      {
        "doc": {
          "_id": "_id",
          "_index": "<viewitem_{2017_04||/M{yyyy_MM|UTC}}>",
          "_type": "_type",
          "_source": {
            "country": "USA",
            "itemId": "1",
            "client": "127.0.0.1",
            "platform": "Web",
```

```
          "timestamp": "2017-04-11T09:02:34.234+07:00"
        },
        "_ingest": {
          "timestamp": "2017-04-12T07:27:42.917+0000"
        }
      }
    }
  ]
}
```

Until now, we used the simulate feature to simulate the pipeline, we can create the pipeline using the _ingest PUT API as shown here:

```
PUT _ingest/pipeline/view_item_pipeline
{
  "description": "Item View Pipeline",
  "processors": [
    {
      "grok": {
        "field": "log",
        "patterns": [
          "%{IP:client} %{TIMESTAMP_ISO8601:timestamp} %{WORD:country}
%{NUMBER:itemId} %{WORD:platform}"
        ]
      }
    },
    {
      "remove": {
        "field": "log"
      }
    },
    {
      "date_index_name": {
        "field": "timestamp",
        "index_name_prefix": "viewitem_",
        "date_rounding": "M",
        "index_name_format": "yyyy_MM"
      }
    }
  ]
}
```

For the complete list of all the processors supported, please visit the official documentation:

https://www.elastic.co/guide/en/elasticsearch/reference/5.1/ingest-processors.html

Let's index a couple of documents using the pipeline we just defined. We would index the logs just like regular documents but specify the pipeline as the query parameter, as follows:

```
POST chapter5/log/?pipeline=view_item_pipeline
{
    "log": "127.0.0.1 2017-04-11T09:02:34.234+07:00 USA 1 Web "
}


POST chapter5/log/?pipeline=view_item_pipeline
{
    "log": "127.0.0.1 2017-04-12T09:02:34.234+07:00 USA 2 Web "
}


POST chapter5/log/?pipeline=view_item_pipeline
{
    "log": "127.0.0.1 2017-04-13T09:02:34.234+07:00 USA 3 Web "
}


POST chapter5/log/?pipeline=view_item_pipeline
{
    "log": "127.0.0.1 2017-04-11T09:02:34.234+07:00 USA 1 Web "
}
```

Let's look at the response of one of the preceding queries:

```
{
    "_index": "viewitem_2017_04",
    "_type": "log",
    "_id": "AVyeUsnSiOAxqKpNGiK7",
    "_version": 1,
    "result": "created",
    "_shards": {
      "total": 2,
      "successful": 1,
      "failed": 0
    },
    "created": true
}
```

From the preceding response, you can see that the document is indexed to the `viewitem_2017_04` index, although the original request is to index the document into the `chapter5` index. We can retrieve the document using the GET API as shown next:

```
GET viewitem_2017_04/log/AVyeUsnSiOAxqKpNGiK7
```

The log message "127.0.0.1 2017-04-11T09:02:34.234+07:00 USA 1 Web" is converted in to the document shown below. The response to the above query is as follows:

```
{
    "_index": "viewitem_2017_04",
    "_type": "log",
    "_id": "AVyeUsnSiOAxqKpNGiK7",
    "_version": 1,
    "found": true,
    "_source": {
      "country": "USA",
      "itemId": "1",
      "client": "127.0.0.1",
      "platform": "Web",
      "timestamp": "2017-04-11T09:02:34.234+07:00"
    }
}
```

Next, we can use the `viewitem` index to run an aggregation query to get the top five most viewed items. We will use the terms aggregation to get the top 5 items.

 Grok processor outputs all the fields as text by default. You can define a index template with mappings if you want to change the default behaviour. Each text field is also indexed as keyword which can be accessed via textfield.keyword. Terms aggregation can only be executed on a `keyword` field due to which we need to use the `itemId.keyword` field instead of `itemId` for the aggregation.

The aggregation query is shown here:

```
POST viewitem_2017_04/_search
{
  "size": 0,
  "aggs": {
    "most_views_items": {
      "terms": {
        "field": "itemId.keyword",
        "size": 5 #No of buckets
      }
    }
  }
}
```

The response of the preceding query is shown here:

```
{
  .....
```

```
    "aggregations": {
      "most_views_items": {
        "doc_count_error_upper_bound": 0,
        "sum_other_doc_count": 0,
        "buckets": [
          {
            "key": "1",
            "doc_count": 2
          },
          {
            "key": "2",
            "doc_count": 1
          },
          {
            "key": "3",
            "doc_count": 1
          }
        ]
      }
    }
  }
```

From the preceding response, you can see that the most viewed item is item ID 1, followed by item ID 2 and 3. We can also run aggregations to first bucket the data by country and then compute the most viewed item for each country and so on. We will discuss aggregations in detail in Chapter 8, *How to slice and dice your data using aggregations*.

Organizing your data

In this section, we will discuss how to divide your data into multiple indices. Elasticsearch provides index aliases, which make it very easy to query multiple indices at once. It also supports index templates to configure automatic index creation. We will also discuss how to deal with time-based data, such as logs, which is a common Elasticsearch use case.

Index alias

An index alias is a pointer to one or more indexes. A search operation executed against an alias is executed across all the indexes the alias points to. The coordinating node executes the request on all indices, collects the results, and sends them back to the client. The index operation, on the other hand, cannot be executed on an alias that points to more than one index. It is recommended to use an alias instead of the actual index name in your application. If the alias needs to point to a different index later, it would be an easy switch.

Due to how the data in stored in the inverted index, mappings of existing fields cannot be changed on the fly. For example, you want to treat a field that is previously indexed as string as a date. To do this, you have to create a new index with the correct mappings and reindex the data. If your application is currently using the index alias named `application_logs` and the alias is currently pointing to the index `index_with_date_as_string`, the alias can be easily changed to use the new index `index_with_date_as_date` as shown here:

```
POST /_aliases
{
  "actions": [
    {
      "remove": {
        "index": "index_with_date_as_string",
        "alias": "application_logs"
      }
    },
    {
      "add": {
        "index": "index_with_date_as_date",
        "alias": "application_logs"
      }
    }
  ]
}
```

Since the application is using an alias, we are able to change the index without any changes to the client code. The response to the preceding query is as follows:

```
{
  "acknowledged": true
}
```

Since an alias can point to multiple indices, we used the _aliases endpoint to switch the index the alias points to. We can also use the _alias endpoint to add an alias. We can add the `index_with_date_as_string` index to the `application_logs` alias in two ways. Using the _alias endpoint as shown here:

```
PUT index_with_date_as_string/_alias/application_logs
```

Or using the _aliases endpoint as shown here:

```
POST /_aliases
{
  "actions": [
    {
```

```
        "add": {
          "index": "index_with_date_as_string",
          "alias": "application_logs"
        }
      }
    ]
  }
```

You can verify the indices the alias points to as shown here:

```
GET /*/_alias/application_logs
```

The response to the preceding query is as follows:

```
{
    "index_with_date_as_string": {
      "aliases": {
        "application_logs": {}
      }
    }
}
```

An index alias can also be used to group one or more indices. This is especially useful when querying for time series data. For example, you are storing the application logs in Elasticsearch. Depending on the volume of the data, you decided to use one index for one month of data. All the logs that are produced in the same month are indexed to the same index. The index that stores the logs for the month of April is named `logs_04_17`. For suppose, you only care about the latest logs, you can create a `logs_last_2_months` alias, which points to indices of the last two months. The user or the application can query the alias rather than figuring out the indices for the last 2 months based on the current date. We will discuss more in the *Managing time-based indexes* section.

The index alias can also be used to view the data with a filter. This is similar to a view in a database. For example, a log document looks like the following:

```
POST logs_04_17/log/
  {
    "level": "ERROR",
    "application": "Service A",
    "timestamp" : "2017-04-13T16:39:00-07:00",
    "message": "Exception in thread java.lang.NullPointerException at
chapter5.main(ServiceA.java:23)"
  }
```

Let's say we just deployed the latest code and want to make sure they are no errors in the application. We can create an alias with a filter for errors as shown here:

```
POST /_aliases
{
  "actions": [
    {
      "add": {
        "index": "logs_04_17",
        "alias": "logs_latest_error",
        "filter": {
          "match": {
            "level": "ERROR"
          }
        }
      }
    }
  ]
}
```

To get only the errors, you can query the `logs_latest_error` index as shown here:

```
GET logs_latest_error/_search
```

You can search for errors that are logged for `Service A` in the last 1 hour as shown here:

```
POST logs_latest_error/_search
{
  "query": {
    "bool": {
      "must": [
        {
          "match": {
            "application": "Service A"
          }
        },
        {
          "range": {
            "timestamp": {
              "gte": "now-1h",
              "time_zone": "-07:00"
            }
          }
        }
      ]
    }
  }
}
```

The response to the preceding query is as follows:

```
{
    "took": 1,
    "timed_out": false,
    "_shards": {
      "total": 5,
      "successful": 5,
      "failed": 0
    },
    "hits": {
      "total": 1,
      "max_score": 1.5162321,
      "hits": [
        {
          "_index": "logs_04_17",
          "_type": "log",
          "_id": "AVtpudeslh63sHCyBgdB",
          "_score": 1.5162321,
          "_source": {
            "level": "ERROR",
            "application": "Service A",
            "timestamp": "2017-04-13T16:39:00-07:00",
            "message": "Exception in thread java.lang.NullPointerException
  at chapter5.main(ServiceA.java:23)"
          }
        }
      ]
    }
}
```

Index templates

When you index a document, if the index doesn't exist already, Elasticsearch will automatically create the index based on the default settings. The mappings of the document are dynamically mapped. You can overwrite the default settings and mapping of the field using the index templates. By default, a new index is created with 5 shards and 1 replica. In the following template, unless specified, a new index created will have 1 shard and 0 replicas:

```
PUT _template/default_template
{
  "template": "*",
  "order": 0,
  "settings": {
    "number_of_shards": 1
```

```
   }
 }
```

Index templates work using the index name. It does a wild card match on the index name. Let's define a template for logs index we discussed in the previous section. A sample log looks like the following:

```
POST logs_04_17/log/
{
   "level": "ERROR",
   "application": "Service A",
   "timestamp" : "2017-04-13T16:39:00-07:00",
   "message": "Exception in thread java.lang.NullPointerException at
chapter5.main(ServiceA.java:23)"
 }
```

When defining an index template, along with the index settings, the mappings of the index can also be defined as shown here:

```
PUT _template/logs_template
 {
   "template": "logs*",
   "order": 1,
   "settings": {
     "number_of_shards": 3
   },
   "mappings": {
     "log": {
       "properties": {
         "level": {
           "type": "keyword"
         },
         "application": {
           "type": "keyword"
         },
         "timestamp": {
           "type": "date",
           "format": "date_optional_time"
         },
         "message": {
           "type": "text"
         }
       }
     }
   }
 }
```

If an index name starts with the word `logs`, the settings and the mappings in the template are automatically applied to the newly created index. Let's delete the existing index and reindex the sample log as follows:

```
#Delete the existing index
DELETE logs_04_17

#Index a document
POST logs_04_17/log/
{
   "level": "ERROR",
   "application": "Service A",
   "timestamp" : "2017-04-13T16:39:00-07:00",
   "message": "Exception in thread java.lang.NullPointerException at
chapter5.main(ServiceA.java:23)"
}
#Verify the index settings
GET logs_04_17
```

The index settings for the `logs_04_17` index are as follows:

```
{
   "logs_04_17": {
     "aliases": {},
     "mappings": {
       "log": {
         "properties": {
           "application": {
             "type": "keyword"
           },
           "level": {
             "type": "keyword"
           },
           "message": {
             "type": "text"
           },
           "timestamp": {
             "type": "date",
             "format": "date_optional_time"
           }
         }
       }
     },
     "settings": {
       "index": {
         "creation_date": "1492140374212",
         "number_of_shards": "3",
         "number_of_replicas": "1",
```

```
        "uuid": "9NjtgYx6Q2uCOWP6Csc95Q",
        "version": {
          "created": "5010299"
        },
        "provided_name": "logs_04_17"
      }
    }
  }
}
```

With the template in place, new indices can be created without worrying about the settings or the mappings. Also, with the settings and mapping, we can define the alias the index belongs to. Once the index is created, the index is automatically added to the alias. We can add the `logs_04_17` index to the `logs_last_2_months` alias as shown next:

```
PUT _template/logs_template
  {
    "template": "logs*",
    "order": 1,
    "settings": {
      "number_of_shards": 3
    },
    "aliases": {
      "logs_last_2_months": {}
    },
    "mappings": {
      "log": {
        "properties": {
          "level": {
            "type": "keyword"
          },
          "application": {
            "type": "keyword"
          },
          "timestamp": {
            "type": "date",
            "format": "date_optional_time"
          },
          "message": {
            "type": "text"
          }
        }
      }
    }
  }
}
```

Using index templates, new indices can be added to the alias, but existing indices cannot be removed. For example, when `logs_04_17` is added to the `logs_last_2_months` alias, the alias now points to more than two indices. You have to manually remove the old indexes or add a filter.

When a new logs index is created, it will be automatically added to the `logs_last_2_month` alias. Any query executed on `logs_last_2_month` will also include the results from the newly created index.

Managing time-based indices

Time series data is a very common Elasticsearch usage pattern. The data is time sensitive; we can only care about the recent data. For example, application logs, the logs beyond a certain time are not relevant anymore. The most recent logs are what we want to query. Since the old logs are not important anymore, to save the disk space and avoid unnecessary compute cycles, we have to remove the old data. The easiest way to deal with time series data is to group the indices based on a time interval so that the older indices can be deleted easily.

In this section, we will summarize the various APIs we discussed so far to manage time-based indexes. For example, we want to store application logs in day-based indices. We will use one index per day. To manage the daily indices, we can do the following:

- Define an index template to set the mappings on index creation automatically
- Use ingest node to transform raw logs into JSON document, index the document into the correct index based on the day
- Define a `logs_last_3_days` alias, which points to the indices that contain logs for the last 3 days
- Remove older indexes from the alias

The application calling Elasticsearch can use the ingest node to transform the data before indexing. We can define a pipeline to perform the necessary transformations. We can use the `date_index_name` processor to read the timestamp from the document and determine the index the document belongs to. If we are using daily indexes, a document with the `2017-04-14T09:02:34.234+07:00` timestamp will be indexed into the `log_2017_04_14` index. A pipeline with `date_index_name` processor for day-based indices is shown here:

```
{
   "pipeline": {
     "description": "Item View Pipeline",
     "processors": [
```

```
      {
        "date_index_name": {
          "field": "timestamp",
          "index_name_prefix": "log_",
          "date_rounding": "d",
          "index_name_format": "yyyy_MM_dd"
        }
      }
    ]
  }
}
```

For more information on how to use ingest node, please refer to the *Ingest Node* section.

Next, let's define an index template to apply the mapping automatically when the index name starts with the word log. When the index is created, it will also be added to the logs_last_3_days alias:

```
PUT _template/logs_template
  {
    "template": "log*",
    "aliases": {
      "logs_last_3_days": {}
    }
  }
```

When the ingest nodes write the document into a new index, the settings/mappings from the template are applied to the index. Please refer to the *Index templates* section for more information.

Next, we will remove the older indexes from the logs_last_3_days alias. When querying the alias, including a date filter for the last 3 days will ensure the data accuracy:

```
POST /_aliases
  {
    "actions": [
      {
        "remove": {
          "index": "log_2017_04_14",
          "alias": "logs_last_3_days"
        }
      }
    ]
  }
```

In the next section, we will discuss the Shrink API, which can be used to reduce the number of shards of an index.

Shrink API

Shrink API is used to shrink an existing index into a new index with a fewer number of shards. If the data in the index is no longer changing, the index can be optimized for search and aggregation by reducing the number of shards. The number of shards in the destination index must be a factor of the original index. For example, an index with 6 primary shards can be shrunk into 3, 2, or 1 shards. When working with time-sensitive data, such as logs, data is only indexed into the current indexes and older indexes are mostly read only. Shrink API doesn't re-index the document; it simply relinks the index segments to the new index.

To shrink an index, the index should be marked as read-only, and either a primary or a replica of all the shards of the index should be moved to one node. We can force the allocation of the shards to one node and mark it as read only as shown next. The shrink_node_name is the name of the node into which all the shards can be allocated.

```
PUT /index_with_six_shards/_settings
{
  "settings": {
    "index.routing.allocation.require._name": "shrink_node_name",
    "index.blocks.write": true
  }
}
```

Once the allocation is finished, we can use the _shrink API to shrink the index as shown here:

```
POST index_with_six_shards/_shrink/index_with_one_shard
{
  "settings": {
    "index.number_of_replicas": 1,
    "index.number_of_shards": 1
  }
}
```

You can monitor the shrink process using the cluster health API as shown here:

```
GET _cluster/health
```

Once all the shards are changed from initializing to the active state, the new index is ready.

Summary

In this chapter, we discussed the various bulk operations Elasticsearch supports. You also learned about Reindex and Shrink APIs, which can be used to the change the index configuration, such as the number of shards, mapping of an existing index and so on without re-indexing the data.

We covered how to organize your data in Elasticsearch using aliases and index templates. We discussed how to use ingest node to pre-process your data before indexing into Elasticsearch. You learned how to use ingest node to transform unstructured log data into JSON documents and automatically index them into a month-based index.

In the next chapter, we will discuss different ways of querying Elasticsearch.

6
All About Search

This chapter dives into search and helps you understand the different types of queries Elasticsearch supports. You will learn how to search, sort, and paginate on your data. Unlike SQL, the query language is based on JSON structure and is very flexible. It is very easy to combine and nest queries. You will also learn how to execute structured queries and full-text queries.

Elasticsearch is a search engine. When you run a query on Elasticsearch, each document in the result is given a relevance score. For example, you are looking for restaurant close by with decent prices, the relevance score in this case is a combination of distance and price. The results are ordered based on how relevant is each document to the query. You will learn the difference between **sorting** and **scoring**. You will learn how relevance is calculated and how to tune the relevance score.

We will discuss how to debug a search query and how it works internally. We will also go through how queries are automatically cached to improve the performance and the different types of cache.

By the end of this chapter, you will learn the following:

- Structured queries
- Full-text queries
- Sort and pagination
- Relevance
- Routing
- Caching

Different types of queries

Elasticsearch queries are executed using the **Search API**. Like anything else in Elasticsearch, request and response are represented in **JSON**.

Queries in Elasticsearch at a high level are divided as follows:

- **Structured queries**: Structured queries are used to query numbers, dates, statuses, and so on. These are similar to queries supported by a SQL database. For example, whether a number or date falls within a range or to find all the employees with `John` as the first name and so on
- **Full-text search queries**: Full-text search queries are used to search text fields. When you send a full-text query to Elasticsearch, it first finds all the documents that match the query, and then the documents are **ranked** based on how relevant each document is to the query. We will discuss relevance in detail in the *Relevance* section

Both structured and full-text search queries can be combined while querying. In the next section, we will describe the overall structure of request and response.

Sample data

To better explain the various concepts in this chapter, we will use the e-commerce site as an example. We will create an index with a list of products. This will be a very simple index called `chapter6` with type called `product`. The mapping for the `product` type is shown here:

```
#Delete existing index if any
DELETE chapter6

#Mapping
PUT chapter6
{
  "settings": {},
  "mappings": {
    "product": {
      "properties": {
        "product_name": {
          "type": "text",
          "analyzer": "english"
        },
        "description" : {
          "type": "text",
```

```
            "analyzer": "english"
          }
        }
      }
    }
  }
}
```

For the `product_name` and `description` fields, the English analyzer will be used instead of the default standard analyzer. Let's index some product documents:

```
#Index Documents
PUT chapter6/product/1
{
  "product_name": "Men's High Performance Fleece Jacket",
  "description": "Best Value. All season fleece jacket",
  "unit_price": 79.99,
  "reviews": 250,
  "release_date": "2016-08-16"
}

PUT chapter6/product/2
{
  "product_name": "Men's Water Resistant Jacket",
  "description": "Provides comfort during biking and hiking",
  "unit_price": 69.99,
  "reviews": 5,
  "release_date": "2017-03-02"
}

PUT chapter6/product/3
{
  "product_name": "Women's wool Jacket",
  "description": "Helps you stay warm in winter",
  "unit_price": 59.99,
  "reviews": 10,
  "release_date": "2016-12-15"
}
```

We will refer to the preceding three documents for different examples used in this chapter.

Querying Elasticsearch

One of most powerful features of Elasticsearch is the Query **DSL** (**Domain specific Language**) or the query language. The query language is very expressive and can be used to define filters, queries, sorting, pagination, and aggregations in the same query. To execute a search query, an HTTP request should be sent to the _search endpoint. The index and type on which the query should be executed is specified in the URL. Index and type are optional. If no index/type is specified, Elasticsearch executes the request across all the indexes in the cluster. A search query in Elasticsearch can be executed in two different ways:

- By passing the search request as query parameters.
- By passing the search request in the request body.

A simple search query using query parameters is shown here:

```
GET chapter6/product/_search?q=product_name:jacket
```

Simple queries can be executed using the URL request parameters. Anything other than a simple query like in the above example should be passed as the request body. The preceding query, when passed as a request body, looks like the following:

```
POST chapter6/product/_search
{
    "query": {
      "term": {
        "product_name" : "jacket"
      }
    }
}
```

The preceding query is executed on the chapter6 index and type named product. The query can also be executed on multiple indexes/types at the same time, as shown here:

```
POST chapter5,chapter6/product,product_reviews/_search
{
    "query": {
      "term": {
        "product_name" : "jacket"
      }
    }
}
```

The HTTP verb we used in the preceding example for the `_search` API is POST. You can also use GET instead of POST. Since most browsers will not support a request body when using GET, we used POST.

The basic structure of the request body is shown here:

```
{
    "size" : //The number of results in the response. Defaults to 10.

    "from" : // The offset of the results. For example, to get the third
page for a page size of 20; you should set the size to 20 and from to 40.

    "timeout" : // A timeout can be specified after which the partial
results are sent back in the response. By default there is no timeout. If
the request times out, the timed_out value in the response will be
indicated as true.

    "_source" : //To select the fields, that should be included in the
response. For example : "_source" : ["product_name", "description"].
    "query" : {
        // Query
    }

    "aggs" : {
        // Aggregations
    }

    "sort" : {
        // How to sort the results
    }
}
```

We will discuss each section of the request, such as pagination, sort, and so on, in the following sections. The structure of the response body is shown here:

```
{
    "took": // Time Elasticsearch took to execute the query.

    "timed_out": // Did the query time out. By default, there is no timeout.

    // Elasticsearch doesn't fail the request if some shards don't respond or
    not available. The response will contain partial results.

    "_shards": {
        "total": // Number of shards the query needs to be executed.
        "successful": // Number of shards the query is successful on.
```

```
    "failed": // Number of shards the query failed.
  },
  "hits": {
   "total": // Total number of hits
   "max_score": // Maximum score of all the documents
   "hits": [
      // Actual documents.
   ]
  }
}
```

Basic query (finding the exact value)

The basic query in Elasticsearch is term query. It is very simple and can be used to query numbers, boolean, dates, and text. Term query is used to look up a single term in the inverted index. Match query, on the other hand, takes care of the mapping and calls term query internally. Match query should be your go-to query. We will describe the differences in detail in the *Term versus Match query* section.

A simple term query looks like the following:

```
POST chapter6/product/_search
{
   "query": {
     "term": {
       "product_name" : "jacket"
     }
   }
}
```

Term query works great for a single term. To query more than one term, we have to use terms query. It is similar to `in clause` in a relational database. If the document matches any one of the terms, it's a match. For example, we want to find all the documents that contain `jacket` or `fleece` in the product name. The query will look like the following:

```
POST chapter6/_search
{
   "query": {
     "terms": {
       "product_name" : ["jacket","fleece"]
     }
   }
}
```

The response of the query is as follows:

```
{
    ....
    "hits": {
        "total": 3,
        "max_score": 0.2876821,
        "hits": [
            {
                "_index": "chapter6",
                "_type": "product",
                "_id": "2",
                "_score": 0.2876821,
                "_source": {
                    "product_name": "Men's Water Resistant Jacket",
                    "description": "Provides comfort during biking and hiking",
                    "unit_price": 69.99,
                    "reviews": 5,
                    "release_date": "2017-03-02"
                }
            },
            {
                "_index": "chapter6",
                "_type": "product",
                "_id": "1",
                "_score": 0.2824934,
                "_source": {
                    "product_name": "Men's High Performance Fleece Jacket",
                    "description": "Best Value. All season fleece jacket",
                    "unit_price": 79.99,
                    "reviews": 250,
                    "release_date": "2016-08-16"
                }
            },
            {
                "_index": "chapter6",
                "_type": "product",
                "_id": "3",
                "_score": 0.25316024,
                "_source": {
                    "product_name": "Women's wool Jacket",
                    "description": "Helps you stay warm in winter",
                    "unit_price": 59.99,
                    "reviews": 10,
                    "release_date": "2016-12-15"
                }
            }
        ]
    }
}
```

```
    }
  }
```

Pagination

In the previous section, we learned about the basic query in Elasticsearch. In this section, we will discuss how to limit the number of results in the response. Pagination is supported using the `from` and `size` fields in the query. The default page size is `10`. A query to limit the number of documents to `2` is shown here:

```
#Pagination
POST chapter6/_search
{
  "from" : 0,
  "size" : 2,
  "query" : {
    "match" : {
      "product_name" : "wool jacket"
    }
  }
}
```

In the preceding query, we are getting the top `2` results. If the page size is `10`, to get the third page, we would use `from` as `20` and `size` as `10`. Pagination in a distributed system is very expensive when compared to a traditional database. The data belonging to an index is spread across multiple shards. For example, if the index consists of five shards, to get the third page, all five shards send the top thirty results to the coordinating node. The coordinating node, in turn, sorts the results from all the shards and sends the results from `20` to `30`. The higher the page number, more expensive is the query.

Sorting based on existing fields

Elasticsearch is a full-text search engine, and the results are ordered by the relevance of each document to the query. We will talk about relevance in detail in the *Relevance* section. In this section, we will only discuss sorting the results based on the existing fields in the document. You can sort the results based on one or more fields. For example, we want to sort the product based on the price. A simple sort query is shown here:

```
#Sort
POST chapter6/_search
  {
    "query": {
```

```
      "match": {
        "product_name": "jacket"
      }
    },
    "sort": {
      "unit_price": {
        "order": "desc"
      }
    }
  }
```

We can also sort using multiple fields. In the following query, we will sort the results by the price and number of reviews:

```
POST chapter6/_search
{
  "query": {
    "match": {
      "product_name": "jacket"
    }
  },
  "sort": [
    {
      "unit_price": {
        "order": "desc"
      }
    },
    {
      "reviews": {
        "order": "desc"
      }
    }
  ]
}
```

 When sorting using multiple fields, the results are first sorted by first field and then by other fields. If the field values for the first field are unique, the other sort will have no effect. Only if two or more documents have the same field value for the first field, the second field is used to sort.

When we sort by multiple fields like in the preceding example, where the documents are first sorted by the price and then by the number of reviews.

Selecting the fields in the response

When you execute a query, by default, the original JSON document which is stored as _source field in the document is returned in the response. Sometimes we want to only include certain fields in the response, especially when the document is big or has lot of fields.

This can be done by specifying the fields in _source field during the query. The fields values are fetched from the document _source. If the source is disabled via mapping, this won't work. The response of the following query will only have the product_name field in the response:

```
POST chapter6/product/_search
  {
    "_source": [
      "product_name"
    ],
    "query": {
      "term": {
        "product_name": "jacket"
      }
    }
  }
```

The response to the preceding query is as follows:

```
{
  ....
  "hits": {
    "total": 3,
    "max_score": 0.13353139,
    "hits": [
      {
        "_index": "chapter6",
        "_type": "product",
        "_id": "2",
        "_score": 0.13353139,
        "_source": {
          "product_name": "Men's Water Resistant Jacket"
        }
      },
      {
        "_index": "chapter6",
        "_type": "product",
        "_id": "3",
        "_score": 0.13353139,
        "_source": {
```

```
          "product_name": "Women's wool Jacket"
        }
      },
      {
        "_index": "chapter6",
        "_type": "product",
        "_id": "1",
        "_score": 0.11867011,
        "_source": {
          "product_name": "Men's High Performance Fleece Jacket"
        }
      }
    ]
  }
}
```

The `_source` field also supports wildcards for the fields names. We can tell Elasticsearch only to include the fields that start with `pr`, as shown here:

```
POST chapter6/product/_search
{
  "_source": [
    "pr*"
  ],
  "query": {
    "term": {
      "product_name": "jacket"
    }
  }
}
```

When returning the fields in the document, scripts can be evaluated on the field value. For example, along with the product price, we want to the return the price including tax. If the sales tax is `10%`, we can use the scripted field to calculate the price with tax and return the field value along the results. The query looks like the following:

```
POST chapter6/product/_search
{
  "_source": [],
  "query": {
    "match_all": {}
  },
  "script_fields": {
    "price_including_tax": {
      "script": {
        "inline" : "params['_source']['unit_price'] * 1.1"
      }
    }
```

```
        }
    }
```

The default scripting language for Elasticsearch is called **Painless**. Using the Painless language, we can access the _source of the document to retrieve the unit_price and multiply with 1.1 to calculate the price including tax. The response to the preceding query is as follows:

```
{
    . . . .
    "hits": {
        "total": 3,
        "max_score": 1,
        "hits": [
            {
                "_index": "chapter6",
                "_type": "product",
                "_id": "1",
                "_score": 1,
                "_source": {
                    "product_name": "Men's High Performance Fleece Jacket",
                    "description": "Best Value. All season fleece jacket",
                    "unit_price": 79.99,
                    "reviews": 250,
                    "release_date": "2016-08-16"
                },
                "fields": {
                    "price_including_tax": [
                        87.989
                    ]
                }
            },
            {
                "_index": "chapter6",
                "_type": "product",
                "_id": "2",
                "_score": 1,
                "_source": {
                    "product_name": "Men's Water Resistant Jacket",
                    "description": "Provides comfort during biking and hiking",
                    "unit_price": 69.99,
                    "reviews": 5,
                    "release_date": "2017-03-02"
                },
                "fields": {
                    "price_including_tax": [
                        76.989
                    ]
```

```
        }
      },
      {
        "_index": "chapter6",
        "_type": "product",
        "_id": "3",
        "_score": 1,
        "_source": {
          "product_name": "Women's wool Jacket",
          "description": "Helps you stay warm in winter",
          "unit_price": 59.99,
          "reviews": 10,
          "release_date": "2016-12-15"
        },
        "fields": {
          "price_including_tax": [
            65.989
          ]
        }
      }
    ]
  }
}
```

The response includes the original price and the price including tax. Although scripting is very powerful, each document has to be parsed to extract the field value, which might come with a performance cost.

Querying based on range

Range query can be used on *numbers* and *dates* to query for all the documents in a given range.

Range query supports the following operators:

- lt: < less than operator
- gt: > greater than operator
- lte: <= less than or equal to operator
- gte: >= greater than or equal to operator

An SQL query to query all the products greater than 70 and less than 100 is shown here:

```
select * from product where unitprice > 70 and unitprice <= 100
```

The preceding query can be written using a range query as shown here:

```
POST chapter6/_search
{
    "query": {
      "range": {
        "unit_price": {
          "gt": 70,
          "lte": 100
        }
      }
    }
}
```

Similarly, a range query can also be used on dates as shown here:

```
POST chapter6/_search
{
    "query": {
      "range": {
        "release_date": {
          "gt": "2017-01-01",
          "lte": "now"
        }
      }
    }
}
```

We will discuss how to query dates in detail in the next section.

Handling dates

Elasticsearch makes it very easy to work with dates. It supports timezones, adding and removing hours/days/months/years to a given date. It also supports `now` as shown in the following example, which returns the current timestamp as datetime value. For example, to find all the documents that were modified within the last hour, the query is shown here:

```
POST chapter6/_search
  {
    "query": {
      "range": {
        "release_date": {
          "gt": "now-1h"
        }
      }
    }
}
```

```
    }
```

A date string or `now` followed by date math can also be specified as follows. The `||` symbol separates the date and date math operation:

```
POST chapter6/_search
{
    "query": {
      "range": {
        "release_date": {
          "gt": "2017-01-11T20:00:00||+1M"
        }
      }
    }
}
```

The following are examples of different date operations supported:

- `now+1M`: This adds one month. You can also use a different date unit, such as an hour, day, month, year, and so on
- `2017-02-01||-1M`: This subtracts one month
- `now/d`: This is used to round to the nearest day
- `now+1M-1d/d`: This adds one month, subtract one day, and round to the nearest day
- `2017-02-01||+1H/d`: This adds one hour to 2017-02-01 and rounds to the nearest day

The following time units are supported:

Time unit	Description
y	years
M	months
w	weeks
d	days
h	hours
H	hours
m	minutes
s	seconds

Analyzed versus non-analyzed fields

To store text values, Elasticsearch supports two mapping types:

- Text: Text fields are analyzed (broken into individual terms) before they are stored in the inverted index
- Keyword: Keyword fields are stored as they are into the inverted index

To better explain text and keyword mapping types, let's use multi-fields to index the same field value as both text and keyword. The mapping for the product_name field is shown next, the mapping for the other fields in the document is irrelevant to this section. Once the mapping is set, we will index a few example documents and run the same query on the product_name and product_name.keyword fields to look at the differences:

```
PUT chapter6/_mapping/fruit
{
    "properties": {
        "product_id": {
            "type": "integer"
        },
        "product_name": {
            "type": "text",
            "analyzer": "english",
            "fields": {
                "keyword": {
                    "type": "keyword"
                }
            }
        }
    }
}
```

Let's index a document:

```
PUT chapter6/fruit/1
{
    "product_id": "1",
    "product_name": "Red Gala Apple"
}
```

Due to multi-field mapping on the product_name, the value of the field is automatically indexed as text and keyword. Since the product_name field has text mapping, it will be analyzed before it is stored in the inverted index. From the preceding example, when the Red Gala Apple text is analyzed using the english analyzer, it is broken down into the red, gala, appl tokens.

You can also use the Analyze API to inspect the list of tokens as shown here:

```
GET _analyze?analyzer=english&text=Red+Gala+Apple
```

You will see a response similar to the following:

```
{
    "tokens": [
        {
            "token": "red",
            "start_offset": 0,
            "end_offset": 3,
            "type": "<ALPHANUM>",
            "position": 0
        },
        {
            "token": "gala",
            "start_offset": 4,
            "end_offset": 8,
            "type": "<ALPHANUM>",
            "position": 1
        },
        {
            "token": "appl",
            "start_offset": 9,
            "end_offset": 14,
            "type": "<ALPHANUM>",
            "position": 2
        }
    ]
}
```

However, the inverted index for the product_name.keyword field will have the exact value (Red Gala Apple) as the mapping type is a keyword. Let's run the same query on the product_name and product_name.keyword fields to see how analyzed and non-analyzed fields are stored differently:

```
POST chapter6/fruit/_search
{
    "query": {
        "term": {
            "product_name": "appl"
        }
    }
}
```

In the preceding query, we are using a term query on the `product_name` field, which is analyzed. The term query will look into the inverted index of the `product_name` field and return the documents that contain the term `appl`. The response will have a document with the `Red Gala Apple` product name.

Let's run the same query on the `product_name.keyword` field, which is not analyzed:

```
POST chapter6/fruit/_search
{
  "query": {
    "term": {
      "product_name.keyword": "appl"
    }
  }
}
```

The response to this query does not contain any result as the inverted index of the keyword field doesn't have an entry with `appl`. Since `product_name.keyword` is not analyzed, the inverted index will only have `Red Gala Apple`. Let's rerun the query:

```
POST chapter6/fruit/_search
{
  "query": {
    "term": {
      "product_name.keyword": "Red Gala Apple"
    }
  }
}
```

You will see a response similar to the following:

```
{
  .....
  "hits": {
    "total": 1,
    "max_score": 0.2876821,
    "hits": [
      {
        "_index": "chapter6",
        "_type": "fruit",
        "_id": "1",
        "_score": 0.2876821,
        "_source": {
          "product_id": "1",
          "product_name": "Red Gala Apple"
        }
      }
```

```
    ]
  }
}
```

The response will contain only one hit as this is an exact match. Similarly, if you query for `apple` in the `product_name.keyword` field, you will not get back any results as the inverted index of `product_name.keyword` only contains `Red Gala Apple`.

Term versus Match query

Term query is the most commonly used query and can be used to query numbers, boolean, dates, and text. Term query looks for the exact search input in the inverted index. Term query is a low-level query and scores the results by default. You can use the term on analyzed or non-analyzed fields. It does not take the mapping type into the account; it just looks for the term in the inverted index.

A match query, unlike term, understands the field mapping. The input query is broken down using the field analyzer. Let's take an example and discuss how match query works:

```
POST chapter6/product/_search
  {
    "query": {
      "term": {
        "product_name": "Women's wool Jacket"
      }
    }
  }
```

When you run the preceding query, you will not see any result in the response as term query looks for `"Women's wool Jacket"` in the inverted index for `product_name` and does not find any matches. Now if we run the same query using a match instead of the term query as shown next, you will see three hits in the result:

```
POST chapter6/product/_search
  {
    "query": {
      "match": {
        "product_name": "Women's wool Jacket"
      }
    }
  }
```

The following happens when you use a match query:

- Match query first looks at the `product_name` field mapping and learns that it is an analyzed field
- It uses the same analyzer used during indexing (if no analyzer is specified during mapping, standard analyzer is default) to break the query term into tokens
- Analyzing the `"Women's wool Jacket"` query term, it will converted into `women`, `wool`, and `jacket` tokens
- Next, it runs a term filter for each token and combines the results. If the match query is run on a non-analyzed field, it will run the term filter without analyzing the query

The response to the match query is as follows:

```
{
    ....
    "hits": {
      "total": 3,
      "max_score": 2.0951898,
      "hits": [
        {
          "_index": "chapter6",
          "_type": "product",
          "_id": "3",
          "_score": 2.0951898,
          "_source": {
            "product_name": "Women's wool Jacket",
            "description": "Helps you stay warm in winter",
            "unit_price": 59.99,
            "reviews": 10,
            "release_date": "2016-12-15"
          }
        },
        {
          "_index": "chapter6",
          "_type": "product",
          "_id": "2",
          "_score": 0.13353139,
          "_source": {
            "product_name": "Men's Water Resistant Jacket",
            "description": "Provides comfort during biking and hiking",
            "unit_price": 69.99,
            "reviews": 5,
            "release_date": "2017-03-02"
          }
        },
```

```
     {
       "_index": "chapter6",
       "_type": "product",
       "_id": "1",
       "_score": 0.11867011,
       "_source": {
         "product_name": "Men's High Performance Fleece Jacket",
         "description": "Best Value. All season fleece jacket",
         "unit_price": 79.99,
         "reviews": 250,
         "release_date": "2016-08-16"
       }
     }
   ]
  }
 }
```

You can see from the response that along with women's wool Jacket, two other documents also matched the query. That's because by default, the match query is converted into a should query, the preceding match query is equivalent to:

```
{
  "query": {
    "bool": {
      "should": [
        {
          "term": {
            "product_name": "womens"
          }
        },
        {
          "term": {
            "product_name": "wool"
          }
        },
        {
          "term": {
            "product_name": "jacket"
          }
        }
      ]
    }
  }
}
```

If you want only the documents that contain all three terms, you can change the operator to and as shown here:

```
POST chapter6/product/_search
  {
    "query": {
      "match": {
        "product_name": {
          "query": "Women's wool Jacket",
          "operator": "and"
        }
      }
    }
  }
```

The response to the preceding query is as follows:

```
{
    ....
    "hits": {
      "total": 1,
      "max_score": 2.0951898,
      "hits": [
        {
          "_index": "chapter6",
          "_type": "product",
          "_id": "3",
          "_score": 2.0951898,
          "_source": {
            "product_name": "Women's wool Jacket",
            "description": "Helps you stay warm in winter",
            "unit_price": 59.99,
            "reviews": 10,
            "release_date": "2016-12-15"
          }
        }
      ]
    }
}
```

Match phrase query

Match phrase query is similar to the match query but is used to query text phrases. Phrase matching is necessary when the ordering of the words is important. Only the documents that contain the words in the same order as the search input are matched.

During the indexing process, along with the token, the position of the word in the text is also saved to the inverted index. The position information is then used in the phrase query. For example, to find an all season jacket, we will use the match phrase query on the description field. The query is shown here:

```
#Match Phrase
POST chapter6/_search
{
  "query": {
    "match_phrase": {
      "description": "All season jacket"
    }
  }
}
```

The preceding query will not match any product as the original field value is `All season fleece jacket` and the words season and jacket are not next to each other. To relax the ordering of the words, you can use the `slop` parameter. The preceding query with a slop value of `1` looks like the following:

```
#Match Phrase
POST chapter6/_search
{
  "query": {
    "match_phrase": {
      "description": {
        "query": "All season jacket",
        "slop": 1
      }
    }
  }
}
```

The response to the preceding query is as follows:

```
{
  ....
  "hits": {
    "total": 1,
    "max_score": 1.6183683,
    "hits": [
      {
        "_index": "chapter6",
        "_type": "product",
        "_id": "1",
        "_score": 1.6183683,
        "_source": {
```

```
        "product_name": "Men's High Performance Fleece Jacket",
        "description": "Best Value. All season fleece jacket",
        "unit_price": 79.99,
        "reviews": 250,
        "release_date": "2016-08-16"
      }
    }
  ]
 }
}
```

Prefix and match phrase prefix query

Prefix query is used to find all the documents with a given prefix. Like term query, phrase query is a low-level query and doesn't take the field mapping into consideration (refer to the *Analyzed versus non-analyzed* section for more details). Terms in the inverted index are sorted in an alphabetical order, and prefix query scans the term dictionary to find the matching terms. For example, if we want to find all the products that start with the prefix ja, the query is as follows:

```
#Prefix
POST chapter6/_search
{
  "query": {
    "prefix": {
      "product_name": "ja"
    }
  }
}
```

Match phrase prefix query combines match phrase and prefix query. Prefix matching is done only on the last term in the query. The number of prefixes that are gathered from the inverted index can be controlled using the max_expansions parameter, which defaults to 50. The Match phrase prefix query looks like the following:

```
#Match Phrase Prefix
POST chapter6/_search
{
  "query": {
    "match_phrase_prefix": {
      "product_name": {
        "query": "Men's High Pe",
        "max_expansions": 10
      }
    }
```

```
    }
  }
```

Wildcard and Regular expression query

Wildcard query is used for wildcard matching on the search input. Just like phrase query, the query term is not analyzed. The following wildcards are supported:

Wildcard	Description
*	Matches any character
?	Matches single character

A sample query looks like the following:

```
#Wildcard
POST chapter6/product/_search
{
  "query": {
    "wildcard" : {
      "product_name" : "j*e?"
    }
  }
}
```

Regex query is used to find the documents based on regular expression matching. Regular expression query can be very expensive depending on the prefix. A sample query looks like the following:

```
#Regular Expression
POST chapter6/product/_search
{
  "query": {
    "regexp" : {
      "product_name" : "jacke."
    }
  }
}
```

The following are the commonly used regex operators:

Operator	Description
.	Matches any character.
?	Matches zero or one character.

*	Matches zero or more characters.
+	To handle repetitions. Pattern `ap+1.` matches, apple.
{min, max}	Min and max repetitions. For example, `ap{2,2}le` matches apple.

To avoid scanning the entire term dictionary, avoid using regex operators (such as `*e`) at the beginning of the prefix.

Exists and missing queries

Exists query is used to find the document that contains a non-null value for the field specified in the query. For example, if you want to find all the document that contain product reviews. The query looks like the following:

```
#Exists
POST chapter6/product/_search
{
    "query": {
        "exists" : {
            "field" : "reviews"
        }
    }
}
```

If you want to find all the products that don't contain reviews, we can use the bool `must_not` query to find the documents that don't contain the field. The query looks like the following:

```
#Missing
POST chapter6/product/_search
{
    "query": {
        "bool": {
            "must_not": {
                "exists": {
                    "field": "reviews"
                }
            }
        }
    }
}
```

Using more than one query

In the relational database world, we would use the and/or clauses to combine different conditions. In Elasticsearch, we would use the **bool query** to achieve the same. Bool query is very powerful; a bool query can have other bool queries. When combining different queries, if matching one query is more important than the other, bool query supports boosting individual queries. We will discuss more in the *How to boost score based on queries* section. The basic structure of bool query is shown here:

```
{
    "query": {
      "bool": {
        "must": [],
        "must_not": [],
        "should": [],
        "filter": []
      }
    }
}
```

The must section of the bool query contains all the must-match queries. The must_not section will contain all the not queries. The should section will contain the or queries. The filter section will contain the must-match queries but in non-scoring mode. For example, an SQL query to find jackets priced under 100$ is shown here:

```
select * from Product where product_name like '%jacket%' and unit_price < 100
```

The preceding SQL query can be rewritten using the bool query as shown here:

```
POST chapter6/_search
{
    "query": {
      "bool": {
        "must": [
          {
            "match": {
              "product_name": "jacket"
            }
          },
          {
            "range": {
              "unit_price": {
                "lt": "100"
              }
            }
          }
```

```
        ]
      }
    }
  }
```

Since the conditions are wrapped in a `must`, only the documents that satisfy both the conditions are returned. Bool query also supports nesting other bool queries, for example, a user is looking for a water resistant jacket but is also okay with a performance fleece that costs less than `100$`. An SQL query to achieve the same is shown here:

```
select * from Product where
product_name like '%Water Resistant Jacket%'
or
(product_name like '%Performance Fleece%' and unit_price < 100)
```

In the preceding SQL query, the `or` condition becomes a `should` clause, and the `and` condition becomes a `must` clause. The SQL query can be written using the bool query as shown here:

```
POST chapter6/_search
  {
    "query": {
      "bool": {
        "should": [ # or
          {
            "match": {
              "product_name": {
                "query": "Water Resistant Jacket",
                "operator": "and"
              }
            }
          },
          {
            "bool": {
              "must": [ # and
                {
                  "match": {
                    "product_name": {
                      "query": "Performance Fleece",
                      "operator": "and"
                    }
                  }
                },
                {
                  "range": {
                    "unit_price": {
                      "lte": "100"
```

```
                  }
                }
              }
            ]
          }
        }
      ]
    }
  }
}
```

The response to the preceding query is shown here:

```
{
    ....
    "hits": {
      "total": 2,
      "max_score": 2.7433372,
      "hits": [
        {
          "_index": "chapter6",
          "_type": "product",
          "_id": "1",
          "_score": 2.7433372,
          "_source": {
            "product_name": "Men's High Performance Fleece Jacket",
            "description": "Best Value. All season fleece jacket",
            "unit_price": 79.99,
            "reviews": 250,
            "release_date": "2016-08-16"
          }
        },
        {
          "_index": "chapter6",
          "_type": "product",
          "_id": "2",
          "_score": 2.0951898,
          "_source": {
            "product_name": "Men's Water Resistant Jacket",
            "description": "Provides comfort during biking and hiking",
            "unit_price": 69.99,
            "reviews": 5,
            "release_date": "2017-03-02"
          }
        }
      ]
    }
}
```

Scoring is an expensive operation, and if scoring the documents is not a requirement, individual queries can be wrapped with the filter, or the entire bool query can also be wrapped with `constant_score`. We will discuss scoring in detail in *Relevance* section below. A bool query wrapped with `constant_score` is shown next:

```
{
    "query": {
      "constant_score": {
        "filter": {
          "bool": {
            "must": [],
            "must_not": [],
            "should": []
          }
        }
      }
    }
}
```

The bool query is very powerful. In the following sections, you will see that bool is the go-to query while using Elasticsearch.

Routing

In the *Routing* section of Chapter 3, *Modeling Your Data and Document Relations*, we discussed how to setup the mapping to use routing and how to index documents using a routing value. In this section, we will discuss using the routing value while running a search query.

Routing can be very handy if you have a way to group your data. For example, you can index all the documents that belong to the same user using the `user_id` as the routing value. All the documents that are indexed using the same `user_id` are indexed to the same shard. When executing a query, if you specify the routing value, Elasticsearch will execute the search request only on one shard; the shard the query has to be executed on is determined based on the routing value. This especially makes sense if the index has a lot of shards. Instead of executing the request on every shard of the index, the search request has to be executed only on one shard.

 Potential downfalls of using routing are hot spots. If some users in the system are much bigger than others, there is a possibility that the all the big users can end up in the same shard. This leads to uneven distribution of data and underutilization of resources and can potentially bring down the entire cluster.

The routing value can be passed as part of the request, as shown here:

```
POST chapter6/order/_search?routing=user1
{
    "query": {
        "match": {
            "shipping_status": "shipped"
        }
    }
}
```

Routing should be used only if there is a way of logically dividing your data by avoiding hot spots.

Debugging search query

If you are ever questioning why a document did not match the query, first check the mapping of the index/type by using the GET mapping API as shown here:

```
GET chapter6/product/_mapping
```

If the mapping is right, verify that the text field value is analyzed correctly. You can use the Analyze API to inspect the list of tokens as shown here:

```
GET _analyze?analyzer=english&text=Men's+Performance+Jacket
```

If the analyzer is behaving as expected, make sure you are using the right kind of query. For example, using a match instead of term query and so on.

If the mapping is not right, you cannot modify the mapping on the fly. You can add a new field with the correct mapping and use the copy_to functionality to the copy the values to the new field. Only the data indexed after the mapping change are copied to the new field. The other option is to re-index the entire data after setting the correct mappings.

Relevance

A traditional database usually contains structured data. A query on a database limits the data depending on different conditions specified by the user. Each condition in the query is evaluated as true/false, and the rows that don't satisfy the conditions are eliminated. However, full-text search is much more complicated. The data is unstructured, or at least the queries are.

We often need to search for the same text across one or more fields. The documents can be quite large, and the query word might appear multiple times in the same document and across several documents. Displaying all the results of the search will not help as there could be hundreds, if not more, and most documents might not even be relevant to the search.

To solve this problem, all the documents that match the query are assigned a score. The score is assigned based on how relevant each document is to the query. The results are then ranked based on the **relevance** score. The results on top are most likely what the user is looking for. In the next few sections, we will discuss how the relevance is calculated and how to tune the relevance score.

Let's query the `chapter6` index we created at the beginning of this chapter. We will use a simple term query to find jackets. The query is shown here:

```
POST chapter6/_search
  {
    "query": {
      "term": {
        "product_name" : "jacket"
      }
    }
  }
```

The response of the query looks like the following:

```
{
    ....
    "hits": {
      "total": 3,
      "max_score": 0.2876821,
      "hits": [
        {
          "_index": "chapter6",
          "_type": "product",
          "_id": "2",
          "_score": 0.2876821,
          "_source": {
            "product_name": "Men's Water Resistant Jacket",
            "description": "Provides comfort during biking and hiking",
            "unit_price": 69.99,
            "reviews": 5,
            "release_date": "2017-03-02"
          }
        },
        {
          "_index": "chapter6",
```

```
      "_type": "product",
      "_id": "1",
      "_score": 0.2824934,
      "_source": {
        "product_name": "Men's High Performance Fleece Jacket",
        "description": "Best Value. All season fleece jacket",
        "unit_price": 79.99,
        "reviews": 250,
        "release_date": "2016-08-16"
      }
    },
    {
      "_index": "chapter6",
      "_type": "product",
      "_id": "3",
      "_score": 0.25316024,
      "_source": {
        "product_name": "Women's wool Jacket",
        "description": "Helps you stay warm in winter",
        "unit_price": 59.99,
        "reviews": 10,
        "release_date": "2016-12-15"
      }
    }
  ]
 }
}
```

From the preceding response, we can see that each document contains a _score value. The scores of the three jackets are as follows:

ID	Product name	Score
2	Men's water-resistant jacket	0.2876821
1	Men's high-performance fleece jacket	0.2824934
3	Women's wool jacket	0.25316024

We can see that the document with the ID 2 is scored slightly higher than documents *1* and *3*. The score is calculated using the BM25 similarity algorithm. By default, the results are sorted using the _score values.

At a very high level, BM25 calculates the score based on the following:

- How frequently the term appears in the document--**term frequency (tf)**
- How common is the term across all the documents--**inverse document frequency (idf)**
- Documents which contains all or most of the query terms are scored higher than the document that don't
- The normalization is based on the document length, shorter documents are scored better than the longer ones

 To learn more about how the BM25 similarity algorithm works, please visit https://en.wikipedia.org/wiki/Okapi_BM25.

Not every query needs relevance. You can search for the documents that exactly match a value, such as status, or search for the documents within a given range. Elasticsearch allows combining both structured and full-text search in the same query. An Elasticsearch query can be executed in a query context or a filter context. In the query context, a relevance _score is calculated for each document matching the query. In a filter context, all the results that match the query are returned with a default relevancy score of 1.0; we will discuss more details in the next section.

Queries versus Filters

By default, when a query is executed, the relevance score is calculated for each result. When running a structured query (such as age equal to 50) or a term query on a non-analyzed field (such as gender equal to male), we do not need scoring. As these queries are simply answering *yes/no*. Calculating the relevance score for each result can be an expensive operation. By running a query in the filter context, we are telling Elasticsearch not to score the results.

The relevance score calculated for a query only applies to the current query context and cannot be reused. Like we discussed in the preceding section, score is based on term and **inverted document frequency (idf)**, due to which the queries are not cachable. On the other hand, filters have no relevance to the query and can be cached automatically. To run a query in the filter context, we have to wrap the query with a constant_score query as shown here:

```
POST chapter6/_search
{
```

```
    "query": {
      "constant_score": {
        "filter": {
          "term" : {
            "product_name" : "wool"
          }
        }
      }
    }
  }
```

The results of the preceding query are not scored, and all the documents will have a score of 1. The query runs in the filter context and can be cached. We will discuss caching further in the *Caching* section. We can also run queries that need scoring in the query context and others in the filter context. We will use the bool query to combine various queries as shown in the following example. We discussed bool query in the *Using more than one more query* section. A sample query is shown here:

```
POST chapter6/_search
{
  "query": {
    "bool": {
      "must": [
        {
          "match": { #Query context
            "product_name": "jacket"
          }
        },
        {
          "constant_score": { #Filter context
            "filter": {
              "range": {
                "unit_price": {
                  "lt": "100"
                }
              }
            }
          }
        }
      ]
    }
  }
}
```

In the preceding query, the match query is executed in the query context, and the range query is executed in the filter context.

How to boost relevance based on a single field

Although the default scoring algorithm (BM25) works for most cases, it is not domain or application specific. The ranking is purely based on the content of the document. Sometimes, a ranking based on just the content may not suffice. For example, for a user looking for a restaurant, along with his preferences, we may also need to factor the distance of a restaurant from the current user location. The restaurants closer to the user are scored better than the ones that are not. In an e-commerce world, we want to factor both price and rating of the product while scoring the products. Maybe the user can compromise on the price of the product, given there are good ratings and so on.

Just like we used the `constant_score` query to not score the results of that query, we can use the `function_score` query to score the results based on a single field or using the functions specified in the query. The basic structure of the `function_score` query is as follows:

```
{
    "query": {
      "function_score": {
        "query": {},
        "functions": [],
        "filter": {},
        "field_value_factor": {}
      }
    }
}
```

Using `field_value_factor`, we can boost the score using one field in the document. In the following example, we want the products with better reviews to show up higher on the list. Along with the full-text score, we can tell Elasticsearch to factor the number of reviews while calculating the score. Higher the number of reviews, better the document score is. See below:

```
POST chapter6/_search
  {
    "query": {
      "function_score": {
        "query": {
          "match": {
            "product_name" : "jacket"
          }
        },
        "field_value_factor": {
          "field": "reviews"
        }
```

```
            }
        }
    }
```

Now, let's look at the response to the query. The actual results will not be different from the regular query, just the ordering of the results will be different:

```
{
    ....
    "hits": {
        "total": 3,
        "max_score": 29.667528,
        "hits": [
            {
                "_index": "chapter6",
                "_type": "product",
                "_id": "1",
                "_score": 29.667528,
                "_source": {
                    "product_name": "Men's High Performance Fleece Jacket",
                    "description": "Best Value. All season fleece jacket",
                    "unit_price": 79.99,
                    "reviews": 250,
                    "release_date": "2016-08-16"
                }
            },
            {
                "_index": "chapter6",
                "_type": "product",
                "_id": "3",
                "_score": 1.3353139,
                "_source": {
                    "product_name": "Women's wool Jacket",
                    "description": "Helps you stay warm in winter",
                    "unit_price": 59.99,
                    "reviews": 10,
                    "release_date": "2016-12-15"
                }
            },
            {
                "_index": "chapter6",
                "_type": "product",
                "_id": "2",
                "_score": 0.66765696,
                "_source": {
                    "product_name": "Men's Water Resistant Jacket",
                    "description": "Provides comfort during biking and hiking",
                    "unit_price": 69.99,
```

```
            "reviews": 5,
            "release_date": "2017-03-02"
          }
        }
      ]
    }
  }
```

You can see from the preceding response that the document with 250 reviews is scored much higher than the document with 10 reviews. That's because when calculating the score, the main query is executed first, and the score is then multiple by the field value.

 Field value factor can only be used to boost the score using one field. To boost the score using multiple fields, you need to use the bool query or functions when using the function_score query.

In the following query, we will use a field_value_factor with a factor of 0.25. The factor controls the effect of the number of reviews on the score. It defaults to 1:

```
POST chapter6/_search
{
  "query": {
    "function_score": {
      "query": {
        "match": {
          "product_name": {
            "query": "jacket"
          }
        }
      },
      "field_value_factor": {
        "field": "reviews",
        "factor": "0.25"
      }
    }
  }
}
```

The score is calculated using the following formula:

```
score = _score + (factor * reviews)
```

We use the factor to normalize the results. Without the factor, we would see very high score values. The scores of the documents are as follows:

Id	Product Name	Reviews	Score
1	Men's high-performance fleece jacket	250	7.416882
2	Men's water-resistant jacket	5	0.33382848
3	Women's wool jacket	10	0.16691424

To better normalize the effect of the number of reviews, we can also use a modifier, such as a logarithmic function. The query with the modifier is shown here:

```
POST chapter6/_search
  {
    "query": {
      "function_score": {
        "query": {
          "match": {
            "product_name": {
              "query": "jacket"
            }
          }
        },
        "field_value_factor": {
          "field": "reviews",
          "modifier": "log1p"
        }
      }
    }
  }
```

The scores of the documents with a logarithmic modifier are as follows:

Id	Product Name	Reviews	Score (Factor 0.25)	Score (log1p modifier)
1	Men's high-performance fleece jacket	250	7.416882	0.28476956
2	Men's water-resistant jacket	5	0.33382848	0.13905862
3	Women's wool jacket	10	0.16691424	0.10390762

You can see from the preceding table that the document with ID 1 has the highest score as it has the most reviews. You may also want to factor both the price and the rating of the product while calculating the relevance. Elasticsearch Query DSL supports custom scoring or boosting individual queries. Boosting the queries enables relevance calculation based on the different signals, such as price or distance from the user location.

How to boost score based on queries

In this section, we will discuss how to use the bool query to combine different queries and boost individual queries. By default, the scores of all the queries are added to calculate the final score. The result documents must match all the `must` queries. The more `should` queries the document matches, the more relevant the document is. For example, we are looking for jackets priced under $100 and have at least 25 reviews. We will use the match query to match the term "jacket" in the must clause, price and reviews in the should clause. The more should clauses the document matches, the higher the score is. Jackets that are over $100 or which have reviews less than 25 can show up in results but are scored very low when compared to the jackets that match one or both the should conditions. This is similar to choosing the preferences on the navigation window, usually on the left, when shopping on an e-commerce site. The bool query to rank the product based on the should clause is shown here:

```
#Boosting queries using bool
POST chapter6/_search
{
    "query": {
      "bool": {
        "must": [
            {
              "match": {
                "product_name": "jacket"
              }
            }
        ],
        "should": [
            {
              "range": {
                "unit_price": {
                  "lt": 100
                }
              }
            },
            {
              "range": {
                "reviews": {
                  "gte": 25
                }
              }
            }
        ]
      }
    }
}
```

The response to the query is as follows:

```
{
  ....
  "hits": {
    "total": 3,
    "max_score": 2.1186702,
    "hits": [
      {
        "_index": "chapter6",
        "_type": "product",
        "_id": "1",
        "_score": 2.1186702,
        "_source": {
          "product_name": "Men's High Performance Fleece Jacket",
          "description": "Best Value. All season fleece jacket",
          "unit_price": 79.99,
          "reviews": 250,
          "release_date": "2016-08-16"
        }
      },
      {
        "_index": "chapter6",
        "_type": "product",
        "_id": "2",
        "_score": 1.1335313,
        "_source": {
          "product_name": "Men's Water Resistant Jacket",
          "description": "Provides comfort during biking and hiking",
          "unit_price": 69.99,
          "reviews": 5,
          "release_date": "2017-03-02"
        }
      },
      {
        "_index": "chapter6",
        "_type": "product",
        "_id": "3",
        "_score": 1.1335313,
        "_source": {
          "product_name": "Women's wool Jacket",
          "description": "Helps you stay warm in winter",
          "unit_price": 59.99,
          "reviews": 10,
          "release_date": "2016-12-15"
        }
      }
    ]
```

```
      }
   }
```

The scores of the document are as follows:

Id	Product Name	Price	Reviews	Score
1	Men's high-performance fleece jacket	79.99	250	2.1186702
2	Men's water-resistant jacket	69.99	5	1.1335313
3	Women's wool jacket	59.99	10	1.1335313

The range query is a structured query. For every range query the document matches, a score of 1 is added to the final score. In the preceding example, both the price and the number of reviews contribute to the score equally. For example, if having more reviews is more important than the price, we can boost the reviews query. In the following query, the score for the reviews query is boosted to 2, and the score from the price query is boosted to 0.5. Only using the bool query, we can control how each query can contribute towards the final score, which is not possible using sort:

```
POST chapter6/_search
  {
    "query": {
      "bool": {
        "must": [
          {
            "match": {
              "product_name": "jacket"
            }
          }
        ],
        "should": [
          {
            "range": {
              "unit_price": {
                "lt": 100,
                "boost": 0.5
              }
            }
          },
          {
            "range": {
              "reviews": {
                "gte": 25,
                "boost": 2
              }
            }
          }
```

```
              }
          ]
        }
      }
    }
```

The scores of the document are as follows:

Id	Product Name	Price	Reviews	Score
1	Men's high-performance fleece jacket	79.99	250	2.1186702
2	Men's water-resistant jacket	69.99	5	0.6335314
3	Women's wool jacket	59.99	10	0.6335314

You can see from the response that due to `0.5` boost on the price, the score for the documents with ID `2` and `3` has been reduced to `0.633` from `1.333`. In the next section, we will factor the release date so that the documents that are released recently are scored more and thereby ranked higher in the results.

How to boost relevance using decay functions

In the previous section, we used the number of reviews and the price of the product to compute the relevance score. In this section, we will promote the recent products using their release date. We want to score the most recently released products higher than the older ones. By the end of this section, we will combine the scores from the main search, the number of reviews, and the release date.

We can start by defining range queries for different time intervals and wrap them in a bool query. Assuming that products released last year are less important than those released in the current year, in the following query, products that are released in the current year are boosted by `1`, the products released in last year are boosted by `0.5`:

```
POST chapter6/_search
  {
    "query" : {
      "bool": {
        "should": [
          {
            "range": {
              "release_date": {
                "gte": "now/y",
                "boost": 1
              }
```

```
              }
          },
          {
            "range": {
              "release_date": {
                "gte": "now-1y/y",
                "lte": "now/y",
                "boost": "0.5"
              }
            }
          }
        ]
      }
    }
  }
```

In the preceding query, `now/y` represents the current date rounded to the year. Please refer to the *Handling dates* section for more details on different date functions that are supported. Using bool queries to score based on different intervals is not very practical. Products that are released in January last year are scored equally as December last year. Regardless of the month a product is released in, it will be classified in the same bucket as all the products in a given year. To calculate a more accurate score for numeric values, dates and geo-location decay functions can be used.

Decay functions work by choosing an origin value and decrease the score as the value moves away from the origin. For example, a user is looking for restaurants close by. We can use his current location as an origin and score the restaurants based on the distance from the origin. The restaurants close by are scored higher than the restaurants further away. By using decay functions, the score is gradually decreased instead of a sudden drop.

In the previous sections, we used the number of reviews to calculate the relevance score; in this section, we will use the release date along with the number of reviews to calculate the score. To use a decay function, we have to specify the origin and scale. The scale parameter defines the rate at which the score is decreased when moving away from the origin, as shown below:

```
POST chapter6/_search
  {
    "query": {
      "function_score": {
        "functions": [
          {
            "gauss": {
              "release_date": {
                "origin": "now",
                "scale": "180d"
```

```
            }
          }
        }
      ]
    }
  }
}
```

 Note how we used `now` as origin and `180d` as the scale. Elasticsearch is calendar aware and will automatically convert these to the appropriate dates.

With the assumption that new products are released every 6 months, we set the scale to 180 days. A product that is released close to the current date receives a score of 1, and a product released six months prior receives a score of 0.5. In the preceding query, we used the Gaussian function. Depending on how you would like the score to decline, whether it be a gradual, continuous curve or a sudden fall, you can choose between linear, exponential, or Gaussian function types.

 Although, Elasticsearch supports different time units, such as year, month, week, day, and hour, at the time of writing, anything beyond days is currently throwing an exception. As an alternative, I represented 6 months as 180 days.

Now is `April 6th, 2017`. The scores of the documents are as follows:

ID	Product Name	Release Date	Score
2	Men's water-resistant jacket	2017-03-02	0.97225076
3	Women's wool jacket	2016-12-15	0.7599717
1	Men's high-performance fleece jacket	2016-08-16	0.30909336

Next, along with the release date, we want to add a function for the price. For example, a user is trying to find products that are priced around $50 and that are recently released. We will the `function_score` query to group the functions for the price and the release date. By default, the scores of the functions are multiplied with each other to calculate the final score. For example, if the product that is just released has a very high price. Multiplying the scores from both the functions uses the scores from both the functions. Other scoring modes such as sum, avg, min, max, and first are also supported, as shown below:

```
POST chapter6/_search
{
  "query": {
```

```
"function_score": {
  "functions": [
    {
      "gauss": {
        "unit_price": {
          "origin": "50",
          "scale": "15"
        }
      }
    },
    {
      "gauss": {
        "release_date": {
          "origin": "now",
          "scale": "180d"
        }
      }
    }
  ]
}
}
}
```

The results to the preceding query are as follows:

```
{
....
"hits": {
  "total": 3,
  "max_score": 0.55876404,
  "hits": [
    {
      "_index": "chapter6",
      "_type": "product",
      "_id": "3",
      "_score": 0.55876404,
      "_source": {
        "product_name": "Women's wool Jacket",
        "description": "Helps you stay warm in winter",
        "unit_price": 59.99,
        "reviews": 10,
        "release_date": "2016-12-15"
      }
    },
    {
      "_index": "chapter6",
      "_type": "product",
      "_id": "2",
```

```
        "_score": 0.28387982,
        "_source": {
          "product_name": "Men's Water Resistant Jacket",
          "description": "Provides comfort during biking and hiking",
          "unit_price": 69.99,
          "reviews": 5,
          "release_date": "2017-03-02"
        }
      },
      {
        "_index": "chapter6",
        "_type": "product",
        "_id": "1",
        "_score": 0.019349905,
        "_source": {
          "product_name": "Men's High Performance Fleece Jacket",
          "description": "Best Value. All season fleece jacket",
          "unit_price": 79.99,
          "reviews": 250,
          "release_date": "2016-08-16"
        }
      }
    ]
  }
}
```

The scores of the document are as follows:

ID	Product Name	Release Date	Price	Score
3	Women's wool jacket	2016-12-15	59.99	0.55876404
2	Men's water-resistant jacket	2017-03-02	69.99	0.28387982
1	Men's high-performance fleece jacket	2016-08-16	79.99	0.019349905

We can also boost the scores of individual functions. If the release date is more important than the price, we can boost the queries as shown next:

```
POST chapter6/_search
{
  "query": {
    "function_score": {
      "query": {
        "match": {
          "product_name": {
            "query": "jacket"
          }
        }
      }
```

```
                },
                "functions": [
                  {
                    "gauss": {
                      "unit_price": {
                        "origin": "50",
                        "scale": "15"
                      }
                    },
                    "weight": 1
                  },
                  {
                    "gauss": {
                      "release_date": {
                        "origin": "now",
                        "scale": "180d"
                      }
                    },
                    "weight": 2
                  }
                ]
              }
            }
          }
```

The result to the preceding query is as follows:

```
{
    ....
    "hits": {
      "total": 3,
      "max_score": 0.14921477,
      "hits": [
        {
          "_index": "chapter6",
          "_type": "product",
          "_id": "3",
          "_score": 0.14921477,
          "_source": {
            "product_name": "Women's wool Jacket",
            "description": "Helps you stay warm in winter",
            "unit_price": 59.99,
            "reviews": 10,
            "release_date": "2016-12-15"
          }
        },
        {
          "_index": "chapter6",
```

```
      "_type": "product",
      "_id": "2",
      "_score": 0.07581205,
      "_source": {
        "product_name": "Men's Water Resistant Jacket",
        "description": "Provides comfort during biking and hiking",
        "unit_price": 69.99,
        "reviews": 5,
        "release_date": "2017-03-02"
      }
    },
    {
      "_index": "chapter6",
      "_type": "product",
      "_id": "1",
      "_score": 0.0045918548,
      "_source": {
        "product_name": "Men's High Performance Fleece Jacket",
        "description": "Best Value. All season fleece jacket",
        "unit_price": 79.99,
        "reviews": 250,
        "release_date": "2016-08-16"
      }
    }
  ]
 }
}
```

The scores of the preceding documents are as follows:

ID	Product Name	Price	Release Date	Score
3	Women's wool jacket	59.99	2016-12-15	0.14921477
2	Men's high-performance fleece jacket	69.99	2017-03-02	0.07581205
1	Men's water-resistant jacket	79.99	2016-08-16	0.0045918548

From the preceding response, you can see that the most expensive jacket, which was released a while ago, was scored the lowest. Relevance calculation entirely depends on your application and domain-specific logic. Depending on what is more important, you can influence the factors that contribute towards the final score.

Rescoring

For a query that matches a lot of documents, scoring all the matching documents can be quite expensive. To reduce this cost and improve the precision, Elasticsearch lets you rescore only the top *N* documents without scoring all the documents that match the query. Expensive scoring queries, such as scripting or using geolocation, can be used in the rescore phrase. The scores from the original query and the rescore query are combined for the final score. For example, you want the distance as one of the factors driving the relevance score, but the geo distance query which is used to calculate the distance is expensive. You can use the main query to calculate the score for all the documents and then use rescoring to order only the top N documents based on the distance. For suppose, we want to score the top 10 products based on the reviews. A rescoring query based on script is shown here:

```
POST chapter6/_search
  {
    "query": {
      "match": {
        "product_name": {
          "query": "jacket"
        }
      }
    },
    "rescore": {
      "window_size": 10,
      "query": {
        "rescore_query": {
          "function_score": {
            "script_score": {
              "script": {
                "inline": "Math.log(params['_source']['reviews'])"
              }
            }
          }
        },
        "query_weight": 0.5,
        "rescore_query_weight": 1.0
      }
    }
  }
```

In the preceding query, the rescore query applies the logarithmic function on the reviews field of each hit. You can see from the following response that the score for the document with 250 reviews is not significantly different from the product with 10 reviews. By applying the log function, we normalized the effect of the reviews on the score.

All the documents that match the original query are scored using the default `BM25` similarity algorithm. Next, for the documents specified in `window_size`(10), the rescore query is executed, and the influence of the rescore query is defined using `query_weight` and `rescore_query_weight`. The default weight is `1` for both the queries. The response to the preceding query is as follows:

```
{
    ....
    "hits": {
        "total": 3,
        "max_score": 5.5807962,
        "hits": [
            {
                "_index": "chapter6",
                "_type": "product",
                "_id": "1",
                "_score": 5.5807962,
                "_source": {
                    "product_name": "Men's High Performance Fleece Jacket",
                    "description": "Best Value. All season fleece jacket",
                    "unit_price": 79.99,
                    "reviews": 250,
                    "release_date": "2016-08-16"
                }
            },
            {
                "_index": "chapter6",
                "_type": "product",
                "_id": "3",
                "_score": 2.369351,
                "_source": {
                    "product_name": "Women's wool Jacket",
                    "description": "Helps you stay warm in winter",
                    "unit_price": 59.99,
                    "reviews": 10,
                    "release_date": "2016-12-15"
                }
            },
            {
                "_index": "chapter6",
                "_type": "product",
                "_id": "2",
                "_score": 1.6762036,
                "_source": {
                    "product_name": "Men's Water Resistant Jacket",
                    "description": "Provides comfort during biking and hiking",
                    "unit_price": 69.99,
```

```
            "reviews": 5,
            "release_date": "2017-03-02"
        }
    }
]
}
}
```

Debugging relevance score

To debug how the relevance score is calculated for the text-search query, you can use the explain query parameter during the search as shown here:

```
POST chapter6/_search?explain
{
    "query": {
      "match": {
        "description" : "hiking"
      }
    }
}
```

The response of the query will have the explanation of the calculation. Each hit along with the source of the document will also contain the details of how the score is calculated. Let's take explanation of a single hit and walk through:

```
"_explanation": {
    "value": 0.98908687,
    "description": "weight(description:hike in 0)
[PerFieldSimilarity], result of:",
```

The explanation will contain the score of the hit, description and the details. The value (0.98908687) is the score calculated for this document. We are searching for term **hike** in the description field. Next are the details on how the score (0.98908687) is calculated:

```
        details": [
          {
            "value": 0.98908687,
            "description": "score(doc=0,freq=1.0 = termFreq=1.0n),
product of:",
            "details": [
              {
                "value": 0.98082924,
                "description": "idf(docFreq=1, docCount=3)",
                "details": []
              },
```

The final score of the document is an outcome of different calculations as shown in the preceding code snippet. The term frequency represents the number of times the term appears in the document. The inverted document frequency represents the number of documents the term appears in. If the term is common in the document and relatively rare in all the documents, it is scored better. The term frequency normalization shown next reduces the effect of term frequency beyond a limit:

```
{
  "value": 1.008419,
  "description": "tfNorm, computed from:",
  "details": [
    {
      "value": 1,
      "description": "termFreq=1.0",
      "details": []
    },
    {
      "value": 1.2,
      "description": "parameter k1",
      "details": []
    },
    {
      "value": 0.75,
      "description": "parameter b",
      "details": []
    },
    {
      "value": 5.3333335,
      "description": "avgFieldLength",
      "details": []
    },
    {
      "value": 5.2244897,
      "description": "fieldLength",
      "details": []
    }
  ]
}
```

Try running some text queries with explain parameter and the explanation will more more sense. The term frequency normalization shown above is the different factors used by BM25 to reduce the effect of parameters like field length.

To learn more about how the BM25 similarity algorithm works, please visit https://en.wikipedia.org/wiki/Okapi_BM25.

Explain is very handy when trying to understand or debug how the relevance score is calculated. Don't let the length of the response scare you; the most important things to watch are the term frequency, inverted document frequency, and term frequency normalization.

Searching for same value across multiple fields

The `multi_match` query is used to match the same value across multiple fields. When a user searches for `biking jacket`, searching just the `product_name` field might not find any matches. To widen the search, we should most probably also search the `description` field along with the `product_name` field. The document that contains both `biking` and `jacket` is shown here:

```
{
   "product_name": "Men's Water Resistant Jacket",
   "description": "Provides comfort during biking and hiking",
   "unit_price": 69.99,
   "reviews": 5,
   "release_date": "2017-03-02"
}
```

Scoring based on a single field is pretty straightforward, scoring based on multiple fields gets tricky. We can't use a match query with an operator as the terms `biking` and `jacket` don't exist in the same field. We need to use a `multi_match` query to search across `product_name` and `description` fields:

```
#Multi Match
 GET chapter6/_search
 {
   "query": {
     "multi_match": {
       "query": "biking jacket",
       "fields": [
         "product_name",
         "description"
       ],
```

```
      "type": "best_fields"
    }
  }
}
```

By default, the `multi_match` query runs as `best_fields`. The score from the best matching field is returned. We can also use a `tie_breaker` to add the scores from the other fields, as shown here:

```
#Multi Match
POST chapter6/_search
{
  "query": {
    "multi_match": {
      "query": "biking jacket",
      "fields": [
        "product_name",
        "description"
      ],
      "tie_breaker": 0.2
    }
  }
}
```

The scores from the other fields are multiplied by `0.2` and added to the best matching field score. `Multi-match` is internally translated into a `dis_max` query. Unlike the `bool` query, which adds all the scores from all the queries, the `dis_max` query returns the score of the best matching query:

```
#Dis max Query
POST chapter6/_search
{
  "query": {
    "dis_max": {
      "queries": [
        {
          "match": {
            "product_name": "biking jacket"
          }
        },
        {
          "match": {
            "description": "biking jacket"
          }
        }
      ]
    }
```

```
        }
    }
```

`Multi-match` also provides some nice shortcuts to boost the score from individual queries. If matching the `product_name` field is more important than matching the `description` field, we can boost the `product_name` using the **caret** (^) symbol as shown here:

```
POST chapter6/_search
  {
    "query": {
      "multi_match": {
        "query": "biking jacket",
        "fields": [
          "product_name^2",
          "description"
        ]
      }
    }
  }
```

Depending on how you want the documents to be scored, three types of `multi_match` queries are supported. The three types differ in how the scores from different fields are used to calculate the final score of each document. In the next sections, we will run the same query using a different type of `multi_match` and look at the how the documents are scored.

Best matching fields

Best matching fields are the default type, and the score of the best matching field is returned. Let's inspect the scores of the documents when running the `multi_match` query as `best_fields`. For example, if you looking the term `jacket` in `product_name` and `description` fields, the `multi_match` query is as follows:

```
#Multi Match (Best Fields)
POST chapter6/_search
  {
    "query": {
      "multi_match": {
        "query": "jacket",
        "fields": [
          "product_name",
          "description"
        ],
        "type": "best_fields",
        "analyzer" : "english"
```

```
            }
        }
    }
```

By default, the query term is analyzed and broken into individual terms based on the field analyzer. For example, we are querying for men's jacket. Using the standard analyzer, the query is broken into `men's` and `jacket`. When using the English analyzer, the query will be broken into `men` and `jacket`. By specifying the analyzer, we are asking Elasticsearch to use the same analyzer for all fields irrespective of their mappings. All the fields are queried for the same terms. The response to the preceding query is as follows:

```
{
    ....
    "hits": {
        "total": 3,
        "max_score": 0.86312973,
        "hits": [
            {
                "_index": "chapter6",
                "_type": "product",
                "_id": "1",
                "_score": 0.86312973,
                "_source": {
                    "product_name": "Men's High Performance Fleece Jacket",
                    "description": "Best Value. All season fleece jacket",
                    "unit_price": 79.99,
                    "reviews": 250,
                    "release_date": "2016-08-16"
                }
            },
            {
                "_index": "chapter6",
                "_type": "product",
                "_id": "2",
                "_score": 0.13353139,
                "_source": {
                    "product_name": "Men's Water Resistant Jacket",
                    "description": "Provides comfort during biking and hiking",
                    "unit_price": 69.99,
                    "reviews": 5,
                    "release_date": "2017-03-02"
                }
            },
            {
                "_index": "chapter6",
                "_type": "product",
                "_id": "3",
```

```
        "_score": 0.13353139,
        "_source": {
          "product_name": "Women's wool Jacket",
          "description": "Helps you stay warm in winter",
          "unit_price": 59.99,
          "reviews": 10,
          "release_date": "2016-12-15"
        }
      }
    ]
  }
}
```

The scores of the documents are as follows:

ID	Product name	Description	Score
1	Men's high-performance fleece **jacket**	Best value. All season fleece **jacket**.	0.86312973
2	Men's water-resistant **jacket**	Provides comfort during biking and hiking.	0.13353139
3	Women's wool **jacket**	Helps you stay warm in winter.	0.13353139

The maximum score between the `product_name` and `description` fields is returned as the final score. The term `jacket` appears in the `product_name` fields of all the documents but only once in the `description` field of document ID 1. Document ID 1 is scored relatively higher because of the inverted document frequency. When querying the `description` field for the term `jacket`, it is a rare term due to which it is scored very high when compared to others.

Most matching fields

The `Multi_match` query, when executed as most matching fields type, it adds the scores from all the fields. We will run the same query in the preceding section but set the type as `most_fields`. The query looks like the following:

```
#Multi Match (Most Fields)
POST chapter6/_search
 {
   "query": {
     "multi_match": {
       "query": "jacket",
       "fields": [
         "product_name",
         "description"
```

```
        ],
        "type": "most_fields",
        "analyzer" : "english"
      }
    }
  }
```

The result to the preceding query is as follows:

```
{
  ....
  "hits": {
    "total": 3,
    "max_score": 0.98179984,
    "hits": [
      {
        "_index": "chapter6",
        "_type": "product",
        "_id": "1",
        "_score": 0.98179984,
        "_source": {
          "product_name": "Men's High Performance Fleece Jacket",
          "description": "Best Value. All season fleece jacket",
          "unit_price": 79.99,
          "reviews": 250,
          "release_date": "2016-08-16"
        }
      },
      {
        "_index": "chapter6",
        "_type": "product",
        "_id": "2",
        "_score": 0.13353139,
        "_source": {
          "product_name": "Men's Water Resistant Jacket",
          "description": "Provides comfort during biking and hiking",
          "unit_price": 69.99,
          "reviews": 5,
          "release_date": "2017-03-02"
        }
      },
      {
        "_index": "chapter6",
        "_type": "product",
        "_id": "3",
        "_score": 0.13353139,
        "_source": {
          "product_name": "Women's wool Jacket",
```

```
            "description": "Helps you stay warm in winter",
            "unit_price": 59.99,
            "reviews": 10,
            "release_date": "2016-12-15"
         }
      }
   ]
   }
}
```

The scores of the documents are as follows:

ID	Product name	Description	best_fields score	most_fields score
1	Men's high-performance fleece jacket	Best value. All season fleece jacket.	0.86312973	0.98179984
2	Men's water-resistant jacket	Provides comfort during biking and hiking.	0.13353139	0.13353139
3	Women's wool jacket	Helps you stay warm in winter.	0.13353139	0.13353139

The score of the document ID *1* is the sum of the scores from the product_name and description fields. The scores for the other documents remain unchanged.

Cross-matching fields

The best fields and most fields execute the query on the different fields and combine the scores to produce the final score. In the previous section, we saw how the score is heavily influenced due to the term frequency of the word jacket. That's because of how the BM25 scoring algorithm works. But if you don't want the score to be influenced because of the term frequencies, you could use cross_fields. Cross fields combine both product_name and description as a single field, and the scores are calculated based on the single field. The query looks like the following:

```
#Multi Match (Cross Fields)
POST chapter6/_search
  {
    "query": {
      "multi_match": {
        "query": "jacket",
        "fields": [
```

```
        "product_name",
        "description"
      ],
      "type": "cross_fields",
      "analyzer" : "english"
    }
  }
}
```

The response to the preceding query is as follows:

```
{
  ....
  "hits": {
    "total": 3,
    "max_score": 0.13353139,
    "hits": [
      {
        "_index": "chapter6",
        "_type": "product",
        "_id": "2",
        "_score": 0.13353139,
        "_source": {
          "product_name": "Men's Water Resistant Jacket",
          "description": "Provides comfort during biking and hiking",
          "unit_price": 69.99,
          "reviews": 5,
          "release_date": "2017-03-02"
        }
      },
      {
        "_index": "chapter6",
        "_type": "product",
        "_id": "3",
        "_score": 0.13353139,
        "_source": {
          "product_name": "Women's wool Jacket",
          "description": "Helps you stay warm in winter",
          "unit_price": 59.99,
          "reviews": 10,
          "release_date": "2016-12-15"
        }
      },
      {
        "_index": "chapter6",
        "_type": "product",
        "_id": "1",
        "_score": 0.11867011,
```

```
    "_source": {
      "product_name": "Men's High Performance Fleece Jacket",
      "description": "Best Value. All season fleece jacket",
      "unit_price": 79.99,
      "reviews": 250,
      "release_date": "2016-08-16"
    }
  }
]
}
}
```

The scores of the documents are as follows:

ID	Product name	Description	best_fields	most_fields	cross_fields
1	Men's high-performance fleece jacket	Best value. All season fleece jacket.	0.86312973	0.98179984	0.11867011
2	Men's water-resistant jacket	Provides comfort during biking and hiking.	0.13353139	0.13353139	0.13353139
3	Women's wool jacket	Helps you stay warm in winter.	0.13353139	0.13353139	0.13353139

When both the `product_name` and `description` fields are combined, the term `jacket` in the combined field is a common term. Due to inverted frequency, it is scored less when compared to others. Depending on the application requirements, choose the correct type of the `multi_match` query.

Caching

In Elasticsearch 5.0, a lot of refactoring has been done to support better caching. The different types of cache available are as follows:

- **Node Query cache**: Queries that run in filter context are cached here
- **Shard request cache**: The results of the entire query are cached here

Node Query cache

Queries, such as numeric or date range, which run in the filter context are great candidates for caching. Since they have no scoring phase, they can be reused. The Node query cache is a smart cache; you do not have to worry about invalidating the cache. Individual queries that run in filter context are cached here. This cache is maintained at a node level and defaults to `10%` of the heap and can be configured using the `elasticsearch.yml` file:

```
indices.queries.cache.size: 10%
```

Frequently used queries are automatically cached, and the eviction from the cache is based on the least recently used queries.

Shard request cache

Shard request cache is used to cache the results of the entire query. Only hits count, aggregation, and suggestions are cached; the actual hits are not. The results are only cached if the size is equal to `0` (when size is set to `0` in the request, the actual hits/documents are not returned as part of the search response). The query JSON is used as a cache key. Just like query cache, shard request cache is smart. The cache is invalidated automatically when there is new data. For data that is not changed frequently, the query can be served directly from the cache avoiding the heavy re-computation. The cache is maintained at a node level and defaults to `1%` of the heap memory and can be configured using the `elasticsearch.yml` file:

```
indices.requests.cache.size: 1%
```

Charts on a dashboard that uses aggregations internally greatly benefit from a shard request cache. If the data is not changing anymore, the request can be served directly from the cache.

Summary

In this chapter, you learned how to query Elasticsearch. We discussed the differences between structured queries and full-text search. We also discussed how to combine different queries using bool query. We learned what relevance means and how it is calculated. We used factors such as price and release date to tune the relevance score.

In the next chapter, we will discuss more advanced features, such as location-based filtering, autocomplete, making suggestions based on the user query, and more.

7
More Than a Search Engine (Geofilters, Autocomplete, and More)

In the previous chapter, we discussed different ways of querying Elasticsearch. For a given query, we looked into different ways of controlling the relevance score to get back the most relevant results at the top. In this chapter, we will discuss how to deal with typos, spelling mistakes, and **auto-completing** the query before the user finishes typing the query. We will talk about how to handle relationships and joins using **nested** and **parent-child** mappings and discuss the advantages and disadvantages of using one versus the other. We will also discuss how to include **geolocation** in your queries. You'll learn about the **percolate query**, which is one of the very popular features of Elasticsearch. The main functionality of percolate query is reverse search; we will explore why it is important and the ways to use it. We will cover the following in this chapter:

- Correcting typos and spelling mistakes
- Autocomplete
- Highlighting
- Handling relations and joins
- Geo and spatial filtering
- Percolate query
- Scripting

Sample data

To better explain the various concepts in this chapter, we will use the e-commerce site as an example. We will create an index with a list of products. We will create a simple index called `chapter7` with type `product`. Our sample data looks like the following:

```
PUT chapter7/product/1
{ "product_name": "Apple iPhone 7"}

PUT chapter7/product/2
{ "product_name": "Apple iPhone Lightning Cable" }

PUT chapter7/product/3
{ "product_name": "Apple iPhone 6"}

PUT chapter7/product/4
{ "product_name": "Samsung Galaxy S7" }

PUT chapter7/product/5
{ "product_name": "Samsung Galaxy S6" }
```

As we progress through the chapter, we will recreate the `chapter7` index with different configurations.

Correcting typos and spelling mistakes

In the previous chapter, we discussed different ways to query documents based on the user search input. But the search input might contain typos and spelling mistakes. Automatically correcting the user's spelling mistakes and typos improves the overall search experience. The term or match query that we discussed in the previous chapter only looks for the exact term in the inverted index. In this section, we will discuss different types of queries Elasticsearch provides to correct the typos.

Fuzzy query

The **fuzzy** query is provided to look for terms that are close to the original term. It looks for terms in the inverted index, which are like the query term based on the **edit distance**. Edit distance is the number of operations required to make two words similar. An operation is either addition, deletion, or substitution. The edit distance between motel and hotel is *1* (*hotel* -> *motel*) as you have to substitute *m* with *h*. The edit distance between Sunday and Monday is 2 (*Sunday* -> *Munday* -> *Monday*) as you have to substitute *s* with *m* and *u* with *o*. Edit distance is also known as **Levenshtein distance**. The fuzzy query is used to automatically **correct typos** and spelling mistakes in the user query.

> Fuzzy query checks the inverted index for possible matches within edit distance of **2**. Most typos and spelling mistakes fall within this. Beyond 2, the probability of two words meaning the same is very less.

All the heavy lifting of calculating edit distance and matching the terms is done by Elasticsearch. For example, if a user queries for `samsund` instead of `samsung`, we can use the fuzzy query to correct the typos automatically, as shown here:

```
#Fuzzy Query
 POST chapter7/_search
 {
   "query": {
     "fuzzy": {
       "product_name": "samsund"
     }
   }
 }
```

The response to the preceding query will contain documents with product names within an edit distance of 2 to `samsund`. The response to the preceding query is as follows:

```
{
  ......
  "hits": {
    "total": 2,
    "max_score": 0.39752966,
    "hits": [
      {
        "_index": "chapter7",
        "_type": "product",
        "_id": "4",
        "_score": 0.39752966,
        "_source": {
          "product_name": "Samsung Galaxy S6"
```

```
              }
           },
           {
             "_index": "chapter7",
             "_type": "product",
             "_id": "3",
             "_score": 0.2169945,
             "_source": {
               "product_name": "Samsung Galaxy S7"
             }
           }
         ]
       }
     }
```

Instead of the fuzzy query, we can also use the **regular match query** and include the fuzziness attribute as shown here:

```
  #Fuzzy Match Query
   POST chapter7/_search
   {
     "query": {
       "match": {
         "product_name": {
           "query" : "samsund galazy",
           "fuzziness": "AUTO",
           "operator": "and"
         }
       }
     }
   }
```

In the preceding query, since we set the fuzziness property to AUTO, the fuzziness is based on the length of the query term as shown in the table here:

Term Length	Fuzziness (Edit Distance)
1-2	0
3-5	1
Greater than 5	2

For example, in the previous query, the length of term `samsund` is greater than 5, so the query looks for terms within the edit distance of 2 in the inverted index. Instead of `AUTO`, you can also specify 0, 1, or 2.

The fuzzy query can be very expensive depending on the number of terms in the inverted index that match the input. To restrict the performance impact, we can limit the number of terms collected from inverted index using the `max_expansions` parameter, which defaults to `50`. In the older versions of Lucene, fuzzy queries are very expensive, as it has to go through the entire inverted index to find the matching terms. The newer version of Lucene calculates the edit distance between two words using much simpler and faster algorithm called **Levenshtein automata**. The algorithm represents each letter in the word as a node in the graph.

Making suggestions based on the user input

In the previous section, we discussed fuzzy query to fix the typos automatically. In this section, we will discuss the **suggest API**, which can provide word or phrase suggestions to the user based on the input query. Fuzzy query automatically corrects the fuzziness; Suggest API simply **makes suggestions**. Suggest API supports the following:

- **Term and phrase suggester:** You can use the term or phrase suggester to make suggestions based on the existing documents in case of typos or spelling mistakes.
- **Completion suggester:** You can use the completion suggester to predict the query term before the user finishes typing. Helping the user with the right search phrases improves the overall experience and decreases the load on the servers.

Implementing "did you mean" feature

The term and phrase suggester uses edit distance just like the fuzzy query to make the suggestions based on the user query. When using Google or other search engines, you often see suggestions as **did you mean** followed by the suggestion.

Elasticsearch supports the following:

- **Term suggester:** This is used to make suggestions based on a single term
- **Phrase suggester:** This is used to make suggestions based on a phrase

Term suggester

The term suggester makes suggestions based on a single term. For example, if a user is looking for `samsung` phones and inputs `samsund` as a search query. Since `samsund` has a spelling mistake, it doesn't exist in the inverted index. We can use `term_suggester` to display suggestions based on the user input. A simple term suggest query would look like the following:

```
#Term Suggester 1
POST chapter7/_search
{
    "suggest" : {
      "term_suggester" : {
        "text" : "samsund",
        "term" : {
          "field" : "product_name"
        }
      }
    }
}
```

Note the following from the preceding query:

- **text:** The query term (term that needs suggestions) is passed as the text field
- **field:** Suggestions are based on this field. In the preceding example, we used `product_name`, but we could also use the `_all` field

The response to the term suggest query is as follows:

```
{
  .....
    "suggest": {
      "term_suggester": [
        {
          "text": "samsund",
          "offset": 0,
          "length": 7,
          "options": [
            {
              "text": "samsung",
```

```
                "score": 0.85714287,
                "freq": 2
            }
        ]
    }
  ]
}
}
```

Each suggestion in the response will have text, score, and frequency:

- **text:** This denotes the suggestion text.
- **score:** This denotes how close the suggestion is to the text we want the suggestion on.
- **freq:** This denotes the frequency of the term in all the documents. In the preceding example, the samsung term has appeared twice.

By default, the suggestions are sorted based on the frequency. Let's take one more example:

```
#Term Suggester 2
POST chapter7/_search
{
    "suggest" : {
        "term_suggester" : {
            "text" : "samsundcd",
            "term" : {
                "field" : "product_name"
            }
        }
    }
}
```

The preceding query will not find any suggestions for samsundcd as there are no terms within an edit distance of 2. The edit distance between samsung and samsundcd is 3.

The suggester makes suggestions irrespective of the query in the request. In the example below, the query for iphone doesn't affect the suggestions for the term samsundd. The scope of the suggester includes all the documents in the index. The following query will result in the same suggestions as in the previous example. The only difference between the previous example and the following query is that the response will contain hits that match the query along with the suggestions as shown here:

```
#Term Suggester with match query
POST chapter7/_search
{
    "query" : {
```

```
      "match" : {
        "product_name" : "iphone"
      }
    },
    "suggest" : {
      "term_suggester" : {
        "text" : "samsundd",
        "term" : {
          "field" : "product_name"
        }
      }
    }
  }
}
```

The response to the preceding query is as follows:

```
{
    .....
    "hits": {
      "total": 2,
      "max_score": 0.9433406,
      "hits": [
        {
          .....
          "_source": {
            "product_name": "iPhone 7"
          }
        },
        {
          .....
          "_source": {
            "product_name": "iPhone 6"
          }
        }
      ]
    },
    "suggest": {
      "term_suggester": [
        {
          "text": "samsundd",
          "offset": 0,
          "length": 8,
          "options": [
            {
              "text": "samsung",
              "score": 0.71428573,
              "freq": 2
            }
```

```
          ]
        }
      ]
    }
  }
```

The suggest API supports more than one suggester in the same query. For example, in the following query, we have two suggesters: one for `samsund` and the other for `iphon`:

```
#More than one suggester
POST chapter7/_search
{
  "suggest" : {
    "suggester1" : {
      "text" : "samsund",
      "term" : {
        "field" : "_all"
      }
    },
    "suggester2" : {
      "text" : "iphon",
      "term" : {
        "field" : "_all"
      }
    }
  }
}
```

The response to the preceding query will have suggestions to both the suggesters as shown here:

```
{
  .....
  "suggest": {
    "suggester1": [
      {
        "text": "samsund",
        "offset": 0,
        "length": 7,
        "options": [
          {
            "text": "samsung",
            "score": 0.85714287,
            "freq": 2
          }
        ]
      }
    ],
```

```
      "suggester2": [
        {
          "text": "iphon",
          "offset": 0,
          "length": 5,
          "options": [
            {
              "text": "iphone",
              "score": 0.6717023
            }
          ]
        }
      ]
    }
  }
```

Phrase suggester

The term suggester is used for a single term. The phrase suggester is used for making suggestions based on a phrase. The phrase suggester builds on the functionality of the term suggester. A simple phrase suggester query would look like the following:

```
#Phrase Suggester
POST chapter7/_search
  {
    "suggest" : {
      "term_suggester" : {
        "text" : "samsund galaxy",
        "phrase" : {
          "field" : "product_name"
        }
      }
    }
  }
```

The phrase suggester is very similar to the term suggester; instead of wrapping the field using the term for the phrase suggester, we wrap it using the phrase attribute. The response to the query is as follows:

```
{
  . . . . .
  "suggest": {
    "term_suggester": [
      {
        "text": "samsund galaxy",
        "offset": 0,
```

```
          "length": 14,
          "options": [
            {
              "text": "samsung galaxy",
              "score": 0.5009329
            }
          ]
        }
      ]
    }
  }
}
```

By default, the maximum number of errors the phrase suggester checks is one. In the following query, we specified the `max_errors` count as 2 to check for a maximum of two errors:

```
#Phrase Suggest with max error 2
POST chapter7/_search
{
  "suggest" : {
    "term_suggester" : {
      "text" : "samsund galaxh",
      "phrase" : {
        "field" : "product_name",
        "max_errors" : 2
      }
    }
  }
}
```

The response to the preceding query is as follows:

```
{
  .....
  "suggest": {
    "term_suggester": [
      {
        "text": "samsund galaxh",
        "offset": 0,
        "length": 14,
        "options": [
          {
            "text": "samsung galaxy",
            "score": 0.47322324
          },
          {
            "text": "samsung galaxh",
            "score": 0.37071815
```

```
      },
      {
        "text": "samsund galaxy",
        "score": 0.36621025
      }
    ]
  }
]
}
}
```

The suggestions as shown in the preceding response are based on the input. Not all suggestions are valid. In the preceding example, along with `samsung galaxy`, two other suggestions are also made. To prune the suggestion that doesn't have any results, Elasticsearch provides **collate**, which excludes suggestions that don't produce any results. The query to check whether the suggestion is valid is passed as a search template. The preceding query with collate is shown next. The field name in the query is passed in the `params`, and the suggestion param is autofilled by the suggester. The preceding query with collate is shown here:

```
#Collate
POST chapter7/_search
  {
    "suggest": {
      "my_suggestion": {
        "text": "samsund galaxh",
        "phrase": {
          "field": "product_name",
          "max_errors": 2,
          "collate": {
            "query": {
              "inline": {
                "match_phrase": {
                  "{{field_name}}": {
                    "query": "{{suggestion}}",
                    "slop" : 1
                  }
                }
              }
            },
            "params": {
              "field_name": "product_name"
            },
            "prune": true
          }
        }
      }
    }
  }
```

```
        }
    }
```

The response to the preceding query is as follows:

```
{
    ....
    "suggest": {
      "my_suggestion": [
        {
          "text": "samsund galaxh",
          "offset": 0,
          "length": 14,
          "options": [
            {
              "text": "samsung galaxy",
              "score": 0.47322324,
              "collate_match": true
            },
            {
              "text": "samsung galaxh",
              "score": 0.37071815,
              "collate_match": false
            },
            {
              "text": "samsund galaxy",
              "score": 0.36621025,
              "collate_match": false
            }
          ]
        }
      ]
    }
}
```

You can see from the preceding response that all the suggestions that produce results will have `collate_match` set to true. You can also remove the `prune` setting in the query or set it to `false` to see only the suggestions that produce query results.

Implementing the autocomplete feature

To support autocomplete, Elasticsearch provides the completion suggester. Unlike the term and phrase suggester, the *speed* of the response for autocomplete is very important. As the user types the next letter, the suggester should make suggestions. To support this, Elasticsearch uses an **in-memory** data structure called **FST** (**Finite State Transducer**).

For information on FST, please visit `https://en.wikipedia.org/wiki/Finite-state_transducer`.

FST is nothing but a graph of all the terms, where each letter in the term is a node linked to the next node. Building FST on the fly is very expensive, and to optimize the performance, FST structure is built **during indexing**, and the files are loaded into the memory for the query execution. Since FST has to be built at indexing time, a special mapping is used to identify the fields that are used by the completion suggester. The completion mapping can be set as shown here:

```
#Delete existing index
DELETE chapter7

#Mapping for Completion
PUT chapter7
  {
    "settings": {},
    "mappings": {
      "product": {
        "properties": {
          "product_name": {
            "type": "text",
            "copy_to": "product_suggest"
          },
          "product_suggest": {
            "type": "completion"
          }
        }
      }
    }
  }
```

In the mapping, we defined a new `product_suggest` field as type completion. In the `product_name` mapping, we used `copy_to` to automatically copy the value to the `product_suggest` field. Let's index the product documents again as shown here:

```
#Sample data
POST chapter7/product/_bulk
{ "index": {}}
{ "product_name": "Apple iPhone 7"}
{ "index": {}}
{ "product_name": "Apple iPhone Lightning Cable" }
{ "index": {}}
{ "product_name": "Apple iPhone 6"}
```

```
{ "index": {}}
{ "product_name": "Samsung Galaxy S7" }
{ "index": {}}
{ "product_name": "Samsung Galaxy S6" }
```

We have set correct mapping and indexed the documents. The user input can be passed as the prefix to the suggest query. We can use the suggest API for autocomplete as shown here:

```
#Completion
POST chapter7/_search
  {
    "suggest": {
      "my_suggestion": {
        "prefix": "a", #input
        "completion": {
          "field": "product_suggest"
        }
      }
    }
  }
```

In the preceding query, when the user input a, we used the suggest API to get the product suggestions. The response to the preceding query is as follows:

```
{
  ....
    "suggest": {
      "my_suggestion": [
        {
          "text": "a",
          "offset": 0,
          "length": 1,
          "options": [
            {
              "text": "Apple iPhone 6",
              "_index": "chapter7",
              "_type": "product",
              "_id": "AVx_cm9WiOAxqKpNCkZB",
              "_score": 1,
              "_source": {
                "product_name": "Apple iPhone 6"
              }
            },
            {
              "text": "Apple iPhone 7",
              "_index": "chapter7",
              "_type": "product",
```

```
                    "_id": "AVx_cm9WiOAxqKpNCkY_",
                    "_score": 1,
                    "_source": {
                      "product_name": "Apple iPhone 7"
                    }
                  },
                  {
                    "text": "Apple iPhone Lightning Cable",
                    "_index": "chapter7",
                    "_type": "product",
                    "_id": "AVx_cm9WiOAxqKpNCkZA",
                    "_score": 1,
                    "_source": {
                      "product_name": "Apple iPhone Lightning Cable"
                    }
                  }
                ]
              }
            ]
          }
        }
```

The response comes back with three suggestions (Apple iPhone 6, Apple iPhone 7, and Apple iPhone Lightning Cable).

Highlighting

Elasticsearch supports highlighting the parts of the response that caused the match. In the following query, the matches in the `product_name` field are highlighted:

```
#Highlighting
POST chapter7/_search
 {
    "query": {
      "match": {
        "product_name": {
          "query": "samsung"
        }
      }
    },
    "highlight": {
        "fields" : {
            "product_name" : {}
        }
    }
 }
```

The response to the preceding query is as follows:

```
{
    ....
    "hits": {
        "total": 2,
        "max_score": 0.7590336,
        "hits": [
            {
                "_index": "chapter7",
                "_type": "product",
                "_id": "AVsC7GDlF21JdiUIl1Q-",
                "_score": 0.7590336,
                "_source": {
                    "product_name": "Samsung Galaxy S7"
                },
                "highlight": {
                    "product_name": [
                        "<em>Samsung</em> Galaxy S7"
                    ]
                }
            },
            {
                "_index": "chapter7",
                "_type": "product",
                "_id": "AVsC7x6WF21JdiUIl1RB",
                "_score": 0.5565415,
                "_source": {
                    "product_name": "Samsung Galaxy S6"
                },
                "highlight": {
                    "product_name": [
                        "<em>Samsung</em> Galaxy S6"
                    ]
                }
            }
        ]
    }
}
```

The query term is highlighted using the em tags. We can change the default tags in the highlight section as shown here:

```
#Highlight with tags
POST chapter7/_search
{
    "query": {
        "match": {
```

```
        "product_name": {
          "query": "samsung"
        }
      }
    },
    "highlight": {
      "pre_tags": [
        "<tag1>"
      ],
      "post_tags": [
        "</tag1>"
      ],
      "fields": {
        "product_name": {}
      }
    }
  }
}
```

The response will now contain `tag1` instead of `em`.

Handling document relations using parent-child

In `Chapter 3`, *Modeling Your Data and Document Relations,* we described how to set the mapping and index parent-child documents. In this section, we will discuss how to query parent-child documents. To manage relationships in Elasticsearch, parent-child and nested mappings are provided. The difference between parent-child and nested is in *how the documents are stored.* The parent-child documents are costly while querying for the data, and nested documents are costly while indexing data. We discussed the differences in detail in `Chapter 3`, *Modeling your data and Document Relations.*

In the previous sections, we indexed product documents for the e-commerce store. In this section, we will use the parent-child relation to index the reviews for the products as the child documents. The product document is the parent document. A new review can be added without modifying the parent document. First, let's set the parent-child mapping in the `chapter7` index as shown here:

```
#Delete existing index
DELETE chapter7

#Mapping
PUT chapter7
{
```

```
      "settings": {},
      "mappings": {
        "product": {
          "properties": {
            "product_name": {
              "type": "text",
              "copy_to": "product_suggest"
            },
            "product_suggest": {
              "type": "completion"
            }
          }
        },
        "product_review": {
          "_parent": {
            "type": "product"
          },
          "properties": {}
        }
      }
    }
```

We set the parent-child mapping. Now let's index some document as shown here:

```
#Parent Documents
PUT chapter7/product/1?refresh=true
{"product_name": "Apple iPhone 6"}
PUT chapter7/product/2?refresh=true
{"product_name": "Apple iPhone 7"}
PUT chapter7/product/3?refresh=true
{"product_name": "Samsung Galaxy S7"}
PUT chapter7/product/4?refresh=true
{"product_name": "Samsung Galaxy S6"}

#Child Documents
POST chapter7/product_review/?parent=1
{"user_id" : "reviewer1",
"comment" : "One of the best phones in the market"}
```

The following are two types of parent-child queries that are supported:

- has_parent
- has_child

The has_parent query

We can use the `has_parent` to query child documents based on a query on the parent. For example, we want to find all the reviews written for a given product. The parent document is `product`, and the child document is `product_review`. The `has_parent` query is shown here:

```
#Has_Parent (Reviews for iphone)
 POST chapter7/product_review/_search
 {
    "query" : {
      "has_parent": {
        "parent_type": "product",
        "query": {
          "term": {
            "product_name": "iphone"
          }
        }
      }
    }
 }
```

The response will contain the product reviews for `iphone`. The response to the preceding query is as follows:

```
{
    ....
    "hits": {
      "total": 1,
      "max_score": 1,
      "hits": [
        {
          "_index": "chapter7",
          "_type": "product_review",
          "_id": "AVsMFvpeF21JdiUIl1RT",
          "_score": 1,
          "_routing": "1",
          "_parent": "1",
          "_source": {
            "user_id": "reviewer1",
            "comment": "One of the best phones in the market"
          }
        }
      ]
    }
 }
```

The has_child query

We will use `has_child` to query parent documents based on a query on children. For example, to find all the products reviewed by `reviewer1`, we can use the `has_child` query as shown here:

```
#Has_Child (Products reviewed by reviewer1)
POST chapter7/product/_search
  {
    "query" : {
      "has_child": {
        "type": "product_review",
        "query": {
          "term": {
            "user_id": "reviewer1"
          }
        }
      }
    }
  }
```

And the response to the preceding query is as follows:

```
{
    . . . .
    "hits": {
      "total": 1,
      "max_score": 1,
      "hits": [
        {
          "_index": "chapter7",
          "_type": "product",
          "_id": "1",
          "_score": 1,
          "_source": {
            "product_name": "Apple iPhone 6"
          }
        }
      ]
    }
}
```

The response contains all the products reviewed by `reviewer1`.

Inner hits for parent-child

In the previous section, we used the `has_child` query on the product document to query for all the products that are reviewed by `reviewer1`. The `has_child` query is executed on its parent mapping type (`product`), and the response will contain the product documents. The actual children (`product_reviews`) that matched the query are not part of the response. To solve this problem, the **inner hits** feature is provided. When the `inner_hits` tag is included in the query, along with the product documents, the product_review documents that matched the query are also included in the response. Inner hits can be used for both the `has_child` and `has_parent` query. The `has_child` query with inner hits is shown here:

```
#Has_Child (Products reviewed by reviewer1)
POST chapter7/product/_search
  {
     "query": {
       "has_child": {
         "type": "product_review",
         "query": {
           "term": {
             "user_id": "reviewer1"
           }
         },
         "inner_hits": {}
       }
     }
  }
```

The response to the preceding query is shown here:

```
  {
     ....
     "hits": {
       "total": 1,
       "max_score": 1,
       "hits": [
         {
           "_index": "chapter7",
           "_type": "product",
           "_id": "1",
           "_score": 1,
           "_source": { # Actual Hits
             "product_name": "Apple iPhone 6"
           },
           "inner_hits": {
             "product_review": {
```

```
    "hits": {
      "total": 1,
      "max_score": 0.2876821,
      "hits": [
        {
          "_type": "product_review",
          "_id": "AVsRR2FzF21JdiUIl1Rk",
          "_score": 0.2876821,
          "_routing": "1",
          "_parent": "1",
          "_source": {
            "user_id": "reviewer1",
            "comment": "One of the best phones in the market"
          }
        }
      ]
    }
  }
}
```

The response contains both the parent (`product`) document and the child (`product_review`) documents that matched the query.

How parent-child works internally

Elasticsearch stores the parent and child documents in the same shard. Having both the parent and child documents in the same shard will make the `has_parent` and `has_child` queries possible. The parent ID is used to determine the shard to which the child document belongs to. To index or retrieve a child document, you need the parent ID. We index a child document (`product_review`) as shown here:

```
#Child Document
POST chapter7/product_review/?parent=1
{"user_id" : "reviewer1", "comment" : "One of the best phones in the
market"}
```

When using parent-child, you are trading **indexing performance** for **query performance**. Internally, Elasticsearch has to maintain a join between the parent documents and child documents. This mapping is lazy loaded the first time the user runs a parent-child query or aggregation. Due to this, parent-child queries are *ten times* slower than corresponding nested queries.

Handling document relations using nested

In the *Document Relations* section in `Chapter 3`, *Modeling Your Data and Document Relations*, we described how to store nested documents. In this section, we will discuss how to query them. To better explain querying nested documents, we will change the mappings of the `chapter7` index to store the variations of a product as nested documents. For example, an `iPhone` is available in several storage options, such as `32GB`, `64GB`, and so on. Each variation has a different price. Each variation of a product will be stored as a **nested document**. A product can have one or more variations. In the following query, we will change the mapping of the type product to include the variations as nested documents:

```
#Delete existing index
DELETE chapter7

#Set mappings
PUT chapter7
  {
    "settings": {},
    "mappings": {
      "product": {
        "properties": {
          "product_name": {
            "type": "text",
            "copy_to": "product_suggest"
          },
          "variations": {
            "type": "nested", #Special Mapping
            "properties": {
              "type": {
                "type": "keyword"
              },
              "value": {
                "type": "keyword"
              },
              "unit_price": {
                "type": "double"
              }
            }
          },
          "product_suggest": {
            "type": "completion"
          }
        }
      },
      "product_review": {
        "_parent": {
```

```
        "type": "product"
      },
      "properties": {}
    }
  }
}
```

Now let's index some products with different variations as shown here:

```
#Parent document with nested variations
PUT chapter7/product/1?refresh=true
{
  "product_name": "Apple iPhone 6",
  "variations": [
    {                         #Variation 1
      "type": "storage",
      "value": "16GB",
      "unit_price": "600"
    },
    {                         #Variation 2
      "type": "storage",
      "value": "64GB",
      "unit_price": "700"
    }
  ]
}

PUT chapter7/product/2?refresh=true
{
  "product_name": "Apple iPhone 7",
  "variations": [
    {
      "type": "storage",
      "value": "128GB",
      "unit_price": "900"
    }
  ]
}

#Child Document
POST chapter7/product_review/?parent=1
{"user_id" : "reviewer1", "comment" : "One of the best phones in the
market"}
```

Suppose that we want to query for phones with at least a 128GB storage. Since variations are nested documents and are stored as separate hidden documents, we have to use a **special nested type** query as shown here:

```
#Nested Query (Query for iPhone with 128GB)
POST chapter7/product/_search
{
  "query": {
    "bool": {
      "must": [
        {
          "term": {
            "product_name": "iphone"
          }
        },
        {
          "nested": {
            "path": "variations",
            "query": {
              "bool": {
                "must": [
                  {
                    "term": {
                      "variations.type": "storage"
                    }
                  },
                  {
                    "term": {
                      "variations.value": "128GB"
                    }
                  }
                ]
              }
            }
          }
        }
      ]
    }
  }
}
```

The response to the preceding query will contain documents that satisfied both the nested query and main parent ("product_name": "iphone") query as shown here:

```
{
  ....
  "hits": {
    "total": 1,
```

```
      "max_score": 1.261772,
      "hits": [
        {
          "_index": "chapter7",
          "_type": "product",
          "_id": "2",
          "_score": 1.261772,
          "_source": {
            "product_name": "Apple iPhone 7",
            "variations": [
              {
                "type": "storage",
                "value": "128GB",
                "unit_price": "900"
              }
            ]
          }
        }
      ]
    }
}
```

Note that the response contains the entire product document, not just the variation. If you need only the variation that matched the query, you can use inner hits, which we will discuss in the next section.

Inner hits for nested documents

The concept of inner hits is best explained with an example. For suppose, we want to find out the price of an iPhone with at least 64GB of storage. Similar to the example in the previous section, we can use a nested query to get the product document with all its variations as shown here:

```
{
  ....
  "hits": {
    "total": 1,
    "max_score": 0.87546873,
    "hits": [
      {
        "_index": "chapter7",
        "_type": "product",
        "_id": "1",
        "_score": 0.87546873,
        "_source": {
          "product_name": "Apple iPhone 6",
```

```
        "variations": [
          {
            "type": "storage",
            "value": "16GB",
            "unit_price": "600"
          },
          {
            "type": "storage",
            "value": "64GB",
            "unit_price": "700"
          }
        ]
      }
    }
  ]
 }
}
```

The response contains the product document with both 16GB and 64GB variation, but what we are looking for is the price of 64GB variation. To get the price of the 64GB variation, you have to add application-side logic to go through the source document and get the unit_price. The **inner hits** feature is provided to solve this problem.

When you include inner hits tag in your query, along with the complete product document, the nested document that matched the query is also shown in the response. In the following query, we will set the source to false to hide the complete product document and use inner hits to get only the 64GB variation document:

```
#Inner hits
POST chapter7/product/_search
 {
    "_source": false,
    "query": {
      "nested": {
        "path": "variations",
        "query": {
          "bool": {
            "must": [
              {
                "term": {
                  "variations.type": "storage"
                }
              },
              {
                "term": {
                  "variations.value": "64GB"
                }
```

```
                }
              ]
            }
          },
          "inner_hits": {}
        }
      }
    }
```

The response to the preceding query is as follows:

```
{
    ....
    "hits": {
      "total": 1,
      "max_score": 0.87546873,
      "hits": [
        {
          "_index": "chapter7",
          "_type": "product",
          "_id": "1",
          "_score": 0.87546873,
          "inner_hits": {
            "variations": {
              "hits": {
                "total": 1,
                "max_score": 0.87546873,
                "hits": [
                  {
                    "_nested": {
                      "field": "variations",
                      "offset": 1
                    },
                    "_score": 0.87546873,
                    "_source": {
                      "type": "storage",
                      "value": "64GB",
                      "unit_price": "700"
                    }
                  }
                ]
              }
            }
          }
        }
      ]
    }
}
```

In the preceding response, you can see that only the `64GB` variation is included in the response. If you want both the complete product document and the variation that matched the query, just remove the `"_source" : false` from the query.

Scripting

Scripting is one of the most powerful features of Elasticsearch. In this chapter so far, we discussed different types of queries Elasticsearch supports. If these queries are not enough, Elasticsearch also provides script query. Scripting allows you to run **user defined scripts** to determine whether a document should be filtered or not. Along with the script query, fields based on a script, sorting based on a script are also supported. In Elasticsearch 5.0, **Painless**, a new scripting language, which is both secure and fast, is introduced. Along with Painless, special-purpose languages, such as Expression, Mustache, and Java are also supported.

Script Query

Script query can be used to evaluate documents against a user-defined script. For example, the product document we discussed so far has a nested field variation, which contains the different variations of each product. We want to query for all the products with more than one variation. Since this cannot be done with already available Elasticsearch queries, we will use a script. The query with a script is shown here:

```
#Script Query
POST chapter7/product/_search
{
    "query": {
        "script": {
            "script": {
                "lang": "painless",
                "inline": "params._source.containsKey('variations') &&
params._source.variations.length > 1"
            }
        }
    }
}
```

In the preceding query, we are using the source of the document to access the `variations` field. We can also use the `doc` values, which is much faster than using a source field. You can access the field value using the `doc` values as shown here:

```
"inline": "doc['numeric_field'].value > 0"
```

Scripts are compiled and cached. To reuse the compiled script, any parameters used in the script should be passed via the `params`. When the parameters are passed via `params`, the compiled script can be *reused* for any number of variations. In the preceding example, the number of variations can be passed as a parameter as shown here:

```
#Script Query
POST chapter7/product/_search
  {
    "query": {
      "script": {
        "script": {
          "lang": "painless",
          "inline": "params._source.containsKey('variations') &&
params._source.variations.length > params.num_of_variations",
          "params": {
            "num_of_variations": 1
          }
        }
      }
    }
  }
```

Executing scripts on a larger index can be very expensive. To minimize the performance impact of scripting, we will discuss post filter in the next section.

Post Filter

You can tell Elasticsearch to run an expensive query, such as a script or geolocation, using post filter. The query in the post filter is only executed **after the main query** is executed so that the number of documents the expensive query has to be executed on is minimum. In the following query, we will run the script query as post filter:

```
POST chapter7/product/_search
  {
    "query": {
      "match": {
        "product_name": "iphone"
      }
    },
    "post_filter": {
      "script": {
        "script": {
          "lang": "painless",
          "inline": "params._source.containsKey('variations') &&
params._source.variations.length > params.num_of_variations",
```

```
      "params": {
        "num_of_variations": 1
      }
    }
  }
 }
}
```

In the preceding example, the main query is executed first, and the script is executed on the documents that match the main query.

Reverse search using the percolate query

The percolate query is one of the popular features of Elasticsearch. Until now, we indexed the documents and used the search API to query the documents. Percolate query is reverse search. The actual queries are stored into an index, and we can percolate a document to get the queries that match the document. By using the percolate query, you are checking whether the document matches any of the **predefined** criteria. Common use cases include alerts and monitoring.

For example, we want to classify the products in an e-commerce store. First, we will add predefined queries to the `chapter7` index and use the `percolate` query to check whether a product matches any predefined queries. The following example will make it more clear. To use the `percolate` query, we need to first add a mapping with the `percolator` type. In the following command, we are adding a new type called `label`, which contains a field named `query`, which is of type `percolator`. We will index the actual queries in the `chapter7` index and type `label`. The mapping for the field query can be added as shown next:

```
#Percolator
 PUT chapter7/_mapping/label
 {
   "properties": {
     "query": {
       "type": "percolator"
     }
   }
 }
```

Now let's add some queries to the new type we just added. The document will contain the actual query and the metadata. In the following command, we will index two labels/tags: one for the products with no variations and the other for the products that are manufactured by Samsung:

```
#No Variations
PUT chapter7/label/no_variations
{
  "query": {
    "script": {
      "script": {
        "inline": "!params._source.containsKey('variations')"
      }
    }
  },
  "metadata": {
    "desc": "Product with no variations"
  }
}

#Samsung
PUT chapter7/label/samsung_product
{
  "query": {
    "match": {
      "product_name": "samsung"
    }
  },
  "metadata": {
    "desc": "Samsung Product"
  }
}
```

Next, imagine we have just added a new product and we want to find out the labels/tags for this product. We will use the percolator query to do that. The product we want to run the percolate query on is shown here:

```
PUT /chapter7/product/4
{
  "product_name": "Samsung Galaxy S7"
}
```

We can run the `percolate` query on the preceding document as shown here:

```
POST chapter7/label/_search
  {
    "_source": false,
```

```
    "query": {
      "percolate": {
        "field": "query",
        "document_type": "product",
        "index" : "chapter7",
        "type" : "product",
        "id" : 4
      }
    }
  }
```

In the preceding query, the following parameters are used:

- `field`: This refers to the field that is of type percolator. This field holds the actual query.
- `document_type`: This refers to the type of the document the percolate query is executed on.
- `index`: This refers to the index of the document.
- `type`: This refers to the type of the document.
- `id`: This refers to the identifier of the document.

The response to the preceding query contains all the labels the document matched. The response is as follows:

```
{
  ....
  "hits": {
    "total": 2,
    "max_score": 1,
    "hits": [
      {
        "_index": "chapter7",
        "_type": "label",
        "_id": "no_variations",
        "_score": 1
      },
      {
        "_index": "chapter7",
        "_type": "label",
        "_id": "samsung_product",
        "_score": 0.25316024
      }
    ]
  }
}
```

You can see from the response that the document matched two labels. One is `no_variations`, and the other is `samsung_product`. In the preceding example, we set the source to false to see only the label _id. You can also set the _source to metadata or other fields you want in the response.

In the previous example, we used the id of an existing document in the request. Instead of the document id, the actual document source can also be used as shown here:

```
POST chapter7/label/_search
{
  "_source": false,
  "query": {
    "percolate": {
      "field": "query",
      "document_type": "product",
      "document": {
        "product_name": "Samsung Galaxy S7"
      }
    }
  }
}
```

Geo and Spatial Filtering

In modern applications, spatial or location-based filtering is a very common requirement, not just for filtering the results based on a location, but also as one of the driving factors of **relevance**. The results that are closer to the user location appear at the top of the list, the results that are not close are **not removed** from the list but simply placed at the bottom of the list. Elasticsearch makes it very easy to work with geographical data by combining full-text search and location-based filtering. Sorting the results based on the distance from the current user location is also supported.

To use geolocation queries, the location information should be indexed using a **special mapping type**. The geolocation can be stored using the `geo_point` mapping type if you want to store the location data in the form of latitude/longitude pairs. If you want to store the location data in form of circles, rectangles, and so on, you can use the `geo_shape` mapping type. Geo shapes are beyond the scope of this book, and we will only discuss how to index and search `geo_point` in this section. We will discuss location-based aggregations in `Chapter 8`, *How to slice and dice your data using aggregations*.

We will continue to use the e-commerce example to demonstrate location-based queries. We will add a new type named `store` to the existing `chapter7` index. The new type will contain documents representing physical stores with the store `name`, `address`, `has_wifi`, and `location` fields. We can add the new mapping as shown here :

```
#GEO
 PUT chapter7/_mapping/store
 {
    "properties": {
      "name": {
        "type": "keyword"
      },
      "address": {
        "type": "text"
      },
      "has_wifi" : {
        "type" : "boolean"
      },
      "location": {
        "type": "geo_point"
      }
    }
 }
```

The mapping type for the `location` field is specified as `geo_point`. The `geo_point` is used to store location information using coordinates.

Now let's index some store documents as shown here:

```
#Index Stores
PUT chapter7/store/1
 {
    "name" : "Store1",
    "address" : "123 High Lane",
    "has_wifi" : true,
    "location" : {
      "lat" : "37.339724",
      "lon" : "-121.873848"
    }
 }

 PUT chapter7/store/2
 {
    "name" : "Store2",
    "address" : "124 High Lane",
    "has_wifi" : true,
    "location" : {
```

```
        "lat" : "37.338495",
        "lon" : "-121.880736"
    }
}
```

As you can see, location information is represented using longitude/latitude pairs. The following variations are also supported:

```
# As an Object
"location" : {
    "lat" : "37.339724",
    "lon" : "-121.873848"
}

# As a String
"location" : "37.339724,-121.873848"

# As an Array
"location" : [37.339724,-121.873848]

# As a Geo Hash
"location" : "9q9k6tqptt03"
```

The following location-based queries are supported:

- Geo Distance
- Geo Bounding Box

Geo Distance

Geo Distance query is used to find the documents that are located within a certain distance from a given location. Let's query for all the stores within 1 mile of the user location. For this example, I'm assuming the user location as follows:

```
"lat": "37.348929", "lon": "-121.888536"
```

In the following Google Maps screenshot, the red pin represents the current user location, and the blue circle represents the 1-mile radius from the user location:

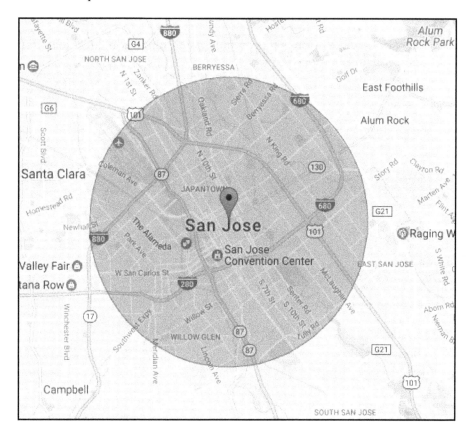

The query would look like the following:

```
POST chapter7/store/_search
   {
     "query": {
       "geo_distance": {
         "distance": "1mi",
         "location": {
           "lat": "37.348929",
           "lon": "-121.888536"
         }
       }
     }
   }
```

The preceding query limits to stores that are within 1 mile from the given location. The response to the query is as follows:

```
{
    ....
    "hits": {
        "total": 1,
        "max_score": 1,
        "hits": [
            {
                "_index": "chapter7",
                "_type": "store",
                "_id": "2",
                "_score": 1,
                "_source": {
                    "name": "Store2",
                    "address": "124 High Lane",
                    "has_wifi": true,
                    "location": {
                        "lat": "37.338495",
                        "lon": "-121.880736"
                    }
                }
            }
        ]
    }
}
```

You can see from the response that there is only one store within 1 mile of the user location.

Using Geolocation to rank the search results

In this section, we will use the Geo Distance query to order the search results based on the distance. The documents closer to the user location are shown higher in the result list. For example, we want to find all the stores that have wifi in them and are within 1 mile of the user location. If none of the stores are within a 1-mile radius, filtering on the location will exclude all the stores in the result. In some cases, the user might be okay with a 2-mile radius. Instead of excluding the stores that are far away, we can *rank them lower* than the stores that are near.

We will use the `bool` query to tune the relevance. We need all the stores that have wifi in them, so we place the `has_wifi` query in the must block. Next, the location query is placed in the `should` block. Stores that match the geolocation query have better relevance than those that don't. The `bool` query simply **adds the relevance** from all the queries. The more queries the document matches, the higher the relevance score is. The `bool` query is shown next:

```
POST chapter7/store/_search
{
   "query": {
     "bool": {
       "must": [
         {
           "term": {
             "has_wifi": "true"
           }
         }
       ],
       "should": [
         {
           "geo_distance": {
             "distance": "1mi",
             "location": {
               "lat": "37.348929",
               "lon": "-121.888536"
             }
           }
         }
       ]
     }
   }
}
```

The response to the `bool` query is as follows:

```
{
   ....
   "hits": {
     "total": 2,
     "max_score": 1.287682,
     "hits": [
       {
         "_index": "chapter7",
         "_type": "store",
         "_id": "2",
         "_score": 1.287682,
```

```
      "_source": {
        "name": "Store2",
        "address": "124 High Lane",
        "has_wifi": true,
        "location": {
          "lat": "37.338495",
          "lon": "-121.880736"
        }
      }
    },
    {
      "_index": "chapter7",
      "_type": "store",
      "_id": "1",
      "_score": 0.2876821,
      "_source": {
        "name": "Store1",
        "address": "123 High Lane",
        "has_wifi": true,
        "location": {
          "lat": "37.339724",
          "lon": "-121.873848"
        }
      }
    }
  ]
 }
}
```

You can see from the preceding response that the score for Store2 is higher than Store1 as Store2 is within 1 mile of the location. The beauty of Elasticsearch is the ability to combine the geolocation-based query with full-text search and structured search as shown in the previous example.

Geo Bounding Box

Geo Bounding Box query is used to find all documents within a bounding box. A bounding box is defined by the coordinates of the `top_left` and `bottom_right`. Unlike the Geo Distance query, which has to calculate the distance of every document from the given location, the Geo Bounding query can quickly check whether the coordinates of the document are within the four corners of the bounding box. The Geo Bounding query is **less expensive** when compared to Geo Distance. A bounding box on Google Maps is shown here:

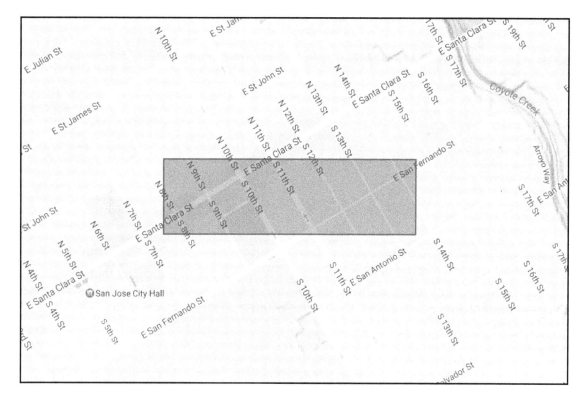

As shown in the screenshot from Google Maps, we are trying to find all the stores within the bounding box. The query would look like the following:

```
#GEO Bounding Box
 POST chapter7/store/_search
 {
   "query": {
     "geo_bounding_box": {
       "location": {
         "top_left": {
```

```
            "lat": 37.340542,
            "lon": -121.877904
          },
          "bottom_right": {
            "lat": 37.339075,
            "lon": -121.871295
          }
        }
      }
    }
  }
}
```

The response to the preceding query is as follows:

```
{
    ....
    "hits": {
      "total": 1,
      "max_score": 1,
      "hits": [
        {
          "_index": "chapter7",
          "_type": "store",
          "_id": "2",
          "_score": 1,
          "_source": {
            "name": "Store2",
            "address": "124 High Lane",
            "has_wifi": true,
            "location": {
              "lat": "37.338495",
              "lon": "-121.880736"
            }
          }
        }
      ]
    }
}
```

The response will contain all the stores within the bounding box.

Sorting

In this section, we will discuss how to sort the results by the distance to the given location. In most cases, **scoring** the results like we did in the *Geo Distance query* section is a better option than sorting the results. The real power of Elasticsearch is combining the different type of queries and **assigning weights** to each query. The query to sort all the stores based on the distance from the current location is shown here:

```
#GEO Sort
POST chapter7/store/_search
{
  "query": {
    "match_all": {}
  },
  "sort": [
    {
      "_geo_distance": {
        "location": {
          "lat": "37.348929",
          "lon": "-121.888536"
        },
        "order": "asc",
        "unit" : "mi"
      }
    }
  ]
}
```

In the preceding query, the result is sorted in ascending ordering of the distance from the given location. And the sort value in the response is shown in miles. The response to the preceding query is as follows:

```
{
  ....
  "hits": {
    "total": 2,
    "max_score": null,
    "hits": [
      {
        "_index": "chapter7",
        "_type": "store",
        "_id": "2",
        "_score": null,
        "_source": {
          "name": "Store2",
          "address": "124 High Lane",
          "has_wifi": true,
```

```
            "location": {
              "lat": "37.338495",
              "lon": "-121.880736"
            }
          },
          "sort": [
            0.8386315194291991
          ]
        },
        {
          "_index": "chapter7",
          "_type": "store",
          "_id": "1",
          "_score": null,
          "_source": {
            "name": "Store1",
            "address": "123 High Lane",
            "has_wifi": true,
            "location": {
              "lat": "37.339724",
              "lon": "-121.873848"
            }
          },
          "sort": [
            1.0273440725719407
          ]
        }
      ]
    }
  }
}
```

You can see from the response that the sort value is the distance of the store from the given location.

Multi search

Multi search allows us to group search requests together. It is similar to the multi-get and the other bulk APIs. By grouping the requests together, we can save the **network round trips** and execute the queries in the request in **parallel**. We can control the number of the requests that are executed in parallel. A simple multi search request is shown here:

```
#Multi Search
GET chapter7/_msearch
{"type" : "product"}
{"query" : {"match_all" : {}}, "from" : 0, "size" : 10}
```

```
{"type" : "product_review"}
{"query" : {"match_all" : {}}}
```

The response of the multi search query is a list of responses. Each request is executed **independently**, and the failure of one request will not affect the others. The response to the preceding query will contain responses to two queries as shown next:

```
{
    "responses": [
        {
            ....
            "hits": {
                "total": 3,
                "max_score": 1,
                "hits": [
                    {
                        "_index": "chapter7",
                        "_type": "product",
                        "_id": "2",
                        "_score": 1,
                        "_source": {
                            "product_name": "Apple iPhone 7",
                            "variations": [
                                {
                                    "type": "storage",
                                    "value": "128GB",
                                    "unit_price": "900"
                                }
                            ]
                        }
                    },
                    {
                        "_index": "chapter7",
                        "_type": "product",
                        "_id": "4",
                        "_score": 1,
                        "_source": {
                            "product_name": "Samsung Galaxy S7"
                        }
                    },
                    {
                        "_index": "chapter7",
                        "_type": "product",
                        "_id": "1",
                        "_score": 1,
                        "_source": {
                            "product_name": "Apple iPhone 6",
                            "variations": [
```

```
                                {
                                    "type": "storage",
                                    "value": "16GB",
                                    "unit_price": "600"
                                },
                                {
                                    "type": "storage",
                                    "value": "64GB",
                                    "unit_price": "700"
                                }
                            ]
                        }
                    }
                ]
            },
            "status": 200
        },
        {
            ....
            "hits": {
                "total": 1,
                "max_score": 1,
                "hits": [
                    {
                        "_index": "chapter7",
                        "_type": "product_review",
                        "_id": "AVx_gfuoiOAxqKpNCloD",
                        "_score": 1,
                        "_routing": "1",
                        "_parent": "1",
                        "_source": {
                            "user_id": "reviewer1",
                            "comment": "One of the best phones in the market"
                        }
                    }
                ]
            },
            "status": 200
        }
    ]
}
```

The number of queries executed in parallel can be controlled using the `max_concurrent_searches` parameter as shown next. The default value depends on the number of nodes in the cluster and the thread pool size. The preceding query with `max_concurrent_searches` equal to 1 is shown here:

```
#Multi Search
GET chapter7/_msearch?max_concurrent_searches=1
{"type" : "product"}
{"query" : {"match_all" : {}}, "from" : 0, "size" : 10}
{"type" : "product_review"}
{"query" : {"match_all" : {}}}
```

Search templates

Search templates are very similar to **stored procedures** in the relational database. Commonly used queries can be defined as a template, and the applications using Elasticsearch can simply refer to the query by its ID. The template accepts parameters, which can be specified at the runtime. Search templates are stored on the server side and can be modified **without changes** to the **client code**. Templates are expressed using the Mustache template engine. For more information on mustache, please visit `http://mustache.github.io/mustache.5.html`.

Let's start by defining a template query to find all the products by their name. The query is as follows:

```
#Define Template
 POST _search/template/find_product_by_name
 {
   "query" : {
     "match" : {
       "product_name": "{{ product_name }}"
     }
   }
 }
```

Once the template is defined, you can execute the template by passing the `product_name` parameter as shown here:

```
#Execute Template
POST chapter7/product/_search/template
{
   "id" : "find_product_by_name",
   "params" : {
     "product_name" : "iphone"
   }
}
```

Applications calling Elasticsearch don't have to worry about the query logic. Any changes to the query can be made on the server side without worrying about changing the client code. Templates are also easy to debug. The result of the preceding query is as follows:

```
{
   . . . .
   "hits": {
     "total": 2,
     "max_score": 0.68640786,
     "hits": [
       {
         "_index": "chapter7",
         "_type": "product",
         "_id": "2",
         "_score": 0.68640786,
         "_source": {
           "product_name": "Apple iPhone 7",
           "variations": [
             {
               "type": "storage",
               "value": "128GB",
               "unit_price": "900"
             }
           ]
         }
       },
       {
         "_index": "chapter7",
         "_type": "product",
         "_id": "1",
         "_score": 0.25811607,
         "_source": {
           "product_name": "Apple iPhone 6",
           "variations": [
             {
               "type": "storage",
```

```
            "value": "16GB",
            "unit_price": "600"
          },
          {
            "type": "storage",
            "value": "64GB",
            "unit_price": "700"
          }
        ]
      }
    }
  ]
}
}
```

You can also store the template as a `.mustache` file in `/config/scripts`. For the preceding example, add the following contents to a `find_product_by_name.mustache` file:

```
{
  "query" : {
    "match" : {
      "product_name": "{{ product_name }}"
    }
  }
}
```

 Before you can execute the template, the `find_product_by_name.mustache` template file should be copied to all the nodes in the cluster. The template file should be placed in the `/config/scripts` folder.

The `find_product_by_name.mustache` template file can be executed as follows:

```
#Execute Template
POST chapter7/product/_search/template
{
  "file" : "find_product_by_name",
  "params" : {
    "product_name" : "iphone"
  }
}
```

Mustache templates also support **conditioning**. For example, in the above template along with the `product_name` we want to pass an **optional** `variation` parameter to filter the products based on storage. The above query with the optional variation parameter is shown here:

```
#Execute Template
POST chapter7/product/_search/template
{
   "file": "find_product_by_name",
   "params": {
     "product_name": "iphone",
     "variation": "128GB"
   }
}
```

Let's update the template query to accept an optional `variation` parameter along with the product name. The updated template looks like the following:

```
{
   "query": {
     "bool": {
       "must": [
         {
           "match": {
             "product_name": "{{ product_name }}"
           }
         }
       ]
       {{#variation}}
       ,
       {
         "nested": {
           "path": "variations",
           "query": {
             "bool": {
               "must": [
                 {
                   "term": {
                     "variations.type": "storage"
                   }
                 },
                 {
                   "term": {
                     "variations.value": "{{ variation }}"
                   }
                 }
               ]
             }
           }
         }
       }
```

```
                    }
                  }
                }
        {{/variation}}
              ]
            }
          }
        }
```

In the preceding query, we have used mustache conditionals to check whether the variation parameter is passed in the request. The variation tags used in the query are shown here:

```
{{ #variation }}    {{ /variation }}
```

Only if the `variation` parameter is provided in the request, the template will conditionally add the nested query to the bool query. Due to how the mustache conditionals are formatted, the preceding template is not a valid JSON and can only be used by saving it as a `find_product_by_name.mustache` file. You don't have to restart the node after adding/updating a script file. Elasticsearch will automatically pick up the script.

 Note that variation is an optional parameter. A template can be executed with or without the variation parameter.

The results of the preceding query are as follows:

```
{
    ....
    "hits": {
      "total": 1,
      "max_score": 1.261772,
      "hits": [
        {
          "_index": "chapter7",
          "_type": "product",
          "_id": "2",
          "_score": 1.261772,
          "_source": {
            "product_name": "Apple iPhone 7",
            "variations": [
              {
                "type": "storage",
                "value": "128GB",
                "unit_price": "900"
              }
            ]
```

```
            }
          }
        ]
      }
    }
```

In the preceding example, since variations is a nested type, a nested query is used. Once the template is defined, the application can simply use the template name to execute the query without worrying about using special type of queries for nested, parent-child, and so on.

Querying Elasticsearch from Java application

In this section, we will discuss how to use a Java client to query Elasticsearch. In Chapter 4, *Indexing and Updating Your Data*, we discussed different types of Java clients and how to use them in your application for indexing. In this section, we will discuss how to use the client to query Elasticsearch. Let's take a simple match query as shown here:

```
#Match Query
 POST chapter7/_search
 {
   "query": {
     "match": {
       "product_name": "iphone"
     }
   }
 }
```

All the queries available via the REST API are also made available via the transport client. To execute the query using the Java client, first set up the client as shown next:

```
TransportAddress node1 = new
InetSocketTransportAddress(InetAddress.getByName("127.0.0.1"), 9300);

Settings setting = Settings.builder().put("cluster.name", "es-dev")
.put("client.transport.sniff", true).build();

TransportClient transportClient = new PreBuiltTransportClient(setting);

// Add the known nodes to the client
transportClient.addTransportAddress(node1);
```

Next, we will use the `QueryBuilders` to build the query. The query builders are available by importing `QueryBuilders` as shown here:

```
import static org.elasticsearch.index.query.QueryBuilders.*;
```

We are using a static import for `QueryBuilder` so that we can use the queries without specifying the class or package. We will use the transport client to execute the query as shown here:

```
// Imports
import org.elasticsearch.action.search.SearchResponse;
import org.elasticsearch.index.query.QueryBuilder;
import org.elasticsearch.search.SearchHit;

// Build a match Query
QueryBuilder matchQuery = matchQuery("product_name", "iphone");

// Execute the query on chapter7 index.
SearchResponse response =
transportClient.prepareSearch("chapter7").setTypes("product")
.setQuery(matchQuery).execute().actionGet();

// Number of hits in the response
long totalHits = response.getHits().getTotalHits();

// Actual Hit
SearchHit searchHit = response.getHits().getAt(0);
```

Once we get the hits from the response, we will use `ObjectMapper` to convert the hit to a `Product` object. The `Product` class definition is shown here:

```
import java.util.List;

import com.fasterxml.jackson.annotation.JsonIgnoreProperties;
import com.fasterxml.jackson.annotation.JsonProperty;

@JsonIgnoreProperties(ignoreUnknown=true)
public class Product {

    @JsonProperty("product_name")
    private String productName;
    private List<Variation> variations;
    public String getProductName() {
        return productName;
    }

    public void setProductName(String productName) {
```

```
            this.productName = productName;
        }

    public List<Variation> getVariations() {
        return variations;
    }

    public void setVariations(List<Variation> variations) {
        this.variations = variations;
    }
    static class Variation {
        private String type;
        private String value;
        @JsonProperty("unit_price")
        private String unitPrice;

        public String getType() {
            return type;
        }

        public void setType(String type) {
            this.type = type;
        }

        public String getValue() {
            return value;
        }

        public void setValue(String value) {
            this.value = value;
        }

        public String getUnitPrice() {
            return unitPrice;
        }

        public void setUnitPrice(String unitPrice) {
            this.unitPrice = unitPrice;
        }
    }
}
```

We can use the `ObjectMapper` to convert the response from Elasticsearch to a `Product`
object as shown next:

```
ObjectMapper mapper = new ObjectMapper();
Product product = mapper.readValue(searchHit.getSourceAsString(),
Product.class);
```

The response using the Java client is very similar to the response from the REST API. The complete application code is shown here:

```
import static org.elasticsearch.index.query.QueryBuilders.matchQuery;

import java.net.InetAddress;
import java.util.ArrayList;
import java.util.List;

import org.elasticsearch.action.search.SearchResponse;
import org.elasticsearch.client.transport.TransportClient;
import org.elasticsearch.common.settings.Settings;
import org.elasticsearch.common.transport.InetSocketTransportAddress;
import org.elasticsearch.common.transport.TransportAddress;
import org.elasticsearch.index.query.QueryBuilder;
import org.elasticsearch.search.SearchHit;
import org.elasticsearch.transport.client.PreBuiltTransportClient;

import com.fasterxml.jackson.databind.ObjectMapper;
import com.learning.elasticsearch.Product;

public class Application {
    public static void main(String[] args) throws Exception {
        //Query Elasticsearch for all the product with iPhone in the
product name.
        List<Product> products = searchProduct("iphone");
    }

    private static List<Product> searchProduct(String productName) throws
Exception {
        List<Product> result = new ArrayList<Product>();
        // Initialize Transport Client
        TransportAddress node1 = new
InetSocketTransportAddress(InetAddress.getByName("127.0.0.1"), 9300);
        Settings setting = Settings.builder().put("cluster.name", "es-
dev").put("client.transport.sniff", true).build();
        TransportClient transportClient = new
PreBuiltTransportClient(setting);
        // Add the known nodes to the client
        transportClient.addTransportAddress(node1);

        // Build a match query
        QueryBuilder matchQuery = matchQuery("product_name",
productName);

        // Execute the query on chapter7 index and product type
        SearchResponse response =
transportClient.prepareSearch("chapter7").setTypes("product").setQuery(matc
```

```
hQuery)
                        .execute().actionGet();

        // Total Hits
        long totalHits = response.getHits().getTotalHits();

        // Initialize Object Mapper
        ObjectMapper mapper = new ObjectMapper();

        for (SearchHit hit : response.getHits()) {
            // Use ObjectMapper to convert the source into Java POJO
            Product p = mapper.readValue(hit.getSourceAsString(),
Product.class);
            result.add(p);
            System.out.println(hit.sourceAsString());
        }
        return result;
    }
  }
```

Summary

In this chapter, we discussed how to implement autocomplete, highlighting, and correcting user typos. Elasticsearch doesn't support traditional SQL joins, and you learned how to use parent-child and nested mapping to handle relationships between different document types. We discussed filtering based on geolocation and how to use location as one of factors driving the relevance score. We also discussed using Painless scripting language to query based on user-defined scripts. We also covered Search Templates and how to query Elasticsearch from your application.

In the next chapter, we will discuss aggregations and how to use them to slice and dice your data.

8
How to Slice and Dice Your Data Using Aggregations

In this chapter, you'll learn how to unleash the analytics power of Elasticsearch. In Elasticsearch 5.0, the aggregation framework has been completely revamped. The query syntax is very simple and easy to understand. The distributed nature of Elasticsearch makes the queries very performant and can easily scale to large datasets. We will go through the different types of aggregations Elasticsearch supports and how easy it is to run these queries. We will discuss how to use Kibana to visualize the data. You will also learn doc values and field data, the internal data structures used to power aggregations.

By the end of this chapter, we will cover the following:

- Different types of aggregations
- Child aggregations
- Aggregation on nested documents
- Aggregation on geolocations
- Doc values
- Memory considerations
- Data visualization using Kibana

Aggregation basics

Aggregation is one of many reasons why Elasticsearch is nothing like anything out there; it is an analytics engine on steroids. Aggregation operations, such as distinct, count, and average on large data sets, are traditionally run on batch processing systems, such as Hadoop, due to the heavy computation involved. As running these kind of queries on a large dataset using a traditional SQL database can be very challenging. Elasticsearch enables these queries to run in real-time sub-second queries. In my first project with Elasticsearch, we solely used Elasticsearch for its aggregation capabilities and few search capabilities.

Aggregations in Elasticsearch are very powerful as you can nest aggregations. Let's take a query from the SQL world:

```
select avg(rating) from Product group by category;
```

To execute the query, the products are first grouped by category. Products that belong to the same category are grouped into the same bucket. The second level of aggregation computes the average ratings of each bucket (category).

Nesting aggregations in Elasticsearch is very simple. These kind of queries are much more performant than SQL and can easily scale. Take the following for example:

- First, you can bucket all the products using their categories.
- Next, for each category, you can further group the products by their manufacturers.
- For each manufacturer, you can compute the average price/rating.
- And you can keep going.

You can use nest any level of aggregations. You can also use pipeline aggregations to use the result of the one aggregation as an input to a different aggregation. Aggregations are **calendar aware**, meaning you can bucket the data by month, year, and so on. Aggregations are **location aware**, meaning you can bucket the data by regions or locations.

In next few sections, we will go through the different types of aggregations that are supported. Once you understand the basic types of aggregations and their syntax, you will be able to use aggregations for any data.

Sample data

Similar to the previous chapters, we will use examples to explain aggregations better. In this chapter, we are going to use aggregations that are useful to an e-commerce site. Our data will be about the products in an e-commerce site.

 In the product mapping, we will use type `keyword` for fields we want to run aggregations on. Keywords are better for running aggregation, sorting and can advantage of doc values. We will discuss doc values further in sections below.

First, let's set the mapping for the `chapter8` index:

```
#Delete existing index
 DELETE chapter8

 #Chapter 8 Mappings
 PUT chapter8
 {
   "settings": {},
   "mappings": {
     "product": {
       "properties": {
         "product_name": {
           "type": "text"
         },
         "manufacturer" : {
           "type": "keyword"
         },
         "category" : {
           "type": "keyword"
         },
         "products_sold" : {
           "type": "integer"
         },
         "variations": {
           "type": "nested",
           "properties": {
             "color": {
               "type": "keyword"
             },
             "storage": {
               "type": "keyword"
             },
             "unit_price": {
               "type": "double"
             }
```

```
                }
              }
            }
          },
          "product_review": {
            "_parent": {
              "type": "product"
            },
            "properties": {}
          }
        }
      }
    }
```

Next, we will index some sample documents:

```
#Parent Documents
 PUT chapter8/product/1?refresh=true
 {
    "product_name": "iPhone 6",
    "manufacturer": "Apple",
    "release_date": "2014-09-12",
    "products_sold" : 25,
    "category": "Cell Phones",
    "variations": [
      {
        "color": "Gray",
        "storage": "16GB",
        "unit_price": "600"
      }
    ]
 }

 PUT chapter8/product/2?refresh=true
 {
    "product_name": "iPhone 7",
    "manufacturer": "Apple",
    "release_date": "2016-08-16",
    "products_sold" : 36,
    "category": "Cell Phones",
    "variations": [
      {
        "color": "Rose Gold",
        "storage": "128GB",
        "unit_price": "900"
      },
      {
        "color": "Rose Gold",
        "storage": "64GB",
```

```
      "unit_price": "800"
    }
  ]
}

PUT chapter8/product/3?refresh=true
{
  "product_name": "Samsung Galaxy S8",
  "manufacturer": "Samsung",
  "release_date" : "2017-04-21",
  "products_sold" : 10,
  "category": "Cell Phones",
  "variations": [
    {
      "color": "Gray",
      "storage": "64GB",
      "unit_price": "750"
    }
  ]
}
PUT chapter8/product/4?refresh=true
{
  "product_name": "Universal cellphone charger",
  "manufacturer": "UniPower",
  "release_date" : "2012-04-21",
  "products_sold" : 10,
  "category": "Cell Phones Accessories",
  "variations": [
    {
      "unit_price": "15"
    }
  ]
}
#Child Documents
POST chapter8/product_review/?parent=1
{
  "user_id": "user1",
  "comment": "One of the best phones in the market"
}
```

In the next few sections, we will use aggregations to analyze the products sold on the e-commerce site.

Query structure

The aggregation query is executed using the search API. You can add a query to restrict the document you want to run the aggregations on. Let's start by looking at a simple aggregation to group all the products by their category. In the SQL world, the query would look like the following:

```
select count(*) from Product
group by category;
```

In Elasticsearch, to achieve the same, we would do the following:

```
POST chapter8/_search
{
  "aggs" :{
    "category_products" : {
      "terms" : {
        "field" : "category"
      }
    }
  }
}
```

The basic structure is as follows:

```
"aggs" :{   // Can be aggs or aggregation.
  "category_products" : { // Name of the aggregation
    "terms" : {  // Type of the aggregation
```

The results of the preceding query are as follows:

```
{
....
  "aggregations": {
      "category_products": { # Name of the aggregation. When you have
multiple levels, the name can used to identify the aggregation.
        "doc_count_error_upper_bound": 0,
        "sum_other_doc_count": 0,
        "buckets": [
          {
            "key": "Cell Phones",
            "doc_count": 3
          },
          {
            "key": "Cell Phones Accessories",
            "doc_count": 1
          }
        ]
```

```
      }
    }
  }
```

It is often not effective to run aggregations on the complete data set. You should filter the data before running the aggregations, for example, if you want to view all the products made by Samsung grouped by their category. The SQL query would look the following:

```
select count(*) from Product
where manufacturer = 'Samsung'
group by category2;
```

In Elasticsearch, to achieve the same, we would do the following:

```
POST chapter8/_search
  {
    "query": {
      "match": {
        "manufacturer": "Samsung"
      }
    },
    "aggs": {
      "category_products": {
        "terms": {
          "field": "category"
        }
      }
    }
  }
```

The results of the preceding query are as follows:

```
  {
  ....
    "aggregations": {
      "category_products": {
        .....
        "buckets": [
            {
              "key": "Cell Phones",
              "doc_count": 1
            }
          ]
        }
      }
  }
```

As you can see from the preceding response, there is only one category for Samsung. If you want only the aggregation results and not the actual documents (hits), you can set the size to zero as shown next:

```
POST chapter8/_search
{
   "size": 0,
   "aggs": {
      "category_products": {
         "terms": {
            "field": "category"
         }
      }
   }
}
```

The response to the preceding query will contain only the aggregations.

Multilevel aggregations

In the previous section, we discussed running aggregation on a single field; the real power of aggregation is nesting multiple levels of aggregations. We want to group all the products by their category and compute the average number of products sold in each bucket. The SQL query would look like the following:

```
select avg(products_sold) from Product
group by category;
```

In Elasticsearch, we need to use two levels of aggregations:

1. The first level of aggregation groups the products by their category. The aggregations used to bucket or group all the documents satisfying a particular criterion are known as **bucket aggregations**.

2. The second level of aggregation, which calculates the average number of products sold for each bucket, is known as **metric aggregation**. Metric aggregation takes one or more values as input and calculates a single-value metric, such as averages, min, and max. The input can be the result of a different aggregation or a field in the document.

In the preceding example, to calculate the average number of products sold, we will use average aggregation, which is a metric aggregation:

```
POST chapter8/_search
  {
    "size" : 0,
    "aggs": {
      "category_products": {
        "terms": { # Bucket Aggregation
          "field": "category"
        },
        "aggs": {
          "products_sold": {
            "avg": { # Metric Aggregation
              "field": "products_sold"
            }
          }
        }
      }
    }
  }
```

The response to the preceding query is as follows:

```
{
   ....
   "hits": {
     "total": 5,
     "max_score": 0,
     "hits": []
   },
   "aggregations": {
     "category_products": {
       "doc_count_error_upper_bound": 0,
       "sum_other_doc_count": 0,
       "buckets": [
         {
           "key": "Cell Phones", // First Level
           "doc_count": 3,
           "products_sold": { // Second Level
             "value": 23.666666666666668
           }
         },
         {
           "key": "Cell Phones Accessories",
           "doc_count": 1,
           "products_sold": {
             "value": 10
```

```
                }
              }
            ]
          }
        }
      }
```

Suppose we want to find out the manufacturers for each category. To do this, we need to use terms aggregation to first group the products by their category and then use nested aggregation to group the products in each category by the manufacturer. The query is as follows:

```
POST chapter8/_search
{
    "size": 0,
    "aggs": {
      "category_products": {
        "terms": {
          "field": "category"
        },
        "aggs": {
          "manufacturer": {
            "terms": {
              "field": "manufacturer"
            }
          }
        }
      }
    }
}
```

The response to the preceding query is as follows:

```
{
    ....
    "hits": {
      "total": 5,
      "max_score": 0,
      "hits": []
    },
    "aggregations": {
      "category_products": { // First Level
        "doc_count_error_upper_bound": 0,
        "sum_other_doc_count": 0,
        "buckets": [ // Buckets in the first level
          {
            "key": "Cell Phones",
            "doc_count": 3,
```

```
"manufacturer": { // Second Level
  "doc_count_error_upper_bound": 0,
  "sum_other_doc_count": 0,
  "buckets": [ // Buckets in the second level
    {
      "key": "Apple",
      "doc_count": 2
    },
    {
      "key": "Samsung",
      "doc_count": 1
    }
  ]
}
},
{
  "key": "Cell Phones Accessories",
  "doc_count": 1,
  "manufacturer": {
    "doc_count_error_upper_bound": 0,
    "sum_other_doc_count": 0,
    "buckets": [
      {
        "key": "UniPower",
        "doc_count": 1
      }
    ]
  }
}
]
}
}
}
```

As you see from the preceding response, the first level, `category_products`, contains products grouped by their category (Cell Phone, Cell Phone Accessories). Each bucket in the `category_products` group is further grouped by the manufacturer (Apple, Samsung, and UniPower).

Types of aggregations

At a higher level, Elasticsearch supports four types of aggregation:

- **Bucket aggregation**: This can be used to group or create buckets. Buckets can be created based on an existing field, custom filters, ranges, and so on

- **Metric aggregation**: This can be used to calculate a metric, such as a count, sum, average, and so on
- **Pipeline aggregation**: This can be used to chain aggregations. The output of other aggregations can be the input for a pipeline aggregation
- **Matrix aggregation**: This can be used to calculate statistics over a set of fields

In this section, we will discuss bucket and metric aggregations. Pipeline and matrix aggregations are still experimental and out of the scope of this book.

Terms aggregations (group by)

Terms aggregation is one of the most commonly used methods of aggregation. Terms aggregation is similar to group by in the SQL world. Terms aggregation creates a bucket for every unique value. A simple terms aggregation is shown here:

```
POST chapter8/_search
{
  "aggs" :{
    "category_products" : {
      "terms" : {
        "field" : "category"
      }
    }
  }
}
```

The response will contain the top buckets.

Size and error

Your index data is spread across multiple shards, so the aggregation query is sent to all the shards, and each shard responds back with its view of the data. Each shard responds with its top buckets, and the coordinating node combines the results and sends them back to the client.

 Each shard only responds with the top buckets, and there is a possibility of error, and the number of documents in each bucket is approximated, which is indicated in the response.

You may go through the following query:

```
"aggregations": {
    "category_products": {
        "doc_count_error_upper_bound" : 0,
        "buckets": [ // Buckets in the first level
            {
```

You can also specify the number of buckets you want in the response by specifying the size as shown here:

```
POST chapter8/_search
{
    "aggs": {
        "category_products": {
            "terms": {
                "field": "category",
                "size": 2
            }
        }
    }
}
```

When the size is specified, each shard is asked to return the number of the buckets equal to the size. If the number of buckets is equal the size, the document count in the buckets will be accurate.

Order

By default, the buckets are ordered in descending order based on the document count. The buckets with the most documents are shown at the top. You can change the order to be ascending, alphabetical, or even based on the value from sub-aggregation. Doing so will increase the possibility of the error. The top buckets will be the most accurate. If the results are calculated based on a single shard due to the use of routing or on a single shard index, the results are always accurate. The terms aggregation with order is shown here:

```
POST chapter8/_search
{
    "size": 0,
    "aggs": {
        "category_products": {
            "terms": {
                "field": "category",
                "order": {
                    "_term": "asc"
                }
```

```
        }
      }
    }
  }
```

In the preceding query, the buckets are ordered alphabetically.

Minimum document count

When you have a large number of buckets, it is possible to filter the buckets that contain documents below a specified threshold value:

```
POST chapter8/_search
{
  "size": 0,
  "aggs" :{
    "category_products" : {
      "terms" : {
        "field" : "category",
        "min_doc_count": 5
      }
    }
  }
}
```

In the preceding query, all the buckets that don't contain a minimum of 5 documents will be excluded from the results.

Missing values

The documents that don't contain the field value are ignored by default. You can assign a default value for the documents missing the value:

```
POST chapter8/_search
{
  "size" : 0,
  "aggs": {
    "category_products": {
      "terms": {
        "field": "category",
        "missing": "Other"
      }
    }
  }
}
```

In the preceding query, all the documents that don't contain the `category` field will fall into the `Other` bucket.

Aggregations based on filters

In the previous sections, we discussed how to run aggregations on an existing field. In this section, we will discuss how to use filters to define the bucket criterion. For example, we want to group the products based on the released date. If we group by the existing `release_date` field, it will result in a lot of buckets. So we will use the filters to group the products that are released before 2016 as *old products* and the ones that are released after 2016 as *new products*. The query is as follows:

```
#Based on Filters
POST chapter8/_search
{
  "aggs": {
    "category_products": {
      "filters": {
        "filters": {
          "new_products": {
            "range": {
              "release_date": {
                "gte": "2016-01-01"
              }
            }
          },
          "old_products": {
            "range": {
              "release_date": {
                "lte": "2016-01-01"
              }
            }
          }
        }
      }
    }
  }
}
```

As shown in the preceding query, we created two buckets using the filters based on the release date. Next, we will use nested aggregation to calculate the average number of products sold in each bucket. We will also modify the preceding query to have three buckets:

- **2016_products**: This comprises products released after 2016
- **2015_products**: This comprises products released in 2015
- **Before_2015**: This comprises products released before 2015

The query is as follows:

```
#Aggs bases on Filters
POST chapter8/_search
{
  "size": 0,
  "aggs": {
    "category_products": {
      "filters": {
        "other_bucket_key": "Before_2015", // Default bucket
        "filters": {
          "2016_Products": {
            "range": {
              "release_date": {
                "gte": "2016-01-01"
              }
            }
          },
          "2015_Products": {
            "range": {
              "release_date": {
                "gte": "2015-01-01",
                "lte": "2016-01-01"
              }
            }
          }
        }
      },
      "aggs": {
        "products_sold": {
          "avg": {
            "field": "products_sold"
          }
        }
      }
    }
  }
}
```

While running the aggregation, a document is placed in one of the filter buckets if it matches the filter criteria. If the document doesn't match any of the filter criteria, a default bucket can be defined using `other_bucket_key`. In the preceding example, products released after 2016 are placed in the 2016_Products bucket. Products released between 2015 and 2016 are placed in the 2015_Products bucket. All the other documents are placed in the Before_2015 bucket.

Once the buckets are created, products_sold, which is a metric aggregation, calculates the average number of products sold in each bucket. The response to the preceding query is as follows:

```
{
    ....
    "hits": {
      "total": 5,
      "max_score": 0,
      "hits": []
    },
    "aggregations": {
      "category_products": {
        "buckets": {
          "2015_Products": {
            "doc_count": 0,
            "products_sold": {
              "value": null
            }
          },
          "2016_Products": {
            "doc_count": 2,
            "products_sold": {
              "value": 23
            }
          },
          "Before_2015": {
            "doc_count": 3,
            "products_sold": {
              "value": 17.5
            }
          }
        }
      }
    }
}
```

You can see from the preceding response that three buckets are created and the average number of products sold in each bucket is calculated.

Aggregations on dates (range, histogram)

Elasticsearch aggregations are calendar aware, which makes working with dates very simple. Let's start with range aggregation. Just like we used filter aggregations to define buckets based on filters, we can use date range aggregation to define buckets based on date ranges. The advantage of using date range aggregation is that it is **calendar aware** and can understand date math (1M, 1h, 1Y).

For example, suppose we want to group all the products based on the product release date. The example used in filter aggregation can be rewritten using range aggregation as shown here:

```
#Date Range
POST chapter8/_search
  {
    "aggs": {
      "range": {
        "date_range": {
          "field": "release_date",
          "ranges": [
            {
              "from": "2016-01-01",
              "to": "now"
            },
            {
              "from": "2015-01-01",
              "to": "2016-01-01"
            },
            {
              "to": "2015-01-01"
            }
          ]
        }
      }
    }
  }
```

The range includes `from` value and excludes `to` value.

Note that `now` in the preceding query is in the UTC time zone. Time zone can be specified using the `time_zone` parameter as shown next:

```
#Date Range with Time zone
POST chapter8/_search
{
  "aggs": {
    "range": {
      "date_range": {
        "field": "release_date",
        "time_zone": "PST8PDT",
        "ranges": [
          {
            "from": "2016-01-01",
            "to": "now"
          },
          {
            "from": "2015-01-01",
            "to": "2016-01-01"
          },
          {
            "to": "2015-01-01"
          }
        ]
      }
    }
  }
}
```

In the preceding example, we are using the Pacific Time zone. You can choose the time zone from the Joda website shown here:

```
http://www.joda.org/joda-time/timezones.html
```

We used range aggregations to divide the data into three buckets. A simpler way to do this is to use date histogram. Date histogram automatically creates the buckets based on the interval specified. The preceding query can be written using data histogram as shown next:

```
#Date Histogram
POST chapter8/_search
{
  "size": 0,
  "aggs": {
    "product_release": {
      "date_histogram": {
        "field": "release_date",
        "interval": "1y",
        "format": "YYYY-MM-dd"
```

```
          }
        }
      }
    }
```

Since we are using the date histogram, it's calendar aware, and the interval can be set to one year. The interval can either be a year, quarter, month, week, day, hour, minute, or second, or a time unit can also be specified as shown in the preceding query. The following time units are supported:

Time unit	Description
y	years
M	months
w	weeks
d	days
h	hours
H	hours
m	minutes
s	seconds

Date internally is stored as a long value, and the format parameter, as shown in the preceding query, can be used to show the bucket keys in the format specified. The response to the preceding query is as follows:

```
{
  . . . .
  "hits": {
    "total": 3,
    "max_score": 0,
    "hits": []
  },
  "aggregations": {
    "product_release": {
      "buckets": [
        {
          "key_as_string": "2014-01-01",
          "key": 1388534400000,
          "doc_count": 1
        },
        {
          "key_as_string": "2015-01-01",
```

```
            "key": 1420070400000,
            "doc_count": 0
        },
        {
            "key_as_string": "2016-01-01",
            "key": 1451606400000,
            "doc_count": 1
        },
        {
            "key_as_string": "2017-01-01",
            "key": 1483228800000,
            "doc_count": 1
        }
      ]
    }
  }
}
```

As you can see, histogram is very handy and one of the most popular features of Elasticsearch. Once the buckets are computed using histograms, you can use a metric aggregation, for example, to get the average number of product sold in each year (bucket) as shown here:

```
#Average products sold each year
POST chapter8/_search
  {
    "size": 0,
    "aggs": {
      "product_release": {
        "date_histogram": { #Bucket Aggregation
          "field": "release_date",
          "interval": "1y",
          "format": "YYYY-MM-dd"
        },
        "aggs": {
          "avg_products_sold": {
            "avg": { #Metric Aggregation
              "field": "products_sold"
            }
          }
        }
      }
    }
  }
```

Aggregations on numeric values (range, histogram)

Just like date range aggregation, range aggregation is used to define buckets based on the ranges specified. In the following example, we will use range aggregation to group the products based on the number of products sold. The query is as follows:

```
#Aggs bases on Filters
POST chapter8/_search
{
  "size": 0,
  "aggs": {
    "price_range": {
      "range": {
        "field": "products_sold",
        "ranges": [
          {
            "to": "10"
          },
          {
            "from": "10",
            "to": "20"
          },
          {
            "from": "20"
          }
        ]
      }
    }
  }
}
```

The response is as follows:

```
{
  ....
  "hits": {
    "total": 5,
    "max_score": 0,
    "hits": []
  },
  "aggregations": {
    "price_range": {
      "buckets": [
        {
          "key": "*-10.0",
          "to": 10,
```

```
                  "doc_count": 0
              },
              {
                  "key": "10.0-20.0",
                  "from": 10,
                  "to": 20,
                  "doc_count": 2
              },
              {
                  "key": "20.0-*",
                  "from": 20,
                  "doc_count": 2
              }
          ]
      }
    }
  }
```

You can see from the preceding response that the keys of the buckets are formed using the from and to values. We can also define the keys for each bucket as shown next:

```
POST chapter8/_search
  {
    "size": 0,
    "aggs": {
      "products_sold": {
        "range": {
          "field": "products_sold",
          "ranges": [
            {
              "key": "Low",
              "to": "10"
            },
            {
              "key": "Medium",
              "from": "10",
              "to": "20"
            },
            {
              "key": "High",
              "from": "20"
            }
          ]
        }
      }
    }
  }
```

The response to the preceding query is as follows:

```
{
    ....
    "hits": {
      "total": 5,
      "max_score": 0,
      "hits": []
    },
    "aggregations": {
      "products_sold": {
        "buckets": [
          {
            "key": "Low",
            "to": 10,
            "doc_count": 0
          },
          {
            "key": "Medium",
            "from": 10,
            "to": 20,
            "doc_count": 2
          },
          {
            "key": "High",
            "from": 20,
            "doc_count": 2
          }
        ]
      }
    }
}
```

Histogram aggregation makes it very easy to bucket the data based on an interval. When using range aggregation, we defined our own buckets; histogram aggregation defines the buckets automatically based on an interval. For example, suppose we want to bucket the number of cell phones sold. We can use histogram aggregation as shown next:

```
POST chapter8/_search
  {
    "size": 0,
    "query": {
      "match": {
        "category": "Cell Phones"
      }
    },
    "aggs": {
      "products_sold": {
```

```
        "histogram": {
          "field": "products_sold",
          "interval": 5
        }
      }
    }
  }
}
```

In the preceding query, we set the interval as 5. The buckets are created in the intervals of 5. The response to the preceding query is as follows:

```
{
  ....
  "hits": {
    "total": 3,
    "max_score": 0,
    "hits": []
  },
  "aggregations": {
    "products_sold": {
      "buckets": [
        {
          "key": 10,
          "doc_count": 1
        },
        {
          "key": 15,
          "doc_count": 0
        },
        {
          "key": 20,
          "doc_count": 0
        },
        {
          "key": 25,
          "doc_count": 1
        },
        {
          "key": 30,
          "doc_count": 0
        },
        {
          "key": 35,
          "doc_count": 1
        }
      ]
    }
  }
}
```

```
    }
```

You can see from the preceding response that the number of products that are sold at least 10 times is `1` and the number of products that are sold at least 35 times is also `1`. The min and max buckets are calculated based on the data.

If we use histogram aggregations to power dashboards, we can ask Elasticsearch to return empty buckets within a start value and an end value. The response can be used to build a chart without modifying the response. We can use extended bounds to show the empty buckets. In the previous example, the first bucket is `10` and the last bucket is `35`. In the following example, we will define min as `0` and max as `50`. Due to extended bounds, the response will contain buckets from `0` to `50`. The query is shown next:

```
POST chapter8/_search
  {
    "size": 0,
    "query": {
      "match": {
        "category": "Cell Phones"
      }
    },
    "aggs": {
      "products_sold": {
        "histogram": {
          "field": "products_sold",
          "interval": 10,
          "extended_bounds": {
            "min": "0",
            "max": "50"
          }
        }
      }
    }
  }
```

The response will now contain six buckets as follows:

```
  {
    . . . .
    "hits": {
      "total": 3,
      "max_score": 0,
      "hits": []
    },
    "aggregations": {
      "products_sold": {
        "buckets": [
```

```
        {
          "key": 0,
          "doc_count": 0
        },
        {
          "key": 10,
          "doc_count": 1
        },
        {
          "key": 20,
          "doc_count": 1
        },
        {
          "key": 30,
          "doc_count": 1
        },
        {
          "key": 40,
          "doc_count": 0
        },
        {
          "key": 50,
          "doc_count": 0
        }
      ]
    }
  }
}
```

As you can see from the preceding response, that empty buckets are added to the response. The response can be now used a input to build a chart.

Aggregations on geolocation (distance, bounds)

In this section, we will discuss how to use geolocation for aggregations. Only fields with explicit geolocation mapping can be used for the geolocation aggregation. The following geolocation aggregations are supported:

- Distance
- Bounds
- GeoHash grid

In this section, we will discuss geo distance and geo bounds aggregation and geohash grid aggregation is out of the scope for this book. To better demonstrate location-based aggregations, let's add a new type named `store` to the existing `chapter8` index. The new type will contain documents representing physical stores with the store name and location fields. We can add the new mapping as shown here:

```
#Store Mapping
 PUT chapter8/_mapping/store
 {
   "properties": {
     "name": {
       "type": "keyword"
     },
     "location": {
       "type": "geo_point"
     }
   }
 }
```

Let's index some store documents:

```
#Index Stores
 PUT chapter8/store/1
 {
   "name": "Store1",
   "location": {
     "lat": "37.339724",
     "lon": "-121.873848"
   }
 }

 PUT chapter8/store/2
 {
   "name": "Store2",
   "location": {
     "lat": "37.338495",
     "lon": "-121.880736"
   }
 }
```

Geo distance

Geo distance aggregation is very similar to range aggregation. It is used to create buckets based on the distance from an origin location. The aggregation calculates the distance between the document value and origin. Depending on the distance, the document is placed to one of the buckets.

For example, suppose you want to group physical stores based on the distance from your current location. In the following query, we will use geo-distance aggregation to define three buckets--within 5 miles, between 5 to 10 miles, and above 10 miles:

```
#Geo Distance
POST chapter8/_search
{
  "size": 0,
  "aggs": {
    "distance": {
      "geo_distance": {
        "field": "location",
        "origin": "37.3382, -121.8863",
        "unit": "mi",
        "ranges": [
          {
            "to": 5
          },
          {
            "from": 5,
            "to": 10
          },
          {
            "from": 10
          }
        ]
      }
    }
  }
}
```

The documents within 5 miles from the origin are placed in the 5 miles bucket and so on. The distance is computed as miles since the unit is specified as **mi** (**miles**). The following distance units are supported:

Unit	Description
Mile	mi or miles
Yard	yd or yards
Feet	ft or feet
Inch	in or inch
Kilometer	km or kilometer
Meter	m or meters
Centimeter	cm or centimeters
Millimeter	mm or millimeters
Nautical mile	NM or nmi or nauticalmiles

Geo bounds

Geo bounds aggregation is used to compute the smallest boundary that encloses all the geo points. Geo bounds is a metric aggregation that takes the documents or buckets (in the case of sub-aggregation) and outputs the boundaries. Take the following for example:

```
#Geo Bounds
POST chapter8/_search
{
   "size": 0,
   "aggs": {
     "boundary": {
       "geo_bounds": {
         "field": "location"
       }
     }
   }
}
```

The result of the response as shown next will be the boundary that can enclose all the geo points:

```
{
    ....
    "hits": {
        "total": 5,
        "max_score": 0,
        "hits": []
    },
    "aggregations": {
        "boundary": {
            "bounds": {
                "top_left": {
                    "lat": 37.33972399961203,
                    "lon": -121.88073601573706
                },
                "bottom_right": {
                    "lat": 37.33849496114999,
                    "lon": -121.87384801916778
                }
            }
        }
    }
}
```

As you can see from the response, the bounds will contain `top_left` and `bottom_right`.

Aggregations on child documents

As defined in the sample data, we have the products as parent documents and the product reviews as children documents. A sample document is shown next:

```
PUT chapter8/product/1?refresh=true
{
    "product_name": "iPhone 6",
    "manufacturer": "Apple",
    "variations": [
        {
            "color": "Gray",
            "storage": "16GB",
            "unit_price": "600"
        }
    ]
}
```

```
#Child Documents
POST chapter8/product_review/?parent=1
{
   "user_id": "user1",
   "comment": "One of the best phones in the market"
}
```

Suppose we want to find the number of product reviews for each manufacturer. The product review is in the child document, and the manufacturer is in the parent document. Due to parent-child mapping, to use the children aggregation, the child document type (`product_review`) should be mentioned explicitly. The query looks like the following:

```
#Children Aggregation
 POST chapter8/_search
 {
    "size" : 0,
    "aggs": {
      "manufacturer": { #First level
        "terms": {
          "field": "manufacturer"
        },
        "aggs": {
          "reviews": {
            "children": { #Children Aggregation
              "type": "product_review"
            },
            "aggs": {
              "product_reviews": {
                "value_count": { #Count
                  "field": "comment.keyword"
                }
              }
            }
          }
        }
      }
    }
 }
```

In the preceding query, we used terms aggregation to group the products by their manufacturer. Next, we used the children aggregation to count the number of comments for each manufacturer. The response to the preceding query is as follows:

```
{
    ....
    "hits": {
      "total": 4,
```

```
      "max_score": 0,
      "hits": []
    },
    "aggregations": {
      "manufacturer": {
        "doc_count_error_upper_bound": 0,
        "sum_other_doc_count": 0,
        "buckets": [
          {
            "key": "Apple",
            "doc_count": 2,
            "reviews": {
              "doc_count": 1,
              "product_reviews": {
                "value": 1
              }
            }
          },
          {
            "key": "Samsung",
            "doc_count": 1,
            "reviews": {
              "doc_count": 0,
              "product_reviews": {
                "value": 0
              }
            }
          }
        ]
      }
    }
}
```

Since we used the `value_count` aggregation, the comments for each manufacturer are counted.

Aggregations on nested documents

Just like children aggregation, aggregation on nested documents is also supported. The product variations are stored as nested documents. A sample product document is as follows:

```
PUT chapter8/product/2?refresh=true
{
  "product_name": "iPhone 7",
  "manufacturer": "Apple",
```

```
    "variations": [ #Nested documents
      {
        "color": "Rose Gold",
        "storage": "128GB",
        "unit_price": "900"
      },
      {
        "color": "Rose Gold",
        "storage": "64GB",
        "unit_price": "800"
      }
    ]
}
```

Suppose we want to find the storage options available for each color. First, we group the products by their color using terms aggregations and then aggregate using the storage. Just like children aggregation, to run aggregation on nested document, the path should be mentioned explicitly. The query looks like the following:

```
#Nested Aggregations
POST chapter8/_search
{
  "size": 0,
  "aggs": {
    "variations": {
      "nested": {
        "path": "variations"
      },
      "aggs": {
        "by_color": {
          "terms": {
            "field": "variations.color"
          },
          "aggs": {
            "by_storage": {
              "terms": {
                "field": "variations.storage"
              }
            }
          }
        }
      }
    }
  }
}
```

We have to specify a nested path, which is then followed by the aggregation. The results of the preceding query are as follows:

```
{
    ....
    "hits": {
      "total": 4,
      "max_score": 0,
      "hits": []
    },
    "aggregations": {
      "variations": {
        "doc_count": 4,
        "by_color": {
          "doc_count_error_upper_bound": 0,
          "sum_other_doc_count": 0,
          "buckets": [
            {
              "key": "Gray",
              "doc_count": 2,
              "storage": {
                "doc_count_error_upper_bound": 0,
                "sum_other_doc_count": 0,
                "buckets": [
                  {
                    "key": "16GB",
                    "doc_count": 1
                  },
                  {
                    "key": "64GB",
                    "doc_count": 1
                  }
                ]
              }
            },
            {
              "key": "Rose Gold",
              "doc_count": 2,
              "storage": {
                "doc_count_error_upper_bound": 0,
                "sum_other_doc_count": 0,
                "buckets": [
                  {
                    "key": "128GB",
                    "doc_count": 1
                  },
                  {
                    "key": "64GB",
```

```
                        "doc_count": 1
                }
            ]
          }
        }
      ]
    }
  }
 }
}
```

You can see from the response that there are two variations (16GB, 64GB) available in the color gray and two variations (64GB, 128GB) in rose gold color.

Reverse nested aggregation

In the previous example, we aggregated on the nested documents. Reverse nested documents will allow you to aggregate on the nested document and then aggregate on the parent documents. The flexibility of running the aggregation on one type and then combining it with the other is the one of the reasons why it is like nothing out there. The following example will make it more clear. A sample product document is shown here:

```
PUT chapter8/product/2?refresh=true
{
  "product_name": "iPhone 7",
  "manufacturer": "Apple",
  "variations": [
    {
      "color": "Rose Gold",
      "storage": "128GB",
      "unit_price": "900"
    },
    {
      "color": "Rose Gold",
      "storage": "64GB",
      "unit_price": "800"
    }
  ]
}
```

For example, we want to query for the manufacturers for each color. The manufacturer field is in the parent document, and the color is in variation stored as a nested document. We first use terms aggregation to group the products by their color and use `reverse_nested` to aggregate on the parent documents:

```
#Reverse Nested Aggregation
POST chapter8/_search
{
  "size": 0,
  "aggs": {
    "variations": {
      "nested": {
        "path": "variations"
      },
      "aggs": {
        "by_color": { //First level
          "terms": {
            "field": "variations.color"
          },
          "aggs": {
            "manufacturer": {
              "reverse_nested": {}, // Parent
              "aggs": {
                "product": {
                  "terms": {
                    "field": "manufacturer"
                  }
                }
              }
            }
          }
        }
      }
    }
  }
}
```

The response to the preceding query is as follows:

```
{
  ....
  "hits": {
    "total": 4,
    "max_score": 0,
    "hits": []
  },
  "aggregations": {
    "variations": {
```

```
        "doc_count": 4,
        "by_color": {
          "doc_count_error_upper_bound": 0,
          "sum_other_doc_count": 0,
          "buckets": [
            {
              "key": "Gray",
              "doc_count": 2,
              "manufacturer": {
                "doc_count": 2,
                "product": {
                  "doc_count_error_upper_bound": 0,
                  "sum_other_doc_count": 0,
                  "buckets": [
                    {
                      "key": "Apple",
                      "doc_count": 1
                    },
                    {
                      "key": "Samsung",
                      "doc_count": 1
                    }
                  ]
                }
              }
            },
            {
              "key": "Rose Gold",
              "doc_count": 2,
              "manufacturer": {
                "doc_count": 1,
                "product": {
                  "doc_count_error_upper_bound": 0,
                  "sum_other_doc_count": 0,
                  "buckets": [
                    {
                      "key": "Apple",
                      "doc_count": 1
                    }
                  ]
                }
              }
            }
          ]
        }
      }
    }
  }
}
```

Going back to the parent document is only possible on nested documents. Using the parent-child document structure, you can only aggregate on the children document. If you need reverse aggregation, you need to use the nested document structure.

Post filter

Post filter is best explained with an example. Suppose in an e-commerce store, a user is looking for a silver-colored cell phone. The products are stored as Elasticsearch documents, and the variations, such as storage and color, are stored as nested documents. To find the cell phone in silver color, the query would look like the following:

```
#Silver Color Cell Phones
POST chapter8/_search
{
  "query": {
    "bool": {
      "must": [
        {
          "match": {
            "category": "Cell Phones"
          }
        },
        {
          "nested": {
            "path": "variations",
            "query": {
              "match": {
                "variations.color": "Silver"
              }
            }
          }
        }
      ]
    }
  }
}
```

The response to the preceding query contains cell phones in silver color. Suppose that along with silver, we want to display all the color variations that are available. To get the list of all the available colors, we can use terms aggregation on the `variations.color` field. We cannot add the aggregation to the existing query as the aggregation is performed on the documents that are a result of the main query. In the preceding example, the result of the main query is cell phones that are in silver color, but we need to run the aggregation on all the cell phones. To do this, we can use post filter. Post filter is executed after the aggregation is run. In the following query, we will use the main query to filter the products to cell phones and the post filter query to filter them to the silver color. When the following query is executed, the order of execution is as follows:

1. First, the top-level query for category cell phones is executed.
2. Next, the `by_color` aggregation is executed on the products that are cell phones.
3. Next, the `post_filter` query is executed to filter the cell phones that are silver in color.

Using post filter, the aggregation is performed on products that belong to the cell phone category. The actual hits in the response are the cell phones in silver, and the aggregation results will include all the available color options:

```
#Post Filter
 POST chapter8/_search
 {
    "query": {
      "match": {
        "category": "Cell Phones"
      }
    },
    "aggs": {
      "variations": {
        "nested": {
          "path": "variations"
        },
        "aggs": {
          "by_color": {
            "terms": {
              "field": "variations.color"
            }
          }
        }
      }
    },
    "post_filter": {
      "nested": {
        "path": "variations",
```

```
        "query": {
          "match": {
            "variations.color": "Silver"
          }
        }
      }
    }
  }
}
```

The response to the preceding query is as follows:

```
{
   ....
   "hits": {
     "total": 0, # No Silver color
     "max_score": null,
     "hits": []
   },
   "aggregations": {
     "variations": {
       "doc_count": 4,
       "by_color": {
         "doc_count_error_upper_bound": 0,
         "sum_other_doc_count": 0,
         "buckets": [ # Other options
           {
             "key": "Gray",
             "doc_count": 2
           },
           {
             "key": "Rose Gold",
             "doc_count": 2
           }
         ]
       }
     }
   }
}
```

You can see from the response that the number of hits is 0. We don't have cell phones in silver, but we can show the user the gray and rose gold color options.

Using Kibana to visualize aggregations

In this section, we will discuss how to use Kibana to visualize aggregations. We will demonstrate a very simple bar chart to represent the terms aggregation. To use an index in Kibana, we have to add the index pattern to Kibana. To do this, perform the following steps:

1. Go to the **Management** tab on the left.
2. Choose **Index Pattern**, and you should see a screen similar to the following:

Input the **index name or index pattern** you would like to run the visualizations on. If you input an index pattern with a wildcard such as `chapter*`, all the indices that start with the name `chapter` are included in the visualization. Once you click on **create**, the next screen should show you the mappings of the index. If the mappings look OK, perform the following steps to create a new visualization:

1. Go to the **Visualize** tab on the left.
2. In the Create New Visualization screen, you can choose the type of visualization you would like. For this example, let's choose a **vertical bar chart**.
3. Next, choose the **index or index pattern** you would like the visualization on.
4. You will be redirected to a screen similar to the following:

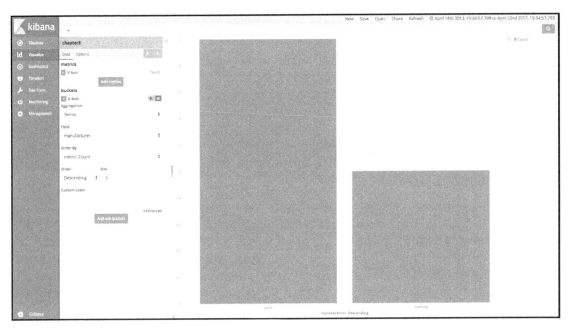

5. For the Y-Axis, we will use the number of documents, which is represented as count.

6. For the X-Axis, we will use terms aggregation on the manufacturer field.

7. For Order By, we will use the default metric count.

8. After everything is set, press the **play** button next to the options tab to display the visualization.

> If you do not see any data in the chart, that is probably because of the date time filter, which is automatically added to every Kibana request. It defaults to the last 15 minutes. The date time filter is based on the date field selected while adding a new index pattern. The date time filter can be changed by clicking on the **clock** icon in the top right corner.

Kibana visualizations are very flexible. For the preceding chart, you can also add sub-buckets to split the bar chart. For example, we first grouped the products by the manufacturer (Apple, Samsung); we can add sub-buckets to further group each bucket by the category (Cell Phone, Cell Phone Accessories).

Caching

When you execute an aggregation query, the node that receives the request sends the query to all the shards of the index. The results from each shard are gathered back and sent to the client. The aggregation results are cached at a shard level. Computing an aggregation is an expensive operation. Caching the response greatly improves the performance and reduces the strain on the system. Elasticsearch cache is smart and is automatically invalidated where there is new data. Since the cache is per shard, the cache is invalidated only for the shards that have new/modified data. Starting Elasticsearch 5.0, the request cache is enabled by default. The query JSON is used as a key.

Cache greatly improves performance for indexes that have static data. For example, if you have a time-based index, the old indexes are not changed anymore. The aggregation results for the old data can be served directly from the cache. By default, 1% of the heap memory is allocated to the request cache. If your data is constantly changing, having a cache may not help at all. If you have dashboards based on aggregations that are refreshed automatically on a schedule, running the entire aggregation every few minutes or seconds can be very expensive. With the request cache, the aggregation needs to be computed only on the recently added data. The request cache can be increased using the `elasticsearch.yml` file as shown here:

```
indices.requests.cache.size: 2%
```

Doc values

Before we jump into doc values, let's quickly refresh what an inverted index is and why it is needed. Let's says we have the following documents:

- **Doc 1**: Apple
- **Doc2**: Apple
- **Doc3**: Samsung

The inverted index for the preceding documents looks like the following:

Term	Doc ID
Apple	1, 2
Samsung	3

To find all the products manufactured by Apple, we would simply use a match query as shown here:

```
{
  "query": {
    "match": {
      "manufacturer": "Apple"
    }
  }
}
```

With the help of inverted index, we can quickly look up all the documents associated with term Apple. But if you want to sort or run the aggregation using the inverted index, we have to go through the entire terms list and collect the document IDs, which is practically not possible. To solve this problem, **doc values** are introduced. Doc values for the preceding documents are as follows:

Doc ID	Terms
1	Apple
2	Apple
3	Samsung

Let's take an example of terms aggregation on the manufacturer:

```
{
  "size" : 0,
  "aggs" :{
    "manufacturer" : {
      "terms" : {
        "field" : "manufacturer"
      }
    }
  }
}
```

The results of the preceding query are as follows:

```
{
  "aggregations": {
    "manufacturer": {
      "buckets": [
        {
          "key": "Apple",
          "doc_count": 2
        },
```

```
        {
          "key": "Samsung",
          "doc_count": 1
        }
      ]
    }
  }
}
```

To execute the preceding aggregation query, Elasticsearch uses the doc values to read the term and create a bucket for each unique term or increment the `doc_count` if the bucket already exists. Similarly, to sort by manufacturer, Elasticsearch uses doc values to get the value of the fields and sort them accordingly. Doc values are also used by the script to access a field value in a document. Doc values are enabled, by default, for all fields except analyzed fields. For analyzed fields, field data can be used, which is turned off by default.

When you index a document, the document in inserted into both inverted index and doc values. Doc values, just like inverted index, are persisted to disk, and Elasticsearch uses the **file system cache** instead of loading them into the JVM memory. By not loading doc values into the JVM heap, less memory can be allocated to JVM, which, in turn, means fewer garbage collections and less heap pressure.

Field data

Only non-analyzed fields are stored in doc values. For aggregations, sorting, and scripting on an analyzed field, an **in-memory** structure called field data is used. Unlike doc values, which live on disk, field data lives in the JVM heap memory due to which it is not very scalable and can cause out-of-memory exceptions. Field data is lazily loaded the first time you try to run an aggregation or sort on an analyzed field. Field data is built from the inverted index of the field, which is an expensive operation and can use significant memory.

Non-analyzed fields are, by default, stored in the doc values, and you can use multi-fields to index the same field as analyzed and non-analyzed fields. You can use the analyzed field for searching and the non-analyzed field for aggregations and so on. Field data is disabled by default, and if you need to run aggregations on an analyzed field, you can enable field data by setting `fielddata` to `true` in the field mapping.

Summary

In this chapter, you learned about the different types of aggregations supported by Elasticsearch. We discussed how to run multilevel aggregations, for example, grouping a document based on a field and computing the average of each bucket. We also discussed how to run aggregations on geolocation, parent-child, and nested documents. You learned how to use Kibana to visualize the aggregations. We also discussed about doc values and field data which power the aggregations internally.

In the next chapter, we will discuss how to configure Elasticsearch.

9
Production and Beyond

This chapter is a flight checklist before going to production. You'll learn about some important Elasticsearch metrics to monitor once you are in production. Since Elasticsearch is an open source, there are a lot of configurable settings. You'll learn about some of the most important settings and how to tailor them to your needs. You'll also learn how to install X-Pack and use the monitoring feature of X-Pack.

In this chapter, we will cover the following topics:

- Configuration
- Cluster API
- Monitoring
- X-Pack
- Thread Pools
- Elasticsearch server logs

Configuring Elasticsearch

Elasticsearch is designed to work out of the box. Most settings can be changed on the fly using the settings API. While in development, the default settings should be sufficient. But for production, depending on your application, you need to modify settings, such as memory, file descriptors, and so on. In this section, we will look at the important settings to configure before going to production. First, let's start by looking at the directory structure of Elasticsearch.

The directory structure

You can choose between `.zip/.tar.gz` or `deb/rpm` to install Elasticsearch. Depending on how you install, the directory structure, location of log files, location of the configuration file, and how you can start/stop Elasticsearch are different.

zip/tar.gz

Let's look at the directory structure when you installed Elasticsearch using a `.zip/.tar.gz` file. By default, when you unzip the `elasticsearch-5.1.2` package, the following directories are within it:

Name	Description
bin	**This contains all the binary files to start Elasticsearch and to install plugins.**
config	This contains configuration files (elasticsearch.yml).
data	This contains all the data files. There is where your data is stored.
logs	This contains all the log files.
plugins	This contains all the plugins.
lib	This contains all the libraries required to run Elasticsearch.

The *data* and *logs* directories are created the first time Elasticsearch was run. We can change the default locations of the directories from the config file. For example, if we want the data folder in a different location, we can modify the location in the configuration file.

DEB/RPM

Let's look at the directory structure when you installed Elasticsearch using the DEB/RPM package:

Name	Description	Location
home	This is the location where Elasticsearch is installed.	/usr/share/elasticsearch
bin	This contains all the binary files to start Elasticsearch and to install plugins.	/usr/share/elasticsearch/bin
conf	This contains configuration files (`elasticsearch.yml`).	/etc/elasticsearch
conf	This contains configuration for environment variables.	/etc/sysconfig/elasticsearch

data	This contains all the data files. There is where your data is stored.	/var/lib/elasticsearch
logs	This contains all the log files.	/var/log/elasticsearch
plugins	This contains all the plugins.	/usr/share/elasticsearch/plugins
script	This contains all the script files.	/etc/elasticsearch/scripts

We can change the default locations of the directories from the configuration file. For example, if we want the data folder in a different location, we can change the location in the configuration file.

Configuration file

The configuration file contains settings specific to a single node. Each node in the cluster has to be configured independently. The configuration files are located in the config directory. Config directory will have the following files:

- `elasticsearch.yml`: This is the Elasticsearch configuration file. It is divided into cluster, node, paths, memory, and so on. Each section contains the defaults, which can be edited.
- `log4j2.properties`: This is the logging configuration.
- `jvm.options`: This is the configuration file to set the JVM settings, such as heap size and so on. If you installed Elasticsearch using a DEB/RPM package, you should configure the environment variables, such as heap size, in `/etc/sysconfig/elasticsearch`.

We will talk about important sections in the configuration file in the sections to follow.

Cluster and node name

In this section, you will learn how to change the cluster and node name. Having a unique cluster name is crucial. By default, Elasticsearch assigns random names to the nodes, and the cluster name defaults to `elasticsearch`. It is very common to have a cluster for development, staging, production, and so on. Without a unique cluster name, a node joining a cluster doesn't know which cluster to join. Also, setting the node name to something such as `node1` or `elasticsearch1` comes in handy when monitoring or debugging.

We can change the node and cluster name by editing the configuration file. Any changes to the configuration file will come into effect only after you restart Elasticsearch. Follow the instructions provided next to modify the cluster and node name:

1. Open the `elasticsearch.yml` file located in the config directory using your favorite text editor.

2. In the config file under the cluster section, change the cluster name shown as follows:

   ```
   cluster.name: es-dev
   ```

3. Under the node section, modify the node name shown as follows:

   ```
   node.name: elasticsearch1
   ```

4. Save the config file.

5. If you have an Elasticsearch instance already running, restart it.

6. Verify the new settings by pointing to `http://127.0.0.1:9200` in your favorite browser, and you should see a response similar to the following:

   ```
   {
       "name": "elasticsearch1",
       "cluster_name": "es-dev",
       "cluster_uuid": "Mp7tziykSjymFwBYozM4RA",
       "version": {
         "number": "5.1.2",
         "build_hash": "c8c4c16",
         "build_date": "2017-01-11T20:18:39.146Z",
         "build_snapshot": false,
         "lucene_version": "6.3.0"
       },
       "tagline": "You Know, for Search"
   }
   ```

You can see from the JSON response that the node name is now `elasticsearch1` and the cluster name is `es-dev`.

By default, all the lines in the configuration file are commented out using the # symbol at the beginning of the line, for example, `#cluster.name: my-application`. You have to remove the # symbol for the setting to come into effect.

Network configuration

Elasticsearch binds to the localhost or `127.0.0.1` by default, which works great for development. When you bind to `127.0.0.1`, only clients running locally will be able to access it. Only after you bind to an external IP address, external clients can communicate with the node.

Elasticsearch assumes it is in the development mode as long as it binds to the default address (`127.0.0.1`). The default address is a loopback address and can't communicate externally. Once an external interface is set, it assumes it is in the production mode and enforces more checks before starting the instance. What previously were warnings while in the development mode will now become errors.

In the configuration file under the network section, you can set the `network.host` to an IP address or a hostname, the node should bind to. For example, if you want to bind the node to `192.168.0.1`, you can do this by the setting the `network.host` as shown next:

```
network.host: 192.168.0.1
```

When you start Elasticsearch with the `network.host` set, you will see in the console/log that Elasticsearch is bound to the new address.

You can also bind Elasticsearch to `0.0.0.0`. In the context of a server, `0.0.0.0` means all IPv4 addresses available. For example, if a server has two IP addresses, `192.168.0.1` and `192.168.0.2`, the Elasticsearch instance can be reached via both the IP addresses. When you bind to `0.0.0.0`, it is also accessible via `127.0.0.1` locally.

If you need more than one node in the cluster, you need to bind Elasticsearch to an external address so that other nodes in the cluster can communicate.

Memory configuration

By default, when you start Elasticsearch, the heap size of the JVM is 2GB. The more memory available to Elasticsearch, the more memory it can use for caching, which improves the overall performance. Also, to run aggregations on your data, there are memory considerations. When you are ready for production, it important to make sure Elasticsearch has enough memory. You can monitor the heap usage and garbage collections using the node stats API. You can configure the JVM settings, such as heap size, garbage collection, and so on in the `jvm.options` file in the config directory.

Let's look at the `elasticsearch1` memory usage using the node stats API as shown next:

```
http://127.0.0.1:9200/_nodes/elasticsearch1/stats/jvm?human&pretty
```

The human flag at the end of the URL makes the numbers in the response more human readable. Let's say we are looking for `heap_used` in the node stats response; without the flag, you will see the following:

```
"heap_used": 349160536,
```

With the flag, you will see the following:

```
"heap_used": "332.9mb",
"heap_used_in_bytes": 349160536,
```

The nodes stats API response is a JSON response as shown next. I've replaced parts of the JSON response with '....' to increase readability as the original response is quite long. We will go through the important sections of the response in the following sections:

```
{
  "cluster_name": "es-dev",
  "nodes": {
      .........
   ],
  "jvm": {
     "mem": {
        .......
     "pools": {
        "young": {
           .....
        },
        "survivor": {
           .....
        },
        "old": {
```

```
          . . . . .
        }
      }
    },
  "threads": {
      "count": 43,
      "peak_count": 50
  },
"gc": {
  "collectors": {
      . . . . . . . . .
    }
  }
 }
}
```

Let's inspect parts of the stats response. First, let's look at the memory section:

```
"mem": {
 "heap_used": "332.9mb",
 "heap_used_in_bytes": 349160536,
 "heap_used_percent": 16,
 "heap_committed": "1.9gb",
 "heap_committed_in_bytes": 2077753344,
 "heap_max": "1.9gb",
 "heap_max_in_bytes": 2077753344,
 "non_heap_used": "58.8mb",
 "non_heap_used_in_bytes": 61673064,
 "non_heap_committed": "62.7mb",
 "non_heap_committed_in_bytes": 65830912
```

You can see from the preceding response that the memory available for this Elasticsearch instance is 1.9 Gb (heap_max). And this Elasticsearch instance is currently using 332.9 MB (heap_used), which is 16% (heap_used_percent) of the total memory. We are currently using only 16% of the available heap since we just started the node. But as we start using it, memory is necessary for caching and aggregations. Depending on the available physical memory, you can monitor the heap usage and increase the heap size. At the end of the section, we will discuss how to increase the heap size.

Another important metric to watch while monitoring memory usage is **garbage collection** (**GC**). Garbage collection and heap size apply to any Java application that runs on JVM. I'll try to describe GC at a very high level as it is beyond the scope of this book. Unlike C and C++, Java does the memory management. It lets developers create new objects without worrying about memory deallocation. The garbage collector automatically claims the memory from the objects that are not being used. JVM pauses the application threads to run the garbage collection, or the application will run out of the memory. This process is also known as stop-the-world as the threads will pause until the garbage collection is done. It is very important to keep the stop-the-world time to a minimum.

Let's inspect the gc section of the node stats:

```
"gc": {
    "collectors": {
        "young": {
            "collection_count": 1,
            "collection_time_in_millis": 24
        },
        "old": {
            "collection_count": 1,
            "collection_time_in_millis": 97
        }
    }
}
```

You can see from the preceding JSON collection_time_in_millis is the time spent in garbage collection. Keeping collection_count and collection_time_in_millis to a minimum is important.

 It is recommended not to have more than 32 GB JVM heap size. Around 32 GB, JVM doesn't compress object pointers. Elasticsearch recommends around 26 GB as a safe cutoff.

Elasticsearch provides a configuration file called jvm.options to configure the JVM settings. You can increase the heap size by setting the -Xms and -Xmx settings. In the jvm.options file, under the JVM Heap Size section, set the following:

```
-Xms4g
-Xmx4g
```

The preceding settings should set the minimum and the maximum heap to `4g`. Once you make these changes, restart your Elasticsearch instance and use the node stats API to verify heap size. You should see the memory section of response similar to the following:

```
"mem": {
 "heap_used" : "245.4mb",
 "heap_used_in_bytes" : 257419688,
 "heap_used_percent" : 6,
 "heap_committed" : "3.9gb",
 "heap_committed_in_bytes" : 4225236992,
 "heap_max" : "3.9gb",
 "heap_max_in_bytes" : 4225236992,
 "non_heap_used" : "57.5mb",
 "non_heap_used_in_bytes" : 60395800,
 "non_heap_committed" : "62mb",
 "non_heap_committed_in_bytes" : 65073152,
```

You can see from the preceding response that the maximum heap memory available is `3.9G`.

When running in production, it is recommended to run Elasticsearch in such a way that it is not sharing the resources with any other applications running on the same machine. Depending on the available memory, set the heap size to not more than `50%` of your physical memory so that Elasticsearch can take advantage of the file system cache. Having enough memory for the file system cache can give you a significant performance boost.

Configuring file descriptors

If you installed Elasticsearch using a DEB/RPM package, this setting is configured automatically. This configuration only applies to Linux and Mac OS. In UNIX operating system, everything is a file including a network connection. A file descriptor is nothing but a handler to the file assigned by the operating system. Once a file is opened, a file descriptor, which is an integer, is assigned to the file. As you index documents, under the covers they are written to Apache Lucene segments. Apache Lucene uses a lot of files to operate. Also, Elasticsearch uses a lot of file descriptors for network communications as the nodes need to communicate with each other. The default number of file descriptors the operating system allows will not be sufficient for Elasticsearch. If the operating system runs out of file descriptors, Elasticsearch might lose data. You need to increase the number of file descriptors for the user running Elasticsearch. Elasticsearch recommends `65,536` or higher.

You can either set the descriptors by running the following command as root before starting Elasticsearch:

```
ulimit -n 655356
```

Alternatively, you can set the limit **permanently** by editing the `/etc/security/limits.conf` and setting the `no file` for the user running Elasticsearch.

Types of nodes

Each Elasticsearch instance can be configured to serve a particular purpose, and you can think of setting the node types once you are ready for production to improve the overall performance and stability.

Following are the different types of nodes:

- **Master eligible node**: Master node is responsible for cluster management, which includes index creation/deletion and keeping track of the nodes that are part of the cluster. For example, adding and removing a node to a cluster are managed by the master node. There will be only one master node at any point of time. A node can act as both master and data nodes. If the master node goes down, one of the data nodes is promoted to master automatically
- **Data node**: Data nodes contain the actual index data. They handle all the index and search operations on the documents
- **Ingest node**: Ingest node is a new type of node added in Elasticsearch 5.0, which can preprocess data before indexing the data
- **Tribe node**: Tribe node can read and write to multiple clusters at a time
- **Coordinating node**: Coordinating node is the node receiving a request. It sends the query to all the shards the query needs to be executed on, gathers the results, and sends them back to the client

 Master node doesn't mean all the requests and responses are channeled through it. You can send a request to any of the nodes in the cluster, and the requests are routed internally by Elasticsearch. The master node is primarily responsible for cluster management and has nothing to do with serving the requests. The nodes communicate with each other internally to serve the request.

A node can be master, data, and ingest node at the same time. Elasticsearch provides these configuration settings to support production environments. Once in production, depending on the criticality of your application, it is important to have a dedicated master node for the overall stability of the cluster. Since the master node performs very lightweight operations when compared to data nodes, the hardware for master nodes can be much lower grade than the hardware used for data nodes. Data nodes are usually CPU and memory intensive.

The type of the node can be configured in the configuration file under the node section as shown here:

```
node.master: true
node.data: true
node.ingest: true
```

By default, a node is master eligible, data, and ingest node. Depending on the application requirements, the configuration can be changed.

Elasticsearch provides cat API to look at different stats about health, pending tasks, nodes, and so on. Unlike the other RESTful API, the cat API response is in a tabular format, which is more human and terminal friendly. You can view all the nodes in the cluster and their roles using the following nodes API. The v at the end of the URL stands for verbose:

```
http://127.0.0.1:9200/_cat/nodes?v
```

You will see a response similar to the following table:

ip	heap.percent	ram.percent	cpu	load_1m	node.role	master	name
127.0.0.1	12	100	10	1.71	mdi	*	elasticsearch1

You can see from the response that there is only one in the cluster right now. And the role of the node is mentioned in the node.role column as mdi, meaning master, data, and ingest node. And since we only have one node in the cluster, it is also the master node indicated by the * symbol in the master column, and the name of the node is elasticsearch1.

Multinode cluster

Elasticsearch is a distributed system, and a cluster contains one or more nodes. In this section, we will discuss how to add a new node to the cluster.

Let's say we have two servers with IP addresses 192.168.0.1 and 192.168.0.2.

Follow the instructions laid down next to start a two-node cluster:

1. Install Elasticsearch in the first server. Please follow the instructions in the *Installing Elasticsearch* section in `Chapter 2`, *Setting up Elasticsearch and Kibana*.
2. Open the configuration file in the first server, and make the following changes:

    1. Change the cluster name under the cluster section:

        ```
        cluster.name: es-dev
        ```

    2. Change the node name under the node section:

        ```
        node.name: elasticsearch1
        ```

    3. Change the host address to bind under the network section:

        ```
        network.host: 192.168.0.1
        ```

    4. Set the address of other nodes in the cluster in the discover section:

        ```
        discovery.zen.ping.unicast.hosts :
        ["192.168.0.1", "192.168.0.2"]
        ```

    5. Start the Elasticsearch instance in the first server.

2. Install Elasticsearch in the second server.
3. Open the configuration file in the second server and make the following changes:
    1. Change the cluster name under the cluster section. Having the same cluster name for both the nodes is important:

        ```
        cluster.name: es-dev
        ```

    2. Change the node name under the node section:

        ```
        node.name: elasticsearch2
        ```

    3. Change the host address to bind under the network section:

        ```
        network.host: 192.168.0.2
        ```

    4. Set the address of other Elasticsearch nodes in the cluster in the discover section:

        ```
        discovery.zen.ping.unicast.hosts :
        ["192.168.0.1", "192.168.0.2"]
        ```

When you start the second instance, it will try to detect the already running Elasticsearch instances from the list of node addresses specified in `discovery.zen.ping.unicast.hosts`. We will discuss discovery further in the *How nodes discover each other* section.

1. Start Elasticsearch in the second server.

2. Make sure both the Elasticsearch instances are started.

Now that we have two nodes in the cluster, we can view the nodes in the cluster and their roles by using the `_cat API` as shown here:

```
http://192.168.0.1:9200/_cat/nodes?v
```

Unlike other APIs, the response of the `_cat API` will be in a tabular format:

ip	heap.percent	ram.percent	cpu	load_1m	node.role	master	name
192.168.0.1	23	100	7	1.40	mdi	*	elasticsearch1
192.168.0.2	21	100	7	1.40	mdi	-	elasticsearch2

From the response, you can see that they are two nodes in the cluster, and `elasticsearch1` is the master node.

Now let's look at the cluster health using the cluster API as shown here:

```
http://192.168.0.1:9200/_cluster/health?pretty
```

The response of the cluster API is as follows:

```
{
  "cluster_name": "es-dev",
  "status": "green",
  "timed_out": false,
  "number_of_nodes": 2,
  "number_of_data_nodes": 2,
  "active_primary_shards": 0,
  "active_shards": 0,
  "relocating_shards": 0,
  "initializing_shards": 0,
  "unassigned_shards": 0,
  "delayed_unassigned_shards": 0,
  "number_of_pending_tasks": 0,
  "number_of_in_flight_fetch": 0,
  "task_max_waiting_in_queue_millis": 0,
  "active_shards_percent_as_number": 100
```

```
}
```

You can see from the response that the number of nodes is `two`, the data nodes are `two` in number, and the cluster status is `green`.

Inspecting the logs

If you are interested in knowing what happens internally when you add a new node, go through the following section. Let's inspect the console/log messages when we start the first Elasticsearch instance. You can find the location of the logs from *Directory Structure* section:

```
[2017-01-21T16:10:03,417][INFO ][o.e.n.Node ] [elasticsearch1] initializing
...
[2017-01-21T16:10:05,681][INFO ][o.e.n.Node ] [elasticsearch1] initialized
[2017-01-21T16:10:05,682][INFO ][o.e.n.Node ] [elasticsearch1] starting ...
[2017-01-21T16:10:05,847][INFO ][o.e.t.TransportService ] [elasticsearch1]
publish_address {192.168.0.1:9300}, bound_addresses {[fe80::1]:9300},
{[::1]:9300}, {192.168.0.1:9300}
[2017-01-21T16:10:08,910][INFO ][o.e.c.s.ClusterService ] [elasticsearch1]
new_master
{elasticsearch1}{xZjyFE19Q0yGxehcys6ydg}{DYY7ZqzcTm-9XXSE7nrKcA}{192.168.0.
1}{192.168.0.1:9300}, reason: zen-disco-elected-as-master ([0] nodes
joined)
[2017-01-21T16:10:08,926][INFO ][o.e.h.HttpServer ] [elasticsearch1]
publish_address {192.168.0.1:9200}, bound_addresses {[fe80::1]:9200},
{[::1]:9200}, {192.168.0.1:9200}
[2017-01-21T16:10:08,926][INFO ][o.e.n.Node ] [elasticsearch1] started
```

This is the first Elasticsearch instance we started. From the console messages, we can see the name of the node as `elasticsearch1`. Let's inspect parts of the console message that are important. First, let's look at the message from the cluster service, which is responsible for cluster management:

```
[2017-01-21T16:10:08,910][INFO ][o.e.c.s.ClusterService ] [elasticsearch1]
new_master
{elasticsearch1}{xZjyFE19Q0yGxehcys6ydg}{DYY7ZqzcTm-9XXSE7nrKcA}{192.168.0.
1}{192.168.0.1:9300}, reason: zen-disco-elected-as-master ([0] nodes
joined)
```

In the console message, you can see that since this is the first Elasticsearch instance, `elasticsearch1` is elected as the new master:

```
[o.e.t.TransportService ] [elasticsearch1] publish_address
{192.168.0.1:9300}, bound_addresses {[fe80::1]:9300}, {[::1]:9300},
{192.168.0.1:9300}
```

In the previous console message, you can see the message from `TransportService`. `TransportService` is the internal communication service. Elasticsearch uses TCP protocol for internal communication between the nodes. From the console message, you can see that transport service for `elasticsearch1` is now running at `192.168.0.1:9300`:

 9200 is the default port for the HTTP service, and 9300 is the default port for transport service.

```
[2017-01-21T16:10:08,926][INFO ][o.e.h.HttpServer ] [elasticsearch1]
publish_address {192.168.0.1:9200}, bound_addresses {[fe80::1]:9200},
{[::1]:9200}, {192.168.0.1:9200}
```

In the previous console message, you can see that `elasticsearch1` HttpServer is now running at `192.168.0.1:9200`. The RESTful API is now available at `http://192.168.0.1:9200`.

Let's inspect the console log when we start the second instance:

```
[2017-01-21T16:10:29,045][INFO ][o.e.n.Node ] [elasticsearch2] initializing
...
[2017-01-21T16:10:31,344][INFO ][o.e.n.Node ] [elasticsearch2] starting ...
[2017-01-21T16:10:31,505][INFO ][o.e.t.TransportService ] [elasticsearch2]
publish_address {192.168.0.2:9300}, bound_addresses {[fe80::1]:9300},
{[::1]:9300}, {192.168.0.2:9300}
[2017-01-21T16:10:34,643][INFO ][o.e.c.s.ClusterService ] [elasticsearch2]
detected_master
{elasticsearch1}{xZjyFE19Q0yGxehcys6ydg}{DYY7ZqzcTm-9XXSE7nrKcA}{192.168.0.
1}{192.168.0.1:9300}, added
{{elasticsearch1}{xZjyFE19Q0yGxehcys6ydg}{DYY7ZqzcTm-9XXSE7nrKcA}{192.168.0
.1}{192.168.0.1:9300},}, reason: zen-disco-receive(from master [master
{elasticsearch1}{xZjyFE19Q0yGxehcys6ydg}{DYY7ZqzcTm-9XXSE7nrKcA}{192.168.0.
1}{192.168.0.1:9300} committed version [3]])
[2017-01-21T16:10:34,716][INFO ][o.e.h.HttpServer ] [elasticsearch2]
publish_address {192.168.0.2:9200}, bound_addresses {[fe80::1]:9200},
{[::1]:9200}, {192.168.0.2:9200}
[2017-01-21T16:10:34,716][INFO ][o.e.n.Node ] [elasticsearch2] started
```

Let's examine the cluster service part of the preceding log. When we started the first instance, it is elected as master. Since we already have a master, the second instance will automatically detect the current master as shown in the following log:

```
[2017-01-21T16:10:34,643][INFO ][o.e.c.s.ClusterService ] [elasticsearch2]
detected_master
{elasticsearch1}{xZjyFE19Q0yGxehcys6ydg}{DYY7ZqzcTm-9XXSE7nrKcA}{192.168.0.
```

```
1}{192.168.0.1:9300}, added
{{elasticsearch1}{xZjyFE19Q0yGxehcys6ydg}{DYY7ZqzcTm-9XXSE7nrKcA}{192.168.0
.1}{192.168.0.1:9300},}, reason: zen-disco-receive(from master [master
{elasticsearch1}{xZjyFE19Q0yGxehcys6ydg}{DYY7ZqzcTm-9XXSE7nrKcA}{192.168.0.
1}{192.168.0.1:9300} committed version [3]])
```

Elasticsearch uses a discovery mechanism it calls **zen discovery** to detect the other nodes in the cluster.

How nodes discover each other

Zen discovery is the discovery module used by Elasticsearch. Since Elasticsearch is a distributed system, you can think of this module as a glue that keeps the cluster together. Cluster management and failure detection are handled automatically by Elasticsearch.

In the configuration file, there is a discovery section dedicated to zen discovery. One of the settings in the discovery section is `discovery.zen.ping.unicast.hosts`. This setting is a list of other hosts Elasticsearch is running, so that the node can join the existing nodes to form a cluster. When we start the `elasticsearch2` instance, this instance will first try to ping the hosts in `discovery.zen.ping.unicast.hosts`. It will scan the ports 9300 to 9305 and find `elasticsearch1` running at `192.168.0.1:9300`. (Note that 9300 is the port for internal communication, 9200 is the HTTP server.) To join the cluster, both the nodes should have the same cluster name. If it cannot find any other Elasticsearch instances running, it elects itself as the master and starts as a single-node cluster.

When you are running Elasticsearch on two different machines, it is important to set the IP address of the two nodes in the `discovery.zen.ping.unicast.hosts` settings. Without this, there is no way for Elasticsearch to discover other nodes. Starting Elasticsearch 5, only unicast is supported and multicast has been removed.

In the discovery section of the config file, set the following:

```
discovery.zen.ping.unicast.hosts : ["node1", "node2"]
```

Node failures

Failure detection is also an important functionality that the discovery module takes care of. Master nodes ping all the nodes in the cluster frequently to make sure they are alive as shown in the following diagram. In the same way, all the non-master nodes ping the master node regularly to ensure the master node is alive. If any failures are detected, they are handled as we described in the *Failure Handling* section in Chapter 1, *Introduction to Elasticsearch*.

 Frequent garbage collections on a node can make it look like a dead node due to the stop_the_world phase. During the stop_the_world phase, the node can't respond to the ping from other nodes; the node might be mistaken for a dead node. In reality, it just couldn't respond due to long garbage collection running on the node. It is important to watch for long running garbage collections.

Master election is the other important functionality the discovery module takes care of. If the master node is dead, the first node to discover that master node is dead initiates the election process, and one of the nodes is elected as the master node. Nodes send ping/heartbeat to the other nodes in the cluster on a regular interval. See below:

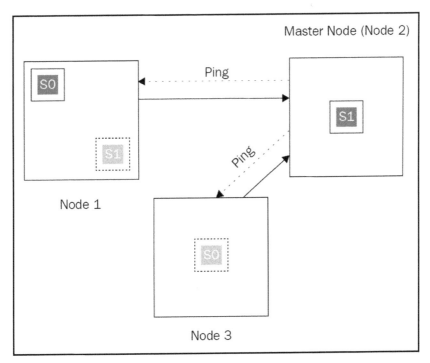

If no communication is received from the node within a certain time, the node is assumed dead. When the cluster detects that the node is dead, it will start copying the shards to a different node to maintain the replication factor as we discussed in the *Failure Handling* section in `Chapter 1`, *Introduction to Elasticsearch*.

Elasticsearch handles all of this internally and is completely transparent to the user.

X-Pack

X-Pack is an elastic offering that enables security, alerting, monitoring, and graph functionality for Elasticsearch. X-Pack requires a paid license to use all the features. When you install X-pack for the first time, you are given a 30-day trial. The basic or free version will provide only monitoring. The other features are available with a paid subscription. In this section, we will install X-Pack and discuss on how to update your license to basic if you are not planning to buy a license. For more details on all the subscription offerings of Elasticsearch, please visit the following link:

```
https://www.elastic.co/subscriptions
```

X-Pack monitoring, which is part of basic or free license, provides UI with easy-to-read graphs to monitor nodes and the indexes. It is available via Kibana. To use X-Pack, you need both Elasticsearch and Kibana. For instructions on how to install Kibana, refer to the *Installing Kibana* section in `Chapter 2`, *Setting up Elasticsearch and Kibana*.

Windows

Using the command prompt, change the directory to where you installed Elasticsearch or `ES_HOME`. And install X-Pack using the following commands:

```
cd C:\elasticsearch-5.1.2
bin\elasticsearch-plugin install x-pack --batch
```

You need to install X-Pack on all the nodes in the cluster and restart the cluster. To install X-Pack on Kibana, follow the commands shown next:

```
cd C:\kibana-5.1.2-windows-x86
bin\kibana-plugin.bat install x-pack
```

Mac OS X

Using the command prompt, change the directory to where you installed Elasticsearch or `ES_HOME`. And install X-Pack using the following commands:

```
cd elasticsearch-5.1.2
bin/elasticsearch-plugin install x-pack --batch
```

You need to install X-Pack on all the nodes in the cluster and restart the cluster. To install X-Pack on Kibana, follow the commands shown next:

```
cd kibana-5.1.2-darwin-x86_64
bin/kibana-plugin install x-pack
```

Debian/RPM

To install X-Pack, follow the commands shown next. The configuration files, by default, are at `/etc/elasticsearch`, as seen below:

```
cd /usr/share/elasticsearch
bin/elasticsearch-plugin install x-pack --batch
```

You need to install X-Pack on all the nodes in the cluster and restart the cluster. To install X-Pack on Kibana, follow the commands shown next:

```
cd kibana-5.1.2-linux-x86_64
bin/kibana-plugin install x-pack
```

Authentication

When you install X-Pack, authentication is enabled by default. You require a username and password to access Elasticsearch and Kibana. The defaults credentials are as follows:

```
username : elastic
password : changeme
```

To disable authentication, set the following in Elasticsearch (`elasticsearch.yml`) and Kibana(`kibana.yml`) configuration files:

```
xpack.security.enabled : false
```

All the nodes in the Elasticsearch cluster, Kibana have to be restarted after you install X-Pack.

X-Pack basic license

When you install X-Pack for the first time, you will have 30 days to either purchase a license or register for a basic license. To continue using the monitoring feature, in this section, we will update the license to basic license. Downgrading to basic license will also remove the authentication. First, you have to register for the basic license by going to the following:

```
https://register.elastic.co/
```

After the registration, you will receive an e-mail with the license file. You can then use the _xpack API to import the basic license. By default, when you install X-Pack, authentication is enabled. You need to pass the username and password as shown next to import the license file:

```
curl -XPUT -u elastic
'http://127.0.0.1:9200/_xpack/license?acknowledge=true' -H "Content-Type:
application/json" -d @license.json
```

You can also use Postman to import the license. When using Postman, in the Authorization tab, you should set the username and password. And in the **body** tab, select the type as **binary**, and choose the license file **elastic** sent you via e-mail:

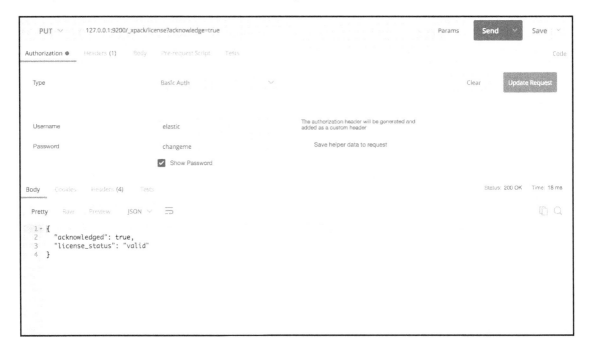

If everything goes well, you should see a response similar to as shown in the preceding screenshot.

Monitoring

Elasticsearch exposes several APIs to monitor cluster health. In this section, we will discuss the native APIs and also X-Pack monitoring, which is available via Kibana. Kibana provides a nice UI and, more importantly, **historical data** to compare the metrics. You can open Kibana by going to the following URL:

```
http://localhost:5601/
```

The default username and password for Kibana are `elastic` and `changeme`. You should a screen similar to this:

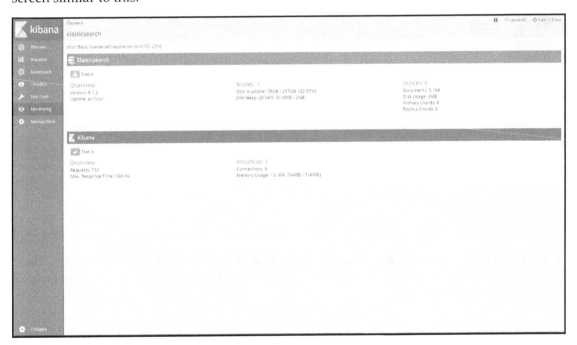

You can see that monitoring is available for both Elasticsearch and Kibana. If you have Logstash installed, you can also monitor Logstash.

Monitoring Elasticsearch clusters

You can use `_cluster` API to retrieve the cluster stats:

```
GET /_cluster/stats/?human&pretty
```

Refer to the *Configuration Elasticsearch* section to understand the important sections in the stats response. You can also monitor cluster-level metric, such as index rate/search rate from the **Monitoring** page as shown here:

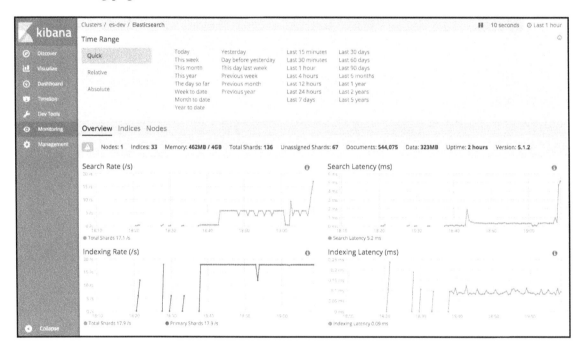

At the top right corner, click on the clock icon to choose the time range for the metrics. The current refresh interval for the charts is 10 seconds. You also change the rate at the which the charts should be updated.

Monitoring indices

You can also monitor individual index stats by going to the following:

```
GET /chapter6/_stats?human&pretty
```

The response contains all the stats of the index. You can also query for particular sections as shown next:

```
GET /chapter6/_stats/indexing
```

You can also look at the index level stats via the Monitoring page as shown here:

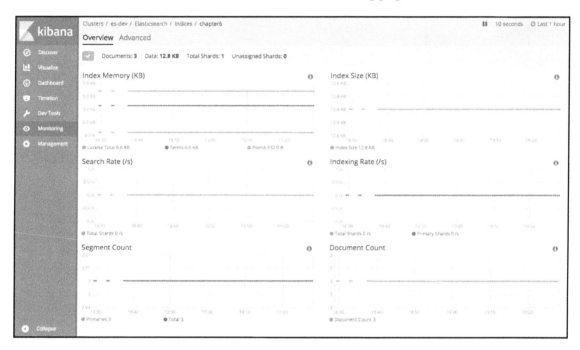

There is also an **Advanced** tab, which contains more advanced metrics, such Lucene memory, disk rate, and so on.

Monitoring nodes

We discussed important node-level metrics to watch for in the *Configuring Elasticsearch* section. Using Kibana, you can get a complete picture of the health of the node. The basic tab has all the important metrics, such as jvm heap size, CPU, load, and so on:

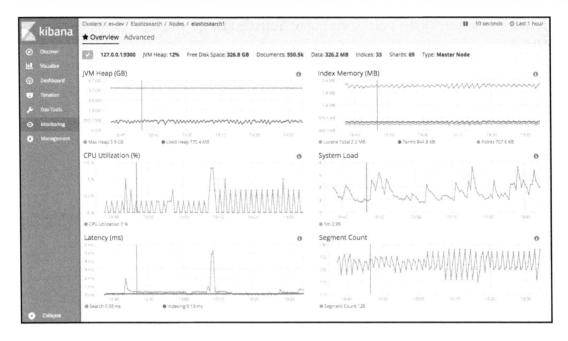

You can also watch for advanced metrics, such as garbage collection and the number of threads in the
Advanced tab:

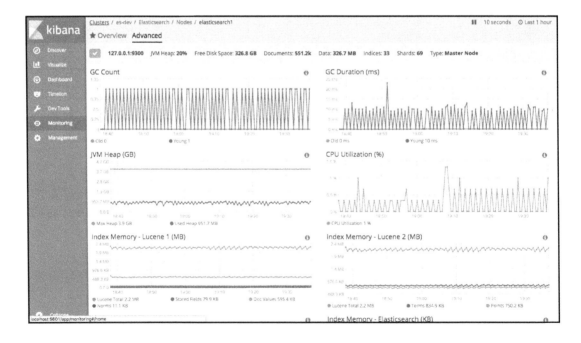

If your current hardware is running hot, most problems can be solved by setting the right mapping types and rethinking the search queries. If all else fails, then you can think of upgrading your hardware.

Thread pools

Elasticsearch has a thread pool for all the major modules. Each thread pool has a queue associated with the pool. For example, if the index thread pool receives more requests than it can process, the requests are queued up. If the queue is full, the request is rejected. Watching for the number of requests in the queue is important. If the requests are frequently queued, the response times are degraded. The pool size is calculated based on the available processors. The important thread pools are as follows:

Thread pool	Description
index	This is used for index and delete operations. It has a queue size of 200.
search	This is used for search operations. It has a queue size of 1,000.
bulk	This is used for bulk operations. It has a queue size of 50.
refresh	This is used for refresh operations.

Note that if the queue is full, the request is rejected with an HTTP 503 error.

You can use cat API to look at the active thread in each pool:

```
GET /_cat/thread_pool?v&h=name,active,queue,rejected,completed
```

The response to the preceding query is as follows:

```
name                active queue rejected completed
bulk                     0     0        0      8067
fetch_shard_started      0     0        0        67
fetch_shard_store        0     0        0         0
flush                    0     0        0       134
force_merge              0     0        0         0
generic                  0     0        0      2777
get                      0     0        0       812
index                    0     0        0         0
listener                 0     0        0         0
management               1     0        0     39531
```

```
refresh               0      0      0     451858
search                0      0      0     103899
snapshot              0      0      0          0
warmer                0      0      0       5765
watcher               0      0      0          0
```

You should watch for the rejected request and queue. You can also use X-Pack monitoring to look at the thread pools in the node stats in the **Advanced** tab:

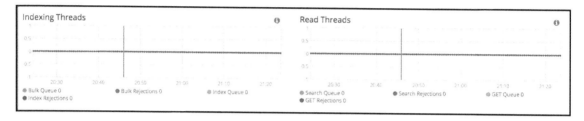

The size of each thread pool is based on the number of processors. Elasticsearch doesn't recommend changing the thread pool size. But the number of threads and the queue size for each pool can be changed in the Elasticsearch configuration file.

Elasticsearch server logs

The server logs should be the go-to place when you are trying to figure out why a node is not starting or why shards are not being allocated. The logs provide insight into what's wrong. Elasticsearch uses `log4j` to handle the logging. The logs are written to the following:

```
ES_HOME/logs/cluster_name.log
```

By default, the logs are rotated every day. If you look at the logs directory, you should find something like this:

```
es-dev-2017-01-21.log                    es-dev-2017-03-23.log
es-dev-2017-01-22.log                    es-dev-2017-03-24.log
es-dev-2017-01-23.log                    es-dev-2017-03-25.log
es-dev-2017-01-25.log                    es-dev-2017-03-26.log
es-dev-2017-01-26.log                    es-dev-2017-03-27.log
es-dev-2017-01-28.log                    es-dev-2017-03-29.log
es-dev-2017-02-01.log                    es-dev-2017-03-30.log
es-dev-2017-02-02.log                    es-dev-2017-04-01.log
es-dev-2017-02-04.log                    es-dev-2017-04-04.log
es-dev-2017-02-13.log                    es-dev-2017-04-05.log
es-dev-2017-02-18.log                    es-dev-2017-04-06.log
es-dev-2017-02-20.log                    es-dev-2017-04-07.log
es-dev-2017-02-24.log                    es-dev-2017-04-08.log
es-dev-2017-02-26.log                    es-dev-2017-04-09.log
es-dev-2017-02-28.log                    es-dev-2017-04-10.log
es-dev-2017-03-02.log                    es-dev-2017-04-11.log
es-dev-2017-03-05.log                    es-dev-2017-04-12.log
es-dev-2017-03-06.log                    es-dev-2017-04-13.log
es-dev-2017-03-11.log                    es-dev-2017-04-14.log
es-dev-2017-03-13.log                    es-dev-2017-04-15.log
```

In the preceding example, the cluster name is `es-dev`. The current logs are written to `es-dev.log`. If you want to change the default log level, you can do so using the cluster setting API as shown next. In the following command, we are changing the logging level for the root logger. Elasticsearch also supports changing the log level for a single module-like discovery:

```
PUT /_cluster/settings
  {
    "transient": {
      "logger._root": "DEBUG"
    }
  }
```

You should see a response similar to the following:

```
{
    "acknowledged": true,
    "persistent": {},
    "transient": {
      "logger": {
        "_root": "DEBUG"
      }
    }
```

```
   }
```

Slow logs

Slow logs are an extremely useful feature, especially when you have a working cluster with a lot of indices. Slow logs are index-level logs, which are logged when the request takes more time than a threshold value. For example, if you want to log all the search queries that are taking more than 5s at the debug-log level. You can enable slow logs for search as shown here:

```
PUT /chapter6/_settings
{
  "index": {
    "search.slowlog.level": "info",
    "search.slowlog.threshold.query.debug": "5s"
  }
}
```

Similarly, you can enable logs while indexing as shown here:

```
PUT /chapter6/_settings
{
  "index": {
    "indexing.slowlog.level": "info",
    "indexing.slowlog.source": "500",
    "indexing.slowlog.threshold.index.debug": "5s"
  }
}
```

Any indexing requests that take more than 5s are logged as debug level. And when logging the indexing request, the first 500 characters of the source are logged. Depending on your application, you can set the preceding values. The slow logs are available in the logs directory. Assuming the cluster name as es-dev, indexing slow logs are logged as es-dev_index_indexing_slowlog.log, and the search logs are logged as es-dev_index_search_slowlog.log.

Summary

In this chapter, we discussed the most important settings to be configured before going to production. You learned about various cluster management APIs to monitor the status of the cluster. We discussed how to use X-Pack monitoring to watch for the important metrics, such as CPU, memory, and so on.

In the next chapter, we will talk about X-Pack premium features, such as graph which can be used to discover relations in your data and alerting which allows you to set up alerts and notifications.

10
Exploring Elastic Stack (Elastic Cloud, Security, Graph, and Alerting)

Elastic, the company behind Elasticsearch, also offers managed cloud hosting and X-Pack which is available as a part of their premium subscriptions. In the previous chapters, we used Kibana to create visualizations of your data. X-Pack adds more functionality, such as graph, **monitoring** to Kibana. The graph will let you discover **relations** in your data. We will discuss how to use **graph** to make recommendations based on the previous purchases in an e-commerce store. Along with graph and monitoring, X-Pack also provides **security**, extremely flexible **alerts**, and a **notification system**. We will briefly talk about the various products in Elastic Stack and Elastic Cloud in this chapter. By the end of this chapter, we will discuss the following:

- Elasticsearch Cloud (Managed Elasticsearch)
- Security
- Graph
- Alerting

Elastic Cloud

Elastic Cloud is the scalable cloud offering by the company that built Elasticsearch. Elasticsearch and Kibana are offered as a service. Your cluster is hosted on Amazon AWS and is completely managed by Elastic Cloud. You can create a new cluster across **multiple data centers** with the click of a button. Once you create a cluster, depending on the application needs, you can scale up or down very easily. The monitoring of clusters is available via Kibana monitoring. X-Pack is automatically included for every cluster running on Elastic Cloud.

> Elastic offers a 14-day trial to new customers to try the service. You can sign up for a trial by going to `https://cloud.elastic.co`

The advantages of Elastic Cloud are as follows:

1. `Monitored and managed by Elastic` - If a node or the cluster goes down, its taken care by the Elastic team. There is no need of a dedicated operations team to monitor and manage you cluster.
2. `Highly available` - Your cluster is span across multiple data centers. Even if couple of nodes or the entire data center goes down, your data is still available.
3. `Automatic data backups` - Data is automatically backed up every 30 mins.
4. `Easy to scale` - Hosted on AWS cloud, you can scale you cluster up and down. For example, you are launching a new product and except more traffic than usual, you can add more resources to your cluster and scale it down later.

> Depending on the number of nodes you need, it can get quite expensive. You can look at the current pricing at `https://www.elastic.co/cloud/as -a-service/pricing`

We will discuss the above features in detail in the sections below.

Once you create a Elastic Cloud account, you can create a new cluster by going to the *Create Cluster* page shown here:

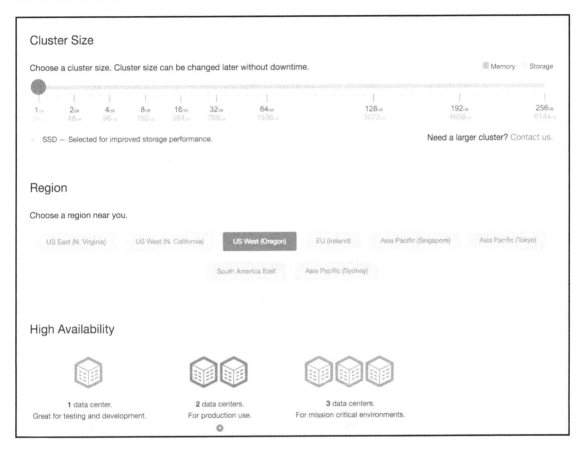

Following are the steps to create a cluster:

1. Choose the memory and storage you would need. You can always scale your cluster up or down later.
2. Choose the region near you (Amazon AWS regions).
3. For high availability, choose 1 or 2 data centers depending on your application needs. We will discuss this in detail in the next section.
4. Once you click on Create, your new cluster will be provisioned.

Once the new cluster is provisioned, the Elasticsearch and Kibana endpoints are available on the *Clusters* page. By default, security is enabled on the cluster. To access Elasticsearch and Kibana, you will need a username and a password. The default username is `elastic`, and you can reset your password by going to the *Security* tab on the left and clicking on the `Reset` button.

High availability

Elastic Cloud supports high availability by spreading the cluster across two or three data centers or AWS availability zones. AWS availability zones are independent zones within an AWS region. Availability zones are connected using low-latency networks. In the case of an availability zone going down, the nodes in the different availability zone will **automatically** take over.

What does this mean in terms of Elasticsearch? Elasticsearch supports high availability by writing your data to both primary and replica shards. When using Elastic Cloud, the primary and replica shards of an index are stored in the nodes that belong to different data centers/availability zones. If a node goes down or an entire availability zone goes down, the replicas in a different availability zone can still support the read/write operations, so that your data is always available.

To look at the shard distribution, let us create a cluster with high availability option of two data centers. Once we have the cluster up and running, let us create an index with 2 shards and 1 replica, the index will have a total of 4 shards. The distribution of shards can be viewed in *Kibana Monitoring* page by the following the steps here:

1. Go to the *Monitoring* page in Kibana.
2. Select indices to get a list of available indices.
3. Choose the index you would like and scroll down to *Shard Legend* at the end of the page.

The shard legend of an index is shown here:

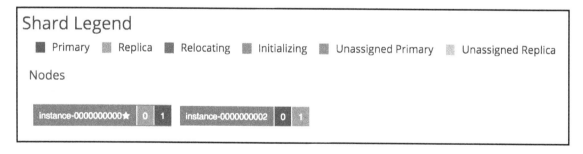

The cluster contains two nodes and they belong to different data centers. The two instances shown in preceding screenshot are the nodes of the cluster. The first instance contains the primary of shard 1 and the replica of shard 0 and the second instance contains the primary of shard 0 and the replica of shard 1. If the first instance goes down, replica of shard 1 in the second instance is promoted to primary and no data is lost. By distributing the shards across nodes that belong to different availability zones, your data is made highly available.

Data reliability

Elastic Cloud supports creating your cluster across three data centers or availability zones. In the case of a node going down, the shards are automatically replicated to different nodes. In the case of all the availability zones going down (which is very rare), you can use the snapshot and restore feature. Elastic Cloud automatically backs up your data every 30 mins to Amazon S3 buckets. You can go to the Snapshots tab on the left to restore a snapshot.

Security

Security is also part of X-Pack gold and premium subscriptions. Security for Elasticsearch is two-fold:

- User authentication to access the cluster using username and password
- Securing the communication between the nodes and the client using SSL

Authentication and roles

X-Pack provides role-based authentication. When you install X-Pack, authentication is enabled automatically. To get started, two default users are created:

Username	Password	Role
elastic	changeme	This is a superuser
kibana	changeme	To access Kibana, the user has the required permissions to talk to Elasticsearch

You can add more users or roles in the Kibana Management Console by going to the Users page. Along with creating new users, you can also add or change roles by going to the Roles page. For example, let's create a new role `chapter10_superuser`. The users in this role have super user permissions to the `chapter10` index only. In the following screenshot, you can see that we restricted the index privileges to only the `chapter10` index:

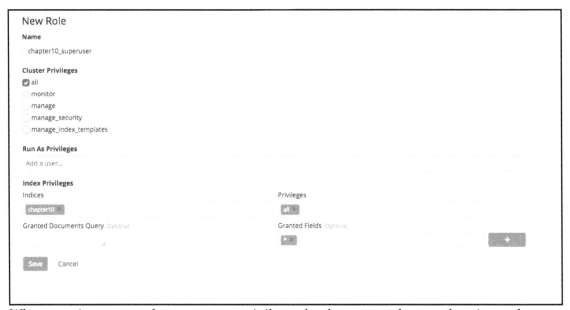

When creating a new role, you can set privileges for the user, such as read, write, and so on. You can also grant access to only certain fields. For example, you can restrict access to a sensitive field, such as credit card information. Once the role is defined, you can add a new user by going back to the Users page as shown here:

When authentication is enabled, requests without username and password are rejected. Anonymous access can be enabled by setting the roles for anonymous access in the Elasticsearch configuration file. You can also completely disable authentication by adding the following to the `elasticsearch.yml` and `kibana.yml` configuration files:

```
xpack.security.enabled: false
```

Securing communications using SSL

If you are storing sensitive information on your cluster, SSL is a must. When SSL is enabled, the internal communication between the nodes and the communication between the client and the cluster are encrypted. SSL is also used to authenticate the nodes before joining the cluster. To enable SSL, you have to generate a private key certificate. For more information, please visit the following URL:

```
https://www.elastic.co/guide/en/x-pack/5.1/ssl-tls.html
```

When talking to a cluster with SSL enabled, the transport client must be configured to use SSL to encrypt/decrypt the communications.

Graph

In this section, we will discuss Graph, which is part of the X-Pack Gold and Platinum subscription. Graph lets you **discover and analyze relationships** in your data. It works on your existing indexes and doesn't require any special configuration. The Graph has two components:

- The functionality required for Elasticsearch to compute the Graph.
- The UI in Kibana to visualize the graphical representation.

To better explain the functionality of Graph, let's build a recommendation system for an online store. We want to know the relations between items frequently bought together and use that information to make suggestions to the users. This information can be very valuable. For example, in a physical store, items frequently bought together can be placed adjacent to each other. We can also use this information to give the user a coupon or e-mail the user about various discounts on those products. We will create an index called `chapter10` and index the user's purchases as documents. First, let's create the index and set the mappings:

```
#Delete existing index
DELETE chapter10

#Mapping
PUT chapter10
{
  "settings": {
    "number_of_shards": 1,
    "number_of_replicas": 0
  },
  "mappings": {
    "order": {
      "properties": {
        "line_items": {
          "type": "keyword"
        },
        "user_id": {
          "type": "keyword"
        },
        "order_creation_date" : {
          "type": "date"
        }
      }
    }
  }
}
```

Next, let's index some documents:

```
PUT chapter10/order/1
{
  "user_id": "1",
  "line_items": [
    "icecream",
    "chocolate",
    "beer",
    "chips",
    "soda"
  ]
}

PUT chapter10/order/2
{
  "user_id": "2",
  "line_items": [
    "icecream",
    "banana",
    "avocado",
    "soda",
    "peanut butter"
  ]
}
PUT chapter10/order/3
{
  "user_id": "3",
  "line_items": [
    "icecream",
    "chocolate",
    "soda",
    "chips"
  ]
}

PUT chapter10/order/4
{
  "user_id": "4",
  "line_items": [
    "icecream",
    "banana",
    "bread",
    "chips"
  ]
}
```

For example, we want to show recommendations for users who bought `soda` and `chips`. We will make the recommendations based on what other users bought along with soda and chips. To do this, we can use a simple terms aggregation and get the count of each line item (items in an order). But the recommendations based on terms aggregation might not be apt as there is no **significance** to soda and chips; the aggregation simply calculates the count for each unique line item. Instead of terms aggregation, we can use the `significant_terms` aggregation to calculate the significance of each term to provide a better recommendation. The following example will better explain why we need to use the `significant_term` aggregation. Let's run the query and look at the results:

```
POST chapter10/_search
{
   "size": 0,
   "query": {
     "bool": {
       "must": [
         {
           "term": {
             "line_items": "soda"
           }
         },
         {
           "term": {
             "line_items": "chips"
           }
         }
       ]
     }
   },
   "aggs": {
     "recommendations": {
       "significant_terms": {
         "field": "line_items",
         "min_doc_count": 1
       }
     }
   }
}
```

The documents that match the preceding query have the following line items:

```
"icecream", "chocolate", "beer", "chips", "soda"
"icecream", "chocolate", "soda", "chips"
```

You can see that the common terms between the two documents are as follows:

```
"icecream", "chocolate", "beer"
```

If you look at the other purchases, all the purchases have ice cream. If you recommend ice cream, you are recommending what anybody would buy in general. But we want to find out what users who bought chips and soda like. **Significant terms aggregation** calculates the significance of each term globally and in the scope of the current query. Terms such as ice cream are significant globally and ranked lower. Let's look at the results of the preceding query:

```
{
    ....
    "aggregations": {
      "recommendations": {
        "doc_count": 2,
        "buckets": [
          {
            "key": "chocolate",
            "doc_count": 2,
            "score": 1,
            "bg_count": 2
          },
          {
            "key": "beer",
            "doc_count": 1,
            "score": 0.5,
            "bg_count": 1
          },
          {
            "key": "soda",
            "doc_count": 2,
            "score": 0.3333333333333333,
            "bg_count": 3
          },
          {
            "key": "chips",
            "doc_count": 2,
            "score": 0.3333333333333333,
            "bg_count": 3
          }
        ]
      }
    }
}
```

You can see from the results that `chocolate` and `beer` are the top recommendations and ice cream is not even recommended. For this example data set, users who bought soda and chips also like chocolate and beer. When we use the Kibana Graph UI, you will see the following graph:

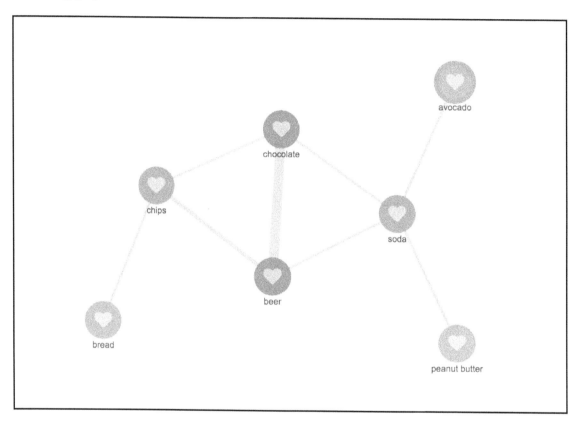

You can see from the preceding graph that the common vertices (also known as nodes) between chips and soda are `chocolate` and `beer`. You can also see vertices and connections (also known as edges) between other products. You can change the input, and a new graphical representation appears instantly. The queries are executed using the query DSL and are very fast. In the next section, we will learn how to use Kibana Graph UI. In a bigger data set with lots of correlations, Graph is very useful in finding hidden relations between the data points.

Graph UI

In this section, we will learn how to use Graph UI to get better insights into user data. To use the `chapter10` index in Kibana, we have to first add the index pattern. If you have Kibana installed locally or on a remote server, you can open Kibana by going to the following URL:

```
http://localhost:5601/
```

 If you are using Elastic Cloud, the Kibana endpoint can be found on the cluster overview page.

Once in Kibana, select the *Management* tab on the left navigation panel, and select *Index patterns* and you will see a screen similar to as shown here:

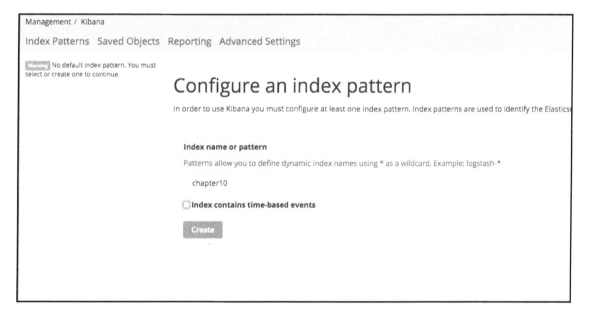

Enter the index name as `chapter10` and unselect the `Index contains time-based events` option as we don't have any date fields in the data set. Click on the `Create` button to use the `chapter10` index in Kibana. Once the index is added to Kibana, let's open Graph by going to the *Graph* tab on the left navigation bar. Once in the *Graph Workspace* page, you will a screen similar to shown here:

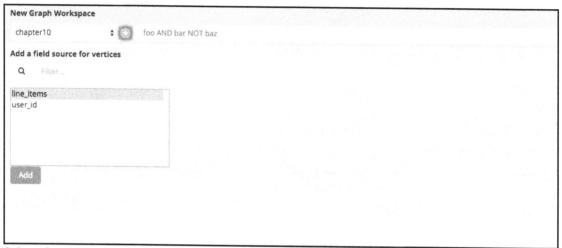

Select the index pattern as `chapter10` and click on the plus (+) button to add `line_items` field to the graph. Input the search text as `chips AND soda` and click on the search button (Magnifying glass icon) to see the graph. Since the dataset has only 4 records, we have to change some settings to execute the graph query. To change the settings, select the *Settings* tab at the top right corner and you will see a screen similar to shown here:

Change the `Certainty` to `1` as the data set is small. You can minimize settings by clicking on the *Settings* tab. Click the search button represented by magnifying glass icon and you will see the graph as shown here:

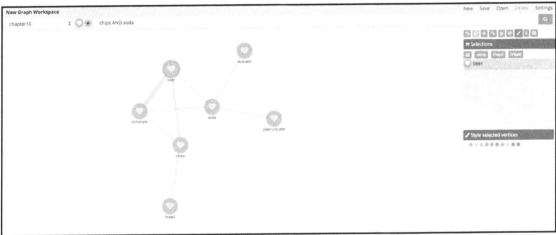

You can select a node and use the advanced options window to change the styling, group nodes together, remove a node, and so on. In the *Settings* tab, you can also view the last request and response.

Alerting

Just like Graph, alerting is a part of X-Pack Gold and Platinum subscription. Alerting was formerly known as . You can define watchers on cluster events and existing indexes. Watcher can be configured to be executed on schedule. Elasticsearch alerting is very **flexible**, and the input can be the response to an HTTP request or a query on existing Elasticsearch index. A watch is triggered if the input matches a predefined condition. For example, the input can be the cluster status and condition is "if the cluster status is red". When a condition is triggered, you can define what action has to be taken. An action can be sending an e-mail, indexing a document, sending a slack message, and so on.

For an e-commerce store, let's define a watcher to alert if less than five orders have been placed within the last 30 minutes. The action we will take when the condition is met is indexing a document. We can also send an e-mail, but in this example, we will index a document instead for further analysis. We want to run the watcher every 30 mins. We can define a schedule as follows:

```
PUT _xpack/watcher/watch/order_count
{
```

```
    "trigger": {
      "schedule": {
        "interval": "30m"
      }
    },
```

Next, let's define the input for the watcher. The input for this watcher is an Elasticsearch query that searches for the number of orders placed in the last 30 minutes:

```
"input": {
    "search": {
      "request": {
        "indices": [
          "chapter10"
        ],
        "types": [
          "order"
        ],
        "body": {
          "query": {
            "range": {
              "order_creation_date": {
                "gte": "now-30m",
                "time_zone": "-07:00"
              }
            }
          }
        }
      }
    }
  },
```

The response of the input is validated against a condition. Let's define the condition, which, in this case, is the number of orders less than five:

```
"condition": {
    "compare": {
      "ctx.payload.hits.total": {
        "lte": "5"
      }
    }
  },
```

If the input matches the condition, an action can be defined. The action we want to take when the number of orders placed is less than five is to index a document into an index named `order_alerts`:

```
"actions": {
    "index_payload": {
        "index": {
            "index": "order_alerts",
            "doc_type": "lte_5",
            "execution_time_field" : "alert_timestamp"
        }
    }
  }
}
```

The complete query is as follows:

```
PUT _xpack/watcher/watch/order_count
  {
    "trigger": {
      "schedule": {
        "interval": "30m"
      }
    },
    "input": {
      "search": {
        "request": {
          "indices": [
            "chapter10"
          ],
          "types": [
            "order"
          ],
          "body": {
            "query": {
              "range": {
                "order_creation_date": {
                  "gte": "now-1m",
                  "time_zone": "-07:00"
                }
              }
            }
          }
        }
      }
    },
    "condition": {
      "compare": {
```

```
        "ctx.payload.hits.total": {
          "lte": "5"
        }
      }
    },
    "actions": {
      "index_payload": {
        "index": {
          "index": "order_alerts",
          "doc_type": "lte_5",
          "execution_time_field" : "alert_timestamp"
        }
      }
    }
  }
}
```

To test the preceding watcher, let's index an order:

```
PUT chapter10/order/5
  {
    "user_id": "5",
    "line_items": [
      "icecream",
      "banana",
      "bread",
      "chips"
    ],
    "order_creation_date": "2017-04-21T16:06:00-07:00"
  }
```

The watcher is scheduled to run every 30 minutes. We can manually execute the watcher using the _execute endpoint as shown here:

```
POST _xpack/watcher/watch/order_count/_execute
```

The results of the execute are as follows:

```
{
  "_id": "order_count_31f37cfc-
e2e0-4e8a-97f2-884a445a614e-2017-04-22T03:07:01.116Z",
  "watch_record": {
    "watch_id": "order_count",
    "state": "executed",
    "trigger_event": {
      "type": "manual",
      "triggered_time": "2017-04-22T03:07:01.116Z",
      "manual": {
        "schedule": {
```

```
                "scheduled_time": "2017-04-22T03:07:01.116Z"
              }
            }
          },
          "input": {
            ....
          },
          "result": {
            "execution_time": "2017-04-22T03:07:01.116Z",
            "execution_duration": 153,
            "input": {
              "type": "search",
              "status": "success",
              "payload": {
                ......
              },
              "actions": [
                {
                  "id": "index_payload",
                  "type": "index",
                  "status": "success",
                  "index": {
                    "response": {
                      "created": true,
                      "result": "created",
                      "id": "AVuToID57yThjPgxn39z",
                      "version": 1,
                      "type": "lte_5",
                      "index": "order_alerts"
                    }
                  }
                }
              ]
            },
            "messages": []
          }
        }
```

You can see from the response that the status of the action is a success. Let's check the order_alerts index to make sure the alert is recorded:

```
POST order_alerts/_search
```

The response to the preceding query is as follows:

```
{
  ....
  "hits": {
    "total": 1,
    "max_score": 1,
    "hits": [
      {
        "_index": "order_alerts",
        "_type": "lte_5",
        "_id": "AVuTekMw7yThjPgxn2f2",
        "_score": 1,
        "_source": {
          "_shards": {
            "total": 1,
            "failed": 0,
            "successful": 1
          },
          "hits": {
            "hits": [],
            "total": 0,
            "max_score": null
          },
          "took": 1,
          "timed_out": false,
          "alert_timestamp": "2017-04-22T03:07:01.116Z"
        }
      }
    ]
  }
}
```

Since this is a test watcher, you can disable the watcher as shown next:

```
POST _xpack/watcher/watch/order_count/_deactivate
```

The preceding example is a very simple watcher. Actions such as slack, email, and hip chat are also supported.

Summary

In this chapter, we discussed Elastic Cloud, which is the scalable cloud offering for Elasticsearch and Kibana. We also discussed various features of X-Pack. With monitoring and alerting, you can make sure your cluster is up and running and that your data is always available.

Although Elasticsearch started as a search engine, it is evolving as an analytics engine. In this chapter, we discussed Graph, which can be used to discover relations in your data. We used the example of an e-commerce store to make recommendations, but this functionality has great potential. For example, for fraud detection or to find out the similarity between customers who like or don't like your product have in common. The graph provides actionable insights into your data.

The alert and notification system that we discussed in this chapter is very flexible. We used alerting to get notified, if the number of orders placed in last 30 minutes are less than five. Think of the possibilities of such a system; you can set up alerts on different trends and get notified. You can do all this without the need of a new system.

Elasticsearch is also working towards including machine learning as part of X-Pack, which supports unsupervised machine learning. The current beta version supports machines learning on time-series data to find data anomalies.

Elasticsearch is a highly scalable analytics and search engine, which is very flexible and high performing. The things Elasticsearch can do are continuously evolving, but the fundamentals discussed in this book will not change.

Index

www.ingramcontent.com/pod-product-compliance
Lightning Source LLC
Chambersburg PA
CBHW062035050326

40690CB00016B/2943